Games That Sell!

Mark H. Walker

Games That Sell!

Mark H. Walker

Wordware Publishing, Inc.

Library of Congress Cataloging-in-Publication Data

Walker, Mark (Mark H.)
    Games that sell! / by Mark H. Walker.
       p.   cm.
    Includes index.
    ISBN 1-55622-950-X (pbk.)
    1. Video games—Marketing.   2. Video games—Evaluation. I. Title.
    GV1469.3.W43 2003
    794.8--dc21   2003010229
                                                                        CIP

© 2003, Wordware Publishing, Inc.
All Rights Reserved

2320 Los Rios Boulevard
Plano, Texas 75074

Printed in the United States of America

ISBN 1-55622-950-X

10 9 8 7 6 5 4 3 2 1
0306

All inquiries for volume purchases of this book should be addressed to Wordware Publishing, Inc., at the above address. Telephone inquiries may be made by calling:

(972) 423-0090

Dedication

To development teams the world over. Putting smiles on faces is never a trivial pursuit.

Contents

Contents

Contents

Acknowledgments

Thanks to Jim Hill for the work, Wes Beckwith for his patience, Heather Hill and Beth Kohler for the great edit, and all of Wordware Publishing, Inc. Thanks also to all the PR reps, designers, editors, gamers, and journalists who contributed to this book.

Introduction

Money makes the world go round. In music, film, and literature—any endeavor, artistic or not—money is what fuels the
fire. Some rail against that, while others accept it. It costs
money to make records. It costs money to make books, produce
films, and design computer games. Accordingly, the people who
fund those endeavors want to make their money back, and that
is what this book is about—making your money back.

There is only one way for investors to make a return on the
dollar they put into game development companies and publishers: The game that those development and publishing
companies make must sell.

Bookshelves are crammed, relatively speaking, with books
about designing, developing, and programming games. However, these books usually concentrate on explaining the coding
end. Even the most altruistic among us hope that their game
sells. So, the underlying theory in these books on programming
and game development seems to be if you make the best game
on the planet, it is going to sell.

That is not true.

Actually, that may be true, but not every design team is capable of making the best game on the planet. The point is that
making a great game does not ensure that it will sell; neither
does making a mediocre game ensure that it won't sell. There
are specific ingredients of games that sell, and that is what this
book is about. In general, good gaming and good sales go hand
in hand. But I will show you where they diverge, and I will show
you the ingredients of what makes up that illusive, good
gaming.

No, this isn't a book about how to design the best game, but rather a book about what makes games sell. Accordingly, we are going to talk to people who see games day in and day out. Although Sid Meier is an excellent game designer, perhaps the best in our industry, he doesn't see and analyze the breadth of games that Jeff Green, the executive editor at *Computer Gaming World*, does or even that a voracious gamer or journalist does. Hence we are going to talk to the editors, journalists, public relation specialists, and yes, even the gamers. These are the people who buy the game. These are the people who have seen which games sell and what makes them unique compared to the games that don't sell. They have the broadest "database" of anyone we can imagine, and hence are the most qualified to explain what makes games sell—in other words, what makes them buy a game.

About This Book

We all know how to read a book. If you didn't, you wouldn't be here. Although I hope you read it cover to cover, perhaps you are looking for a specific part or section of the book. Let's briefly go through what this book is about and how to use it. There are five factors common to every good-selling game. The first factor is topic (Part One: Topic—Setting the Stage)—in other words, what the game is about. Part One covers topics in detail including game genre, licensing and franchising, and the choice of topics and genres that makes games successful. The second part of the book covers quality. Great games don't necessarily sell well, but if the game isn't good, it probably won't sell at all. I take a look at quality game play and the air of quality given to a game by first-rate documentation and strategy guides. Part Three is titled Marketing and Public Relations. This part discusses public relations, how to get press, and marketing the product. Games must not only be well promoted but well marketed. There must be buzz, and there must be stores to sell the game. Part Four is called Range of Appeal and Cool Factor. Some niche games have sold well, but they are the exceptions. To sell well, a game must have a broad range of appeal. Although darn near intangible, "cool factor" is oh so important. If a game is to sell, it must be cool. The coolness may be beautiful graphics, neat weapons, or Lara Croft's tight shorts. Whatever it is, games must have it.

It must be something unique; if not unique, it must be something done well—something that pulls gamers into the game. Included in Part Four is cool factor analysis from fans, journalists, developers, and publishers.

Part Five is titled Been There and Back—A Few Games that Have Sold and Some that Haven't. This part takes some of the best-selling games from the past two years and with the help of industry insiders analyzes why the game sold well. It is here that the previously discussed points will be used to figure out why these games sold. Also included in this section is a chapter on a handful of great games that haven't sold well and why they haven't.

In the final part, Speaking Out, there are numerous interviews with editors, public relations specialists, marketers, producers, fans, and writers. I asked them what they believe makes a game sell and what their favorite games are and why. In short, from the people buying the games and analyzing the games, we find out what they feel makes games sell.

The End of the Beginning

So that's what the book is about. I hope it is interesting, and I hope you learn something to boot. Most of all, I hope that you learn how to make games that sell.

About the Author

Mark H. Walker is a veteran journalist, writer, and game designer. He has written over 40 books about computer gaming, including *The Video Game Almanac* and *A Parent's Guide to PlayStation Games*. He designs board and computer games, and his latest game (Mark H. Walker's Lock 'n Load) has been called "a landmark in tactical boardgaming" by The Wargamer (www.wargamer.com), a top 100 Internet site. Mark lives in the foothills of the Great Smokey Mountains with his wife and three daughters.

Chapter 1

What Makes Games Sell

A s I mentioned in the introduction, this isn't a book about programming or developing games. Certainly there are developmental elements in the book, but I don't pretend to be a coder. What I am is a journalist (with ten years of experience) in the electronic entertainment field. That experience has given me access to hundreds of games. I have seen good games, bad games, mediocre games, and everything in between. I've seen what's worked, what hasn't worked, what has sold, and what hasn't sold.

If you aren't interested in selling your game, then put down this book now. This isn't a book on designing innovative, creative, or even great games, but rather a book on how to design games that sell. Frequently, a great game and a game that sells are one and the same, but such is not always the case. "We've had experiences with games that were really good (i.e., they were nominated for numerous awards and even won several of them)," says Christina Ginger, former director of communications at Strategy First. "But without a large marketing budget or retail support, the games did not sell as well as they could have."

What I hope to do in this book is show you how to design a game that sells, a game that lives up to your expectations. It is up to you to make that salable game a great game.

There are five properties, items, thingies, or whatever you would like to call them that make games sell: topic, quality, marketing and public relations, range of appeal, and the cool factor. We will look at each in detail in Parts One through Four of the book.

Topic

Topic is what the game is all about. Some topics are hotter than others. A game based on *Saving Private Ryan* (can you say Medal of Honor: Allied Assault?) will sell much better than a game based on an unknown movie. "I definitely think such licenses can enhance a game's sales; again, the reason being reputation," says Kelly Ekins of Strategy First. "This reputation will create the feeling for the consumer that they are in a way guaranteed quality if the game is based on a license. If not quality, they can assume that if they like the *Scooby-Doo* TV show, then they will most likely enjoy the game based on it."

But of course, topic is about more than the subject of the game. Topic is also about the genre of the title. During the real-time strategy craze of the late '90s, publishers could just about guarantee that a solid real-time strategy game would sell 100,000 units. On the other hand, a turn-based game needed to be marketed, promoted, and designed to perfection to crest that magical 100,000-unit mark.

If choosing a popular topic and genre is important, franchising and licensing is critical. Name recognition sells games, and when you sell a game with a popular movie tie-in, such as *Blair Witch*, *Star Trek*, or *Harry Potter*, you already have the name recognition that will sell the game.

"Absolutely, franchises sell games," states Bonnie James, former executive editor at Electric Playground. "Especially for more casual buyers or those buying for others. For instance, Mom knows that her kid loves Harry Potter. If she sees a Harry Potter game, you bet she picks it up."

But by the same token, franchises may also be built on the name recognition garnered by the early releases. It is no coincidence that Blizzard decided to design Warcraft II and Warcraft III rather than make an equally entertaining real-time strategy game on separate subjects for each one of their subsequent releases. Not only could they work in a universe with which they were familiar, but they could expand on the name recognition garnered by the previous games.

Quality

Great games don't necessarily sell well, but if the game isn't good, it probably won't sell at all. Quality is a key ingredient of any product, be it an automobile or a computer game. If you give gamers a high-quality product (a game that works the first time, every time, with a well thought-out spoken tutorial, excellent and easily understood user manual, and a top-notch strategy guide), you will convince potential buyers that they are buying a quality product—a product that won't disappoint them and gives them their $49 worth.

Marketing and Public Relations

Games must not only be well made but well promoted and well marketed. There must be buzz, good public relations, and games in the store to sell. "Development people like to think that we don't play that much of a role in a success of a game," adds Ginger. "Rather, it is the quality of the game that makes it sell. I am big on quality of game play too, but the gaming community would not know about a good game if it wasn't for PR and/or marketing. It is, after all, the press announcements, screen shots, developer diaries, interviews, advertising, POS materials, and packaging that allow the public to learn about the game and then hopefully encourages them to go to the store and purchase it."

Make no mistake, public relations and marketing is the key to selling a quality game. Discount bins are littered with well-made and critically acclaimed games that lacked the PR focus or widespread marketing needed to reach big sales.

Range of Appeal

Some niche games have sold well, but they are the exceptions. To sell well a game must have a broad range of appeal. In some ways, range of appeal overlaps topic; in other ways, it is different. Range of appeal has more to do with making a game on a subject that has a broad appeal to many gamers. "I think the game has to appeal to some part of a gamer's mind," states Dan Clarke, owner of Gaming Nexus. "The genre and topic have to be something of interest to the gamer in order for them to buy it. You are never going to make a non-sports gamer buy a football game."

3

By the same token, range of appeal considers the genre of the game—including the mixing of genres. For example, a real-time strategy game will by nature of the genre sell reasonably well, but a real-time strategy game that incorporates role playing and action elements, could, theoretically, sell very well. So range of appeal is not only about the topic but about making a game that appeals to a broad audience and, once that game is made, ensuring that it is accessible to that audience—by being easy to learn and entertaining.

Cool Factor

This is darn near intangible but oh so important. If a game is to sell, it must be cool. Whatever coolness there is, games must have it. "Novelty and accessibility sell a game," claims Jason Bell, senior vice president of creative development at Infogrames, Inc.

Nothing can create that elusive buzz as well as a game with a high cool factor. That cool factor can be that "Bullet Time" of Max Payne or the engrossing story of StarCraft, but whatever it is, games that are to sell well must have the cool factor.

The Final Topic

So there you have it—the five things that I believe make games sell. For the rest of the book, I will discuss some in depth and get opinions from editors, writers, and even some developers, and definitely from the gamers themselves. Hopefully by the time you finish reading you will have that in-depth understanding necessary to make a game that sells.

Part One

Topic—Setting the Stage

The topic can make or break a game. Choosing a hot topic or one that will soon become hot and cashing in on a popular genre, license, or franchise can mean the difference between success and failure.

Chapter 2

Game Genres

Creating a quality game that is fun to play with a sweet cool factor and solid public relations/marketing efforts will sell a game. Games will sell even quicker if they are part of a strong-selling genre. "Genres affect sales because many casual fans self-define their interests," claims Bill Mooney, a game producer at Simon & Schuster Interactive. "Casual gamers will say 'I only like first-person shooters or turn-based strategy games.' Thus, genres matter in terms of customer-created expectations and definitions. Of course, this is problematic—particularly for games that straddle genres...."

"Many consumers know beforehand that they want a strategy game or a first-person shooter," adds Randy Sluganski, founder of Just Adventure (www.justadventure.com). "Unfortunately, this predetermination also negatively affects sales of certain genres, such as adventure, as many consumers still have a narrow viewpoint of what constitutes a specific genre and are unaware that some genres, like adventure and role-playing games, have evolved to encompass key elements of other genres, and what once may not have been to their liking would now be a welcome addition to their gaming collection."

Yet this doesn't mean that designers should abandon their dream games—the games they have always desired to make, a game with innovation, fun, and imagination. "There are plenty of niche markets for all the game genres, and there is still money in them," states Raymond Lee, editor in chief at Game-Surge. "Few games make it big no matter what genre, so there are plenty of opportunities in the less developed areas."

No, designers shouldn't abandon their dreams, but some genres sell better than others. If, for example, you have an equal passion for real-time strategy and chess simulators, you will be financially rewarded by choosing to design a real-time strategy game instead of a chess simulator. "Most people I know have particular game genre preferences," continues Lee. "For example, I know plenty of first-person shooter aficionados who would never touch Warcraft III. On the other hand, there are lots of people who would blindly buy Warcraft III just because it is a real-time strategy game." Yet, before we discuss which genres are the hot sellers, let's talk about the genres and define them (just so we are on the same page, so to speak).

Figure 2-1: Warcraft III attracts legions of fans. ©2002 Blizzard Entertainment, All Rights Reserved.

Genres

Action

Action games are reflex-oriented games with an emphasis on the player's ability to shoot, move, or dodge more quickly than his enemy can. The category is broken into several sub-genres, including first-person shooters such as Unreal Tournament and Quake II, third-person action games such as the Tomb Raider series, and even horror survival games such as Resident Evil. Also included in the genre are the fighting games such as Mortal Kombat.

Figure 2-2: Unreal Tournament is an excellent action game.

9

Strategy

Strategy games are games that force a player to make decisions. Although that is the key to the genre, it is a somewhat shallow explanation. The decisions and the world in which the decisions occur must be interesting, and actual mechanics of the game must be enjoyable. There are also several sub-genres in the strategy genre.

Real-time strategy involves strategy games with an element of action. The gamer must not only make decisions but make them under time and occasionally space constraints. Examples are Blizzard's Warcraft III and Microsoft's Age of Empires series.

Another branch of the strategy genre is turn-based strategy. These games are usually more complex than their real-time strategy brethren. Gamers may take their time as they contemplate strategy and move their markers about the board. When they are done with their turn, they click a button and it's the computer's turn.

Figure 2-3: Age of Empires II

Some strategy games are also about war. Many of these are realistic simulations of the decisions and challenges that face commanders. Conversely, other strategy games have no connection to violence whatsoever. For instance, PopTop Software's Railroad Tycoon II lets players strategize while building a railroad empire. On the other hand, some games, such as Microsoft's Zoo Tycoon, blur the line between simulation and strategy. In Zoo Tycoon gamers must grow the zoo and take care of the animals and people that come to see them while making sound business decisions that will grow the beastly endeavor.

Adventure

Adventure games are the closest thing to fiction in the computer entertainment industry. A gamer works his way through a complex story line, interacting with the elements of the world in which the game designer has placed him. The emphasis in an adventure game is on the story and the player's interaction with the story. Myst is the most famous adventure game of all time and the reason this genre led sales through the '90s.

Figure 2-4: Myst, a huge seller

Role-Playing Games

Role-playing games are somewhat like adventure games. Yet in a role-playing game the emphasis is not only on the story, which may or may not be a linear story. In fact, the story may branch off into several sub-stories. In role-playing games the emphasis is on the play, developing the characters, the tactical combat between the characters, and the enemies they may meet. Interplay's Baldur's Gate series is an excellent example.

Sports

Sports games are just what they would seem to be—games about sports (whether it's FIFA Soccer 2002, John Madden Football 2003, or High Heat Baseball 2003). Normally, sports games put the gamer in the shoes of the athlete—the running back carrying the ball, the quarterback throwing the pass, the batter smashing a home run—but there is a small sub-category that has more in common with strategy than sports games. These are sport statistic

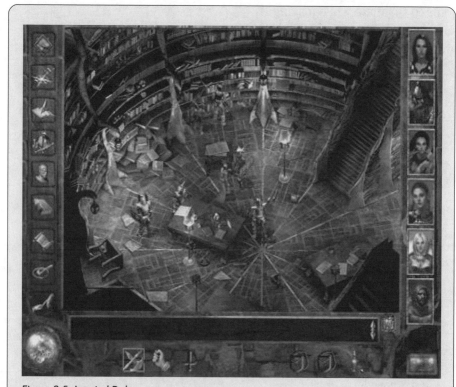

Figure 2-5: Icewind Dale

games, such as Stratomatic Baseball. These games emphasize managing the athletic team rather than fielding the ball or smashing the puck.

Simulations

Simulations are an odd hybrid of games. On one hand, these can be games that simulate the act of doing something such as flying a jet, firing a tank cannon, or driving a racecar. On the other hand, simulations can also simulate the act of building a city (as in SimCity) or managing a person's life (as in The Sims).

Puzzle or Classic Games

Last but not least are puzzle or classic games. These are games that present the gamer with a puzzle, such as Tetris, or bring a classic game, such as Monopoly or chess, to the computer screen.

Console Games

I focus on PC games in this book, but console games are similar. There are significant games/genres in the console industry that either do not exist in the PC side of things or make

Figure 2-6: The Sims lets you manage someone else's life.

much more money in their console iterations. Platform or arcade games, such as Sony's Crash Bandicoot or Nintendo's Super Mario, are great examples of a genre that does well on the living room TV but less than well (or not at all) on the computer

screen. On the flip side of the sales coin are console strategy games. With the exception of classics such as SquareSoft's Final Fantasy Tactics, strategy is a genre best left to the computer.

So, What's the Point?

So now that we have discussed what the computer game genres are, what's the point? Which of those genres sell? Do all the games in those genres sell? Well, the best-selling genre according to NPD FunWorld for the last decade of the 20th century was adventure games. Strange as it seems, they outpace all the rivals. Much of this has to do with the wildly popular Myst. The second best-selling games were strategy games, led by the real-time strategy games Warcraft and Command & Conquer. So should your company's next game be an adventure game? No, it shouldn't, not unless that is your designers' area of expertise and you have the business model that will allow you to turn a profit on a game that will sell (even if successful) much less than 100,000 units.

Real-time strategy, however, is a financial horse of an entirely different color. Although it is no longer the real-time boon days of the late '90s, real-time strategy games are more likely to sell out of the gate than

most other genres. That isn't a surprising revelation, nor are the reasons for those sales.

Companies spend millions on licenses and subsequently making games based on those licenses. They also spend buckets of money creating franchises and game series with sequels, and add-on packs continue for years. The reason is simple; buyers feel more comfortable purchasing a game with which they are familiar. If a gamer spots a title on Harry Potter and she is an avid Harry Potter fan, she can assume she will enjoy the game. Hence, she purchases it. By the same token, if a player has enjoyed the first iterations of the Lara Croft or Resident Evil series, he can assume there is a good chance he will enjoy the current iteration on the shelf.

Genres are no different. If gamers have enjoyed playing Warcraft, Command & Conquer, or Age of Empires, they can assume that they will enjoy playing other games in the real-time strategy genre. Accordingly, there is a baseline of sales in each genre—a number of units that can be expected to sell for a solid quality game. That basis of sales for real-time strategy is higher than that of most other genres. Game publishing companies believe a solid real-time strategy game will sell a minimum of 75,000 units.

And the Winner Is...

Does that mean you should develop a real-time strategy game? Yes and no. There are other genres that sell well and even sell fantastically well. Who would have foreseen the boon of sales that Deer Hunter presaged?

"Publishers should choose games that make money and are fun...," says Simon & Schuster's Mooney. "Thus, if a small-genre game is cheap enough and fun, it may be worth the risk...most of the really successful games redefined genres anyway, á là The Sims, which is hardly a normal 'simulation.'"

In addition to real-time strategy games, action games have been consistently big since their inception. Currently hot are survival/horror titles. That may not last, but a good action game that incorporates both story and thrilling action sequences will always sell.

The bottom line is this: You must design what you know, and your heart must be in what you design. We will spend most of this book taking what could be termed a "mercenary" look at game design. As I have stated many times, the point of this book is not to teach game design but to show designs that have been financially successful. As I have said before and will say again, great games do not necessarily make financially successful games. Yet at the same time, discount bins are littered with games that were designed with little heart and nothing but an eye toward whatever the currently hot genre was.

So certainly look to genre. Real-time strategy is going to sell well. Action games are going to sell well. For sure, the next big-time seller is probably not going to be a turn-based game, but then again, look at Civilization, a turn-based game that is one of the best selling games of all time. Design with soul, make an early working prototype to determine if the game is fun, and then you will have a game that will at least have a chance for success.

15

Chapter 3

Licensing and Franchising

Game sales are linked to the quality of the game, the marketing effort, the public relations effort, the cool factor, and other facets of game design that we talk about in this book. It's a well-known fact that much of a game's sales can be attributed to how much exposure the game has with media and gamers, and almost everything associated with the game determines how much exposure it receives. Leading the way are the public relations and marketing efforts; these campaigns will put the game in front of prospective buyers. Simply put, the more gamers that know about the game, the more gamers are likely to buy the game. This has been a recognized fact in the movie, book, and electronic entertainment industries for years. One of the best ways, however, to get gamers to know about your game is to use licensing and franchises.

Let's start by getting ourselves on the same page. Licenses, when used in the context of this book, are the rights bought to use well-known characters, stories, or themes from pre-existing media. For example, when I talk about the Star Trek license, I mean the right to use the characters, ships, people, and events from the Star Trek universe.

Figure 3-1: Starfleet Command III

Franchises, however, are different. Franchises use immediately recognizable characters, universes, and backgrounds in a manner similar to licenses. A franchise, however, has built its own universe, its own characters, and its own story. Hence, there are no licensing fees to be paid to Paramount Studio, Simon & Schuster, or whomever.

An example of a famous franchise is Tomb Raider, the game that put Eidos Interactive on the electronic entertainment map. A game that wildly exceeded Eidos' original expectations, Tomb Raider and its buxom star created such a splash that Ms. Croft was once named as one of *People Magazine's* 50 most influential people of the year. Yet this is a story, a background, and a character that Eidos made, instead of one they had to buy or license from a pre-existing universe. Hence the game had a higher per unit profit margin.

To License or Not To License

Licensing brings a pre-existing audience to the game. So, it would seem that licenses are always a good deal. After all, if you have a pre-existing audience, you have a pre-existing market. In other words, licenses would appear to be a marketer's dream, but such is not always the case.

Louise Castle of Westwood Studios states, "I don't believe any game or license is well served by attaching a license to the game. I think a game must be developed around the property you are licensing. Before deciding what to license, I would encourage anyone to find a reason to bring a license to a new medium like a computer. If you have no reason, the chances are that you should not use the license. The type of game should have as much to do with the license as the license has to do with the game."

Succinctly put, slapping a Star Trek license on a baseball game probably won't do any good. The game and the license must fit hand in glove. If you have an excellent real-time tactical spaceship battle engine such as Starfleet Command, then using the Star Trek engine only enhances what is already a great game. On the other hand, placing legendary home run champ Barry Bond's endorsement on your hockey game probably won't pump up the game's sales.

If you have decided to go with a license, there are several things to consider. Primary among these are the restrictions the licenser places on the development team. More than one game has been ruined by an inflexible licenser. Ensure that you understand what the restrictions are and what you can develop in the game universe before you sign on the dotted line.

Another thing to consider is the type of fan base that the license draws. If the fan base is casual and somewhat unsophisticated, an in-depth, strategy game will probably not sell well within the franchise.

Make sure you understand what type of review and sign-off privileges the licenser requires. Ensure that you understand how quickly this turnaround will be and how it will affect your deadlines. For example, NASCAR often takes weeks to review and sign off on their myriad of NASCAR-related licenses.

Discuss with the licenser their concerns and how they wish to see their product portrayed. When a major publisher was developing a critically acclaimed science-fiction role-playing game, it was originally slated to use a famous role-playing system. Accordingly, the role-playing system's designer was given sign-off rights to the game. The designer felt like this included all aspects of the game, and when he objected to the introduction video, he and the publisher were at an impasse. Don't let this happen to you.

Ascertain exactly what you are getting when you sign the contract. Do you have free license, so to speak, to use the license in subsequent games, or is this a one-time-only deal? Also, determine how much help you will have from the licenser. Will they freely provide background material? Will they provide art support? Will they contribute new art to the project? These are all critical issues that must be ironed out before you sign your licensing contract.

To Franchise or Not to Franchise

This truly is a no-brainer. If you can build a franchise, there is no downside to it. Mark Barret, a scripter and level design expert with over 20 years of experience in the industry, says, "A franchise is simply a

Figure 3-2: Jagged Alliance 2. Franchising even works with turn-based strategy games.

self-sustaining license with subsequent products feeding off the success of the original. A good franchise can be even more successful than a good license because it doesn't have to go through the risky process of being translated into a computer game from another medium. The downside of a franchise is an elevation of player expectations, which can be hard to satisfy."

Yet there can be no mistake: A franchise is a selling sweet spot. Franchises breed instant marketability, recognition, and a fan base that guarantees sales.

Look toward a franchise in every game you sell. The computer entertainment industry is ripe with examples—from action games such as Tomb Raider through simulations such as Rainbow 6 to turn-based strategy games such as Jagged Alliance. All genres support franchises; the important thing to recognize when building a franchise is to make either a character, a system, or a story (preferably all three) that catches gamers' attention and pulls them into your gaming universe. When you have done this, you have made a game that will sell.

What the Industry Says about Franchises and Licenses

You have heard my opinion on the power of franchises and licensing. Let's look at what a couple of other folks have said. Jason Bell, senior vice president of creative development at Infogrames, states, "Anything imprimatur that increases the customer's perception of value or coolness in a title will enhance sales. Cross-medium identification is usually a benefit—unless the license has been slapped on a generic product—but that product probably wouldn't succeed anyway."

Jeff Vitous, veteran freelance writer and director of partnership development at the Wargamer (www.wargamer.com), says, "Sure, official licenses are a good thing.

Familiarity with the subject makes it much easier to become involved with the game." He continues with a few words on franchises: "Branding breeds familiarity. People know what to expect with those series (in other words, franchises). It is the same basic effect as license material."

Ben Smith, former director of marketing for CDV Software, chimes in, "Yes, licenses definitely increase sales if they are marketed properly. However, the market is fussy. What is trendy one day can be gone the next. So you best be sure you are not holding a license that has gone out of style or may do more harm for the title than good. In addition, some licenses are just played out (e.g., there have been so many bad Star Trek games that putting a Star Trek label on it does not close the deal anymore)."

Dan Clarke, owner of Gaming Nexus, states, "I think franchises continue a buzz and generate additional sales. I think that many people buy the franchise game based on the original game looking to recreate some of the magic that brought the people to the game in the first place."

The Final License

Licenses, when appropriate to the game and not too expensive, can be a good thing. Though hard to afford for a small-time developer, there are less well-known licenses available that can be built into enormous game sales. Be creative, look around, go to the movies, look at what could be hot in a year or two, and think about how it could help the game you are working on. Remember, don't slap a license on a game but rather build a game into a license. Franchises, as I have said before, are the sweet spot in software sales. Look not to build one game, but look to build a franchise. Look for ways to attach the gamer to your characters, story, and universe and, once attached, build that universe.

Topic—Your Gaming World, Cool or Not

When was the last time you played Race the Nags? How about Grand Prix Manager? Have you heard of either of them? Both were pretty good games but covered obscure topics. On the other hand, Sum of All Fears and Hidden & Dangerous were also *just* pretty good games, but covered two very popular topics—one was associated with a best-selling book and the other took place during World War II. Accordingly, most everyone has heard of them, and they sold fairly well.

Figure 4-1: Hidden & Dangerous

All things being equal, games on popular topics will sell better than games on less-than-popular topics. In fact, over 50 percent of the 100+ gamers who took the *Games That Sell!* survey stated that topic was a primary reason behind their purchase of a game.

"Topic is everything," says Vince Savelli, a longtime, hard-core gamer. "I'm a history buff, and I'm keenly interested in World War II. I'll buy any half-decent game on the subject. It doesn't matter if it's real-time strategy, turn-based strategy, or first-person shooter. If it's in the Second World War, I'm all over it."

If one-half of the gamers out there buy because of topic, that's a strong incentive to design a game with a popular topic. Yeah, topic is important. It almost goes without saying, nevertheless, that every year "on-topic" games are released that make reviewers write, "What the hell were they thinking when they made this?"

Thinking with Your Heart

In the movie *The Land Before Time*, Littlefoot's mother said, "Some things you see with your eyes. Some things you see with your heart." The same can be said for game design and development. Gaming journalists can usually see right through a heartless design, a game designed to "fill a slot," something put together to take advantage of the latest gaming fad. Such games usually lack the attention to detail present in labors of love. Believe me, after writing about games for 11 years, I know that *every* game's goal is to make money. There is no sin in that, but games designed with passion stand apart from those that are not.

You can't be passionate about a topic that leaves you cold. Of course, therein lays the rub. Developers/ publishers want their games to sell well and the topic helps to sell games, but developers develop and design better games when working on a topic that interests them.

The solution is to find common ground, a compromise so to speak. In the gaming world of swords, bows, and arrows, fantasy games usually sell better than historical ones (Medieval: Total War *excepted*). If medieval war is a designer's passion, perhaps he could slightly shift that passion to a medieval fantasy setting and not only create a game that he is crazy about but also a game that will sell well enough to finance future projects.

For example, simulating modern (i.e., very recent) conflict has always fascinated me. The color and challenge (at least in the gaming world) of small 100- to 200-man (and

Figure 4-2: Dungeon Siege—a medieval game in a fantasy setting

-woman) battles interested me. My recently released tactical gaming system, Mark H. Walker's Lock 'n Load, simulates those small battles, but when I considered working the game into an ultra-modern setting, such as Desert Storm, market analysis threw some pretty discouraging sales projections on my desk. I wanted to keep Lock 'n Load modern, but it looked like my target audience—wargamers—wanted a conflict with a bit more history behind it. Hmmm… I wanted modern, but my audience wanted historical.

I could have designed Lock 'n Load for Germany's eastern front in the Second World War—a favorite with wargamers, but those battles currently do nothing for me. Finally, I hit on a compromise—Vietnam, a war that holds significant historical interest in the United States but one that has many of the features of modern conflict that grab my attention. It was a good compromise, and I was able to throw myself into the game.

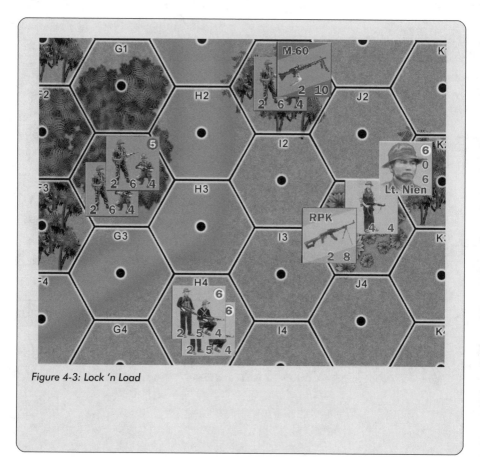

Figure 4-3: Lock 'n Load

Tradition Says

Gaming tradition says that you'll do better if you stick to specific topics in specific genres. Certainly there have been exceptions. Computer role-playing games have long sold well when the era/topic is the age—however it is modified—of swords and sorcery, yet Interplay's Fallout and several iterations of the Final Fantasy series have sold very well when set in a science-fiction universe. Nevertheless, the following topics have historically sold better than other topics within the same genre:

- Role-playing games—medieval swords and sorcery

- First-person shooters—science fiction universe (Medal of Honor and Wolfenstein are exceptions)

- First-person, squad-based, tactical shooters (Ghost Recon, etc.)—modern era

- Real-time strategy—science fiction (Warcraft series is a notable exception.)
- Turn-based strategy—grand strategic (Civilization)
- Turn-based war—World War II
- Flight simulation—World War II or present day
- Racing simulation—NASCAR in the United Sates, Formula One anywhere else
- Platform game—cute animal (You have to have a cute animal.)
- Sports—baseball, football, basketball, soccer (Stay away from horse racing.)

Find the Golden Nugget

Unfortunately, developers cannot always switch a medieval passion for a fantasy setting or a love of current era military operations for Vietnam. In such cases, developers can motivate themselves with a golden nugget. Let me explain. Several years ago I was discussing game design with a designer at a smaller design house who was working on a game that he wasn't completely into. He was, however, completely immersed in his work, and the design released to rave reviews and solid sales. I asked him how he stayed motivated. He smiled and said, "I've found a golden nugget."

He went on to explain that the golden nugget was something, anything within the design that he could be passionate about. He then used that passion to fuel his fires and keep focus. It's not a bad idea—both in game design and in life at large.

Insiders Talk

What would a chapter on topic be without a couple of quips from folks inside the industry?

Mario Kroll
Vice President of U.S. Marketing and Business Development, The Wargamer Network
I think a game's topic is a huge factor in game sales. It's kind of like the saying, "Blondes have more fun." Packaging is not everything, but good packaging and a good theme can help, while the lack thereof certainly can hurt. The appropriate theme can hugely influence impulse purchases and sales made in the retail environment, where buyers can only judge a game by the packaging and the impact that the underlying theme has. Look at games like Harry Potter. A good movie or book tie-in with a decent

game can make all the difference. Likewise, if particular topics are "hot" for external factors or current events, there is a significantly increased interest in all things involving those topics, including games. While this doesn't necessarily impact longevity of a game, a good theme or topic can certainly help get games sold well initially, until players have a chance to discover that the game under the theme may not be so interesting or well made. Conversely, games that choose obtuse or other topics that are off the beaten path and seem uninteresting are likely to have a tough sell and must rely on the solidity of the gaming

experience and subsequent word of mouth to sell more copies.

Bill Mooney
Producer, Simon & Schuster
Topicality can be very important, particularly with smaller budgets and "niche" markets. Value software on a PC is a perfect example.

Jonah Falcon
Entrepreneur, United Gamers Online
[Topic influences gamers' purchases] to an extent. I think topic doesn't have as much weight as brand name because pre-sale hype and press and box graphic art are more important.

Cool Factor

Bullet Time! Enough said. Those two words have become so closely linked with Max Payne as to almost be synonymous with the name. Bullet Time is perhaps the most prominent cool factor of the last few years, but there have been others:

- Age of Empires realism/real-time strategy mix
- StarCraft's story
- Rainbow 6's realistic one-shot-one-kill damage model
- The ambience and unexpected booby traps in Vietcong
- The photorealistic graphics in NASCAR Racing 4

This is just to name a few. Usually when we reminisce about a game, the thing we recall most vividly is the cool factor. In a world of look-alike, play-alike games, the breakout factor can often be that cool factor that wows the gamers.

"There's no doubt that the elusive cool factor is often what captures gamers' imagination, influences reviewers, and creates buzz," claims Bart Farkas, former magazine editor and author of more than 50 computer gaming books.

As we know, both buzz and positive game reviews help generate sales. It is interesting, however, that

Max Payne (tm) coming from 3D Realms and Remedy Entertainment. www.maxpayne.com

Figure 4-4: Max Payne's Bullet Time, the ultimate cool factor

only 10 percent of the gamers who took the *Games That Sell!* survey cited cool factor as a reason for buying games. There are mitigating circumstances. Many of the respondents were strategy gamers, and these people have traditionally been less influenced by cool factors than other gamers.

Another explanation is that although cool factor is a contributing reason that gamers buy games, it is not the primary reason. In other words, a game with a neat cool factor won't make a dyed-in-the-wool turn-based wargamer give up The Operational Art of War for Crash Bandicoot; it will influence a platformoholic to buy Crash Bandicoot over Frogger.

"Above all else the cool factor creates buzz," says George Jones, former editor of *Computer Gaming World*. And buzz is one of those semi-intangibles that sets one game apart from another.

"You can't create a cool factor," a designer once told me. She went on to explain that the inspiration for something really cool within the game comes from outside of the game. To tell the truth, it often comes from outside of the industry. Such is the case with Bullet Time, which owes its heritage to the gunplay we have witnessed in hundreds of action movies during our lives.

So the trick to a developer finding a cool factor is staying focused on the game but also experiencing life and pondering how she could put the cool things she sees into the game.

The Final Topic

So, topic and cool factors are important to any game that is going to sell. That much is obvious. What isn't so obvious is how to choose a topic that sells well and motivates the design team and how to pluck that elusive cool factor from the world around us and throw it into the game.

Part Two

Quality

Quality is a game's foundation. As I point out in this
book, it isn't necessary to make a great game in
order to sell it. It is, however, necessary to make a
quality game. This part discusses the facets of a quality game and examines what editors and gamers are
looking for.

Chapter 5

Ambience

L ong a buzzword in the entertainment industry, *immersion* is what producers, product managers, and public relations agents dream of. It doesn't take a nuclear scientist to understand that an immersed gamer is a happy gamer. Happy gamers buy more games from the companies that made them happy.

Figure 5-1: *Warcraft III completely immerses the gamer; hence, it sells well.*
©2002 Blizzard Entertainment, All Rights Reserved.

In fact, it can be said that much of this book is no more than a discussion about how to immerse the gamer, and ambience is an important part of immersion. In this book's connotation, ambience is a holistic term. It is a sum of the visual, aural, and—to a lesser extent—touch stimuli that involves a gamer in an environment.

As I alluded to above, there are two parts—three if you count touch stimuli—of a game's ambience. The first are the game's graphics or visuals. These can be further subdivided into in-game graphics and full motion video (FMV) or full motion animation (FMA). Second are the aural effects, which can further be reduced to music, voice acting, and sound effects of the game. Finally there is the physical stimuli such as force feedback steering wheels and vibrating gamepads, etc. Each side of this ambience triangle has an effect on the game's ambience, so let's take a moment to look at each and how they impact your game.

Graphics

A game's visuals or graphics are an integral part of its message and the ambience that it creates. Even more importantly, they are the most important selling feature of the game. Dave Kosak, the creative director at GameSpy (www.gamespy.com), says, "Most people have very little to judge a game by when they go out to make the purchase, and that is where graphics come in. Those beautiful screen shots laid out in magazines or posted to the web, the game play shots on the back of the box, the brief glimpse gamers get of a game running on a TV screen above the store—often that is where a person's first and last impression of a game originates. That is why graphics have always been a selling point and will continue to be for years to come. In short, graphics have a great deal to do with a title's initial sales, although long-term, sustained sales (such as with the PC game The Sims, for example) are usually dependent on the game play underneath."

Martin Turewicz, designer, writer, business manager, and all-around handyman at Battlefront.com, agrees. "Good graphics make it easier to market and successfully sell a game (at least when you do so through the traditional retail channels). No questions about it. Visuals are a strong marketing tool, so they're always a plus. This is true for pretty much any game and genre, but obviously it's more important for some (like, say, sports games) and less for others (like, ahem, Go). Visuals are also more important for retail distribution because games move so fast off the shelf that there is very little time for people to actually try out a game or demo and have a game 'grow' on them before retailers issue RMAs (return merchandise authorization) to the distributor. For us in Internet sales, the situation is much better."

Bonnie James, editor at Electric Playground, a web site owned and operated by veteran soundman Tommy Tallarico, echoes both sentiments. "Graphics have become more important to games over the last several years. While it is still possible to have a great game with less than stellar graphics, most companies spend significant time working on the 'aesthetics' of their game.

"I do think there is a correlation between good graphics and good sales. Companies use screen shots and video clips to hype games long before they hit the shelves, so that's what consumers have to base their desire for a game on."

Finally, Randy Sluganski, the owner of Just Adventure, the Internet's largest gaming site devoted to adventure games, adds,

"For the mainstream buying public, graphics are very important and greatly influence sales but the hard-core gamers, especially when talking about PC games, know that graphics are secondary to a good story and, more importantly, a fun game."

There can be no doubt that graphics are a valuable marketing tool. Internet sites receive million of hits a month, most of them focused on the screen shot pages of upcoming games. Gamers eagerly tear open the latest copy of *Computer Gaming World* and flip to the screen shots of the featured preview game. Most players can tell what type of game and how it plays by just the screen shots… and that's a great way to catch an audience.

Graphics are a great marketing tool but only if the graphics are done right. To do it right artists agree that the graphics must be consistent; there must be a common thread that runs through the entire game. If the game is macabre, you can't have a level that is dominated by sunlit gardens… at least not normally.

Figure 5-2: Clive Barker's Undying wouldn't work if the scenes were bright and well lit.

Artists also agree that early in the game's development, the design teams need to decide what style they want and stick with it. For example, is the game going to be 3D or 2D? 3D games can be beautiful, allow the gamer to roam the world and look at it from multiple perspectives, and infuse the world with life. That, however, doesn't mean that 3D games are a graphic cure-all. Although it is only viewable from one direction, 2D games frequently have a higher degree of detail. Games such as Eidos' Commandos 2, Infogrames' Desperado, and Strategy First's Robin Hood incorporate highly detailed 2D environments to bring their world to life.

Figure 5-3: Strategy First's Robin Hood uses lush 2D environments to bring the game to life.

In-game graphics are not the only visuals that design teams must concern themselves with. Most games use cut-scenes or some form of video between missions or at the beginning of the game to introduce and move the story along. Scenes that are well done—such as SquareSoft's Final Fantasy series or the introduction to MechWarrior 2 —can place the gamer in the game world and create an ambience that he or she enjoys.

Audio

Yet graphics are only one part of the ambience puzzle. Despite their ability to sell games and convey a wealth of information about the game in one picture, graphics may not be the most important sensory element in the game. A study by the Massachusetts Institute of Technology provides interesting insight about the impact of sound in computer games. Briefly put, the MIT media lab showed two groups two video clips (one with bad audio content and one with really great audio content). The overwhelming feedback received indicated the clip with the better audio track looked better to the subjects. Obviously, this seems to imply the better sound in a game, the better looking it will appear to be.

Again, Martin Turewicz from Battlefront.com speaks. "When gauging the impact of the different ambionic effects on gaming from my personal experience, I'd say—and this might be a surprise to some—it's the sound first. Simple test—horror game. Imagine a black monitor and some scary, creepy voice talking to you. Great ambience—no graphics needed. Another example is Medal of Honor: Allied Assault (Electronic Arts). The game is touted as [being] so full of ambience and atmosphere. Well, the graphics ain't all that spectacular, at least not so much ahead of other FPS [first-person shooters]

games nowadays and possibly even behind Castle Wolfenstein 3D. But it's the sound that enhances this experience. Take two games with the same graphics/visuals but one has better (i.e., more real, more rich) sound—this one will be the winner."

Sound engineers and developers both agree that the music must match the mood. If the game's mood is somber, slow ominous music is the order of the day. When the action speeds up, so must the music. On the other hand, when there is a lull in the game, the music should be used to show that lull and ease the gamer's tension.

But of course, aural ambience is about more than just music. There are also sound effects, which must closely model the real event that they are depicting in addition to blending with the graphics and music to enhance the feel of the game.

Voice acting is another key part of any game. Dave Kosak says, "When it comes to voice acting, it can only be as good as the script of a game, so it starts there. Good voice acting can somewhat help create the atmosphere for a game; really what's more important is to stay away from *bad* voice acting, which destroys the player's sense of immersion faster than anything else. Games with no voice acting can sometimes be the most immersive of all. For instance, the developers of the PC game

Half-Life chose not to have the main character speak at all. Instead of breaking up the action with 'cutscenes,' they allowed the action to play out in front of the character. Players could stop and listen or walk away as they saw fit. Not many games have the guts to take this approach, but it does wonders for immersion and flow!"

Kosak continues, "Music and sound effects are always underrated when compared to graphics, when in fact these two can completely throw a gamer into another world when done correctly. More resources devoted to deep, rich, well-integrated sounds pay rich dividends when it comes to the overall game experience."

Bonnie James agrees. "Voice acting and music combine to enhance the ambience of a game. Poor voice work can quickly rip you out of a game, but realistic voices go a long way toward helping you suspend your disbelief and become drawn into the story that you are playing. A lot of times you don't even notice the music in a game, but if it is done well it can manipulate your emotions and create tension in all the right places."

Physical Stimuli

Last, but certainly not least, in the triangle of ambience is physical stimuli. Although in their infancy in both computer and video games, these stimuli can significantly enhance the gamer's immersion.

These include vibrating controllers, force feedback steering wheels, and not much else. These are only the tip of the iceberg, and many more are sure to come. When properly employed they will transmit the thump of the rocket launcher that the player is carrying or shudder his arms when his stock car slams Daytona's wall.

The Last Ambience

Nevertheless, whether the ambience is provided by force feedback steering wheels, voice acting, or lush graphics, it is an important part of constructing a great game. A game that will sell.

Chapter 6

Story

Everyone loves a good story. Tom Clancy earns millions, and so do Dean Koontz and George Lucas. It does not matter if the story is in print or film; people love to jeer bad guys and cheer for the good guys. They love to see the underdog win and good triumph over evil. Computer games are no different; story creates immersion, and immersion creates fun, and games are all about fun. If your game creates immersion, whether through story, quality game play, graphics, or a combination of all of the above, you have created a game that will sell.

In this chapter I take a look at the importance of story and how it makes the game better, which in turn makes the game sell. I'm a writer, so you might think that I am naturally inclined to do some chest thumping here. Perhaps you'll be surprised. A good story isn't the critical piece of most games' puzzle, and rarely will story alone sell a game. It is, however, an important ingredient. I've talked with some writers in preparing this chapter, and we get their opinion as we move along. So, let's get on with it.

Who Needs Story?

That's a good question. Does every game need an epic story? Should every development team hire a full-time writer for 18 months (assuming a game can be completed that quickly)? The answer is no. Some genres are more conducive to story than others, and it almost goes without saying (but I'm going to say it anyway) that games such as puzzle games, racing games, or arcade games need no story. By the same token, massively multiplayer online role-playing games require little in the way of a linear plot, but need massive (pun intended) amounts of back story to set up the universe in which the game exists.

No, all games don't require a story, but story will enhance most games. The games that have a strong story will most often sell better than those that don't.

There are two genres that live and die by the story: adventure games and role-playing games. In both of these genres a good story—although not *the* most important element of the game—lends a crucial degree of immersion to the gaming experience. However, in the electronic entertainment industry of today, there is a great deal of bleed over between the genres. As part of that bleed over, there are many first-person shooters, third-person action games, and real-time (and even turn-based) strategy games that have strong adventure or role-playing elements. Accordingly, story can also be important in any of these genres. For

Figure 6-1: Half-Life has a strong story element.

example, Blizzard's real-time strategy opus, StarCraft, had an excellent story, as did Valve's first-person shooter, Half-Life.

In the words of Neal Hallford, who wrote the story for Gas Powered Games' Dungeon Siege, "In an entirely black and white analysis, adventure gamers and traditional role-playing gamers are the people who tend to have the greatest demand for story. Simulation, action, and real-time strategy players tend to be attracted to story-lite or story-free design structures."

Mark Barrett, an industry veteran who has written stories and designed missions for numerous games including Fighter Squadron: The Screamin' Demons Over Europe, says, "The most story-centric genre has always been adventure games, many of which derived a great deal of their entertainment value from story. In the past decade or so many adventure game features, including strong story, character, and puzzle elements, have been added to a number of other genres, including role-playing games, first-person shooters, and third-person action-adventures."

So, we've determined that role-playing games and adventure games are the genres that most rely on story, but their first-person action, third-person action, and real-time strategy progeny can also benefit from clever storytelling.

But what is the difference between writing a computer game story and other fiction? Barrett again chimes in. "The primary difference between computer games and other fictional entertainment is that fictional works in other mediums need make no allowance for player input of any kind. Movies, books, TV, and the vast majority of theatrical plays are entirely predetermined expressions of authorial craft. Interactive entertainment, on the other hand, expressly involves the audience (the player) making choices which determine (or appear to determine) outcomes."

Hallford agrees with the assessment. "To understand the difference, you need to understand the difference between puzzles and problems. In a puzzle, there is only one 'real' answer. Every time that you put that jigsaw puzzle together, it's always going to create the same picture because that is the way that those pieces are designed... To only 'fit' one way... Novels follow the same principle. Novels are all about the 'picture' that the creator holds, and everything in the book is going to be designed in such a way that piece A always fits into piece B... Games— or at least good games—are about solving problems. [Game designers/writers] have to be more creative and allow for divergent tastes of different kinds of players. Let's say that the designer puts a quest in front of a player to rescue a spy from a maximum security prison… One kind of player is going to want to blast their way in, which means they are going to need enough weaponry and ammunition to fight their way into (and back out of) the prison. Another player might want to find a non-violent way inside instead. They might prefer to bribe guards, or find passwords, or have an ability to scale sheer walls."

What makes plotting and scripting for games even more difficult is that a set of rules has yet to be established for what creates a successful plot. According to Mark Barrett, it's like hitting a moving target.

"Unlike screenplays, or even novels, there are few hard-and-fast rules about either the formatting or formulation of computer game narratives. Invariably the product's game play,

genre, budget—even its platform—will determine in large part which narrative efforts can be made from a design and technical point of view. These constraints will in turn go far in determining the format and structure of the document or documents that need to be created.

"For example, where the script for an adventure game could easily come in at well over 250 pages and include multiple plot branches and dialogue trees, the cut-scenes between missions in a first-person shooter might only encompass 50 pages of non-branching scenes and dialogue. In games with little narrative content, such as some strategy games, the text or dialogue accompanying mission briefings might fit on a few pages, particularly if the product is aimed at the console market."

Why Not?

If the folks in the know agree that a story can enhance the sales of games, why doesn't every game have a great story? There are several reasons, not the least of which is the economic reality of the gaming market. Design firms only have so much money—money that must be doled out for artists, coders, marketers, public relations personnel, etc. As Hallford says, "There generally speaking isn't enough work to keep a writer on a project busy for two

years, so it's cheaper and easier to have someone already on staff handle the writing. In the instances where professional, full-time writers are hired, they don't tend to get paid what they would get paid working outside of the industry. So, the caliber of writers you get stepping up to the plate isn't as high as you'd like. As long as Hollywood is paying more, why write for the computer gaming industry?"

Barrett seems to agree, citing four reasons that professional writers are not always used to pen computer and video game scripts/stories. Barrett says that economic realities (there isn't enough money for writers), development realities (there isn't enough work for writers), production realities (short-notice changes in a game's ship date can make working with outside writers difficult), and personal vanities (designers don't want anyone to mess with their vision of the game) are the reasons that development firms shy away from hiring professional writers.

But the bottom line is that a strong story will help sell the games of the future.

Neal Hallford states, "Game makers want to make games that sell more copies. Game consumers want high-quality products that compete with television and motion pictures. In order to get to that place, the gaming companies will ultimately have to start hiring ace writers with the same zeal that they now hire ace programmers and ace artists. If they don't, their competitors ultimately will, and the market will go with whatever company is cranking out the best stuff."

Making the Story

We've discussed the impact of story on games. Let's takes a couple of pages to discuss how to make a story that will impact your game. Great stories don't just happen; they are the intersection of planning and talent. Often, for every word that makes it into a game there will be ten others that remain on the writer's hard drive. These other words are character descriptions, the game-world history, or just words that didn't work. Quality story creation is a demanding and intricate task, a task that would take a book to teach. Instead, let's hit the high points.

Write It Down

Before you begin with a script, you develop the world. World creation is a key point in developing your story. Not only must you be able to script the words the characters will speak to move your game along, but you must understand the character's motivation in speaking. That understanding comes from not only creating a detailed and believable world in which the characters live but detailed and believable characters as well.

Figure 6-2: Dungeon Siege included an excellent story with buckets of character detail.

What does your world look like? What are the weather patterns? What is the social structure and history? Think through each of your characters. What are their motivations, fears, and desires? How old are they, and what are their hobbies? The deeper you delve into a character's personality, the more real the character will feel to your audience.

Write it down! Above all else, write it down. You need to document your world's history and your character's desires so that you may refer to them later and share your work.

Conflict

After you have created a believable world and inhabited that world with breathing characters, you need to set the plot in motion. Understand that epic tales of long quests do not make a story. Listen to me when I say that neither do twists and turns intrigue a gamer. Every story must have one element and one only, and upon that element the story is built. That element is conflict—conflict between the protagonist and antagonist, the protagonist and his or her lover, the protagonist and the boss monster, or whatever. Establish characters the gamer may relate to and then place them in conflict with each other, and the story will pull the players inside the game.

The Right Tool for the Job

Does all this character building and conflicting sound difficult? It is.

"It's a near-universal notion that writers are non-technical," says Neal Hallford. "Folks think that just about anybody who can string a sentence together can do the job properly. I get people all the time who come up to me and say, 'Hey, I've got this great idea for a story,' and then proceed to rattle off whatever claptrap they came up with in the shower that morning."

Writing well is difficult work. If someone on your team has experience, you'll be a step ahead of the crowd. If not, consider hiring a writer. There are listings of qualified writers at the National Writer's Union's web site (www.nwu.org), or ask a fellow developer. Placing a writer on staff is the best way to guarantee quality. The writer will work closely with your team and that interaction will enhance the story. Unfortunately, your budget may not support another full-timer. In that case, look to the freelance writer community. Freelance writers may often be found by posting on game site bulletin boards, through http://www.Gamasutra.com and http://www.gamedev.net, or through writing sites such as http://www.writeronline.us.

The Final Word

Story alone may not sell your game. In fact, the value of story is genre dependent. Adventure and role-playing games benefit the most from a well-crafted story. Story alone will not sell your game, but an intriguing story will enhance sales, and that, after all, is what we hope to do.

Chapter 7

Documentation and Strategy Guides

U ser manuals and strategy guides are an important aspect of any game's success. As I have said throughout this book, a game must not only make the player feel good about the game but feel good about themselves as well. A frustrating experience, especially a frustrating experience that stems from a lack of understanding of how the game is to function or an inability to solve a specific puzzle, can turn off a gamer. A turned-off gamer stops playing the game, and even worse, he tells other gamers about his bad experience, which reduces the game's future sales. Add these things together and you have created a negative buzz about your game that can seriously hinder sales.

"A well-written strategy guide can add to the luster and enjoyment of a great game," claims Bart Farkas, noted strategy guide writer and author of the official Warcraft III strategy guide. "It can even add to the game's sales (especially when they are bundled for sale together)."

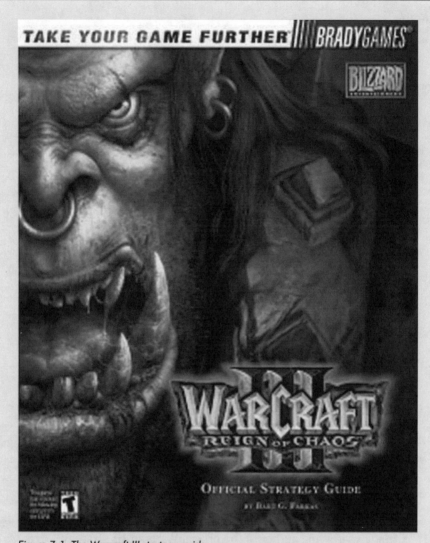

Figure 7-1: The Warcraft III strategy guide

Additionally, an excellent user manual can enhance a gamer's experience. A strategy guide that is both well written and informative can excite the gamer, inducing him to continue playing. That is why I have devoted an entire chapter to both user manuals and strategy guides in this book. So without further ado, let's get started.

User Manuals

User manuals should explain how to play the game. No one would debate that fact, yet few user manuals adequately do their job. There are numerous problems that keep user manuals from doing their job. Poor writing is foremost, but lack of focus and lack of space are two other prominent problems.

The Writer

As I said elsewhere in this book, writers are an important part of a successful game. You need a good writer to write the game's story. You need a good writer to write the in-game dialogue. You also, however, need a good writer to write the user manual. Too often the user manual writing is left to whomever on the development or production staff has a bit of extra time. Although these people may be familiar with the game, they may not be familiar with how to convey meaning to a reader with the minimum amount of verbiage. In other words, they may not be able to write well.

Obviously, you wouldn't ask an underutilized programmer to do art for the game, nor would you ask a sound technician to program the game's AI on his weekend off. Neither should you ask these people to write the user manual. Writing is a skill, a skill that must be learned and practiced through years of hard

work. Simply put, a successful user manual must be well written.

It takes more, however, than hiring a writer and telling him (or her) to "get to it" to create a quality user manual. The writer must have access to key personnel on the production or developmental staff. Who the key personnel are will change from company to company. But whoever it is must be available. The writer needs questions answered and guidance in order to write a quality user manual.

Guidance is an important concept, for it is an oft-overlooked piece of the user manual. The game's producer should decide what information and style is important to be in the user manual and convey both of these visions to the writer. Rarely is a production team given sufficient space to have everything they would like to have documented about their game in their user manual. This is especially true with smaller game boxes and escalating publishing costs. It is hard for a developer to convince the game publisher to fund a thick manual.

Hence, the producer must decide what is key to the game and convey that to the writer. If the game has complex interrelated strategies (for example, the production strategies in Stronghold or the research and development strategies in Civilization III), the producer must make sure that the writer understands that these strategies must be clearly explained to the gamer. Don't skimp on important game elements and then fill in the manual with history or back story.

Always important is the interface. Gamers want to know what each button does and how the different functions within the game interact. If the game includes unique components—whether they are warriors, weapons, buildings, or units of monetary exchange—explain those components to the gamer.

Once the manual is written, make sure the manual is tested as if it were a piece of software. All too often the producer, even a diligent producer, will read through the draft manual and then send it off to the printer. That's good, but it isn't good enough. The person who needs to take a look at the manual is the person who has never seen the game. This newbie reads through the manual, attempts to play the game, and then writes down the questions that spring to his mind. Those are the questions that need to be answered in the manual because those are the questions that the typical gamer is going to have as he plays the game.

The Strategy Guide

The strategy guide business began in the early '90s and peaked the last half of the decade. Although not as strong as it once was, strategy guides are still a multi-million dollar business, one that not only can enhance the gamer's enjoyment of your game, but also can enhance your game's image.

"The size and scope of some [computer and video] games is so vast that in some cases hundreds of hours are required to complete the mammoth tasks they put before the gamer," states Farkas. "In the last decade it has become clear that many games can benefit from having a separate strategy guide that can enable the gamer to get past particularly difficult portions of the game with ease. These guides also usually contain background information and details that cannot be found anywhere else, thus adding to the gaming experience."

Gamers have come to expect strategy guides to accompany important releases. If a publisher's game doesn't have a strategy guide, the game comes across looking like a grade B title. Grade B titles on store shelves crammed with "triple-A" games are going to come out on the short end of the selling stick.

Strategy guides are also a means to advertise your game; not only is your game promoted through the typical public relations channels associated with the game, but the strategy guide company also, in advertising their strategy guide, advertises your game.

So, you understand the importance of the strategy guide, but how do you ensure that your game gets the best strategy guide? First, be sure you get a good strategy guide writer. Once your game publisher has signed with a strategy guide publishing firm such as Brady Games or Prima, make sure the writer assigned to your project is experienced and skilled.

The game's product manager may ask the strategy guide company for the name of the author. Take a minute to look up the author on the Internet. See the other strategy guides he has written. Go to Amazon.com and see how those strategy guides have been reviewed.

Another way to check a writer's credentials is to check with game publishers who have worked with him or her. Was he easy to work with? Was he professional? Does he have experience in the field? If your game is a real-time strategy game, you want a writer who has a history of writing real-time strategy guides or reviewing real-time strategy games. Bottom line: If you are not satisfied with the writer assigned by the strategy guide publisher, request that the publisher assign a new author.

Once you are satisfied with the author, make sure that you support him. Too many game publishers look at the strategy guide as an afterthought rather than the marketing tool/game-enhancement device that it actually is. Answer the writer's questions quickly. The key to answering them quickly is to provide a liaison that knows the game. Frequently, a strategy guide author's liaison is the product manager—a person who only has cursory knowledge of the game. Ideally, the liaison would be the game's QA lead or somebody else with a solid knowledge of the game. These people can answer minor questions quickly with little impact on their time.

Once the strategy guide is written, take a minute to look at it. Demand that it is done right. All the strategy guide publishers I have worked with want a quality product.

> **Note:**
>
> The reviewers on Amazon.com are not professionals. These reviews are written by amateurs who can be planted by other strategy guide companies, people who enjoy digging at authors, or people who are not qualified to write the reviews. Hence, take Amazon.com reviews with a grain of salt.

Nevertheless, it takes time to make quality, and time is not a strategy guide publisher's friend. To maximize their profits, a strategy guide publisher must be "day and date" with the game. In other words, they must have the strategy guide on the shelves the day that the game is on the shelves. Accordingly, strategy guide publishers are forced to choose speed over perfection.

It is the game publisher's responsibility to make sure that the game's strategy guide is perfect. Assign someone who knows the game to go through the strategy guide with a fine-tooth comb. Have two or three people on the team go through it. Correct things that are wrong. Make suggestions for things you would like to see put in the guide. Supply the information to the strategy guide publisher to make sure the process of revision is easy. Do your revision quickly; that way, the strategy guide publisher can get their guide out on time.

The Last Manual

In the final analysis, if you take time with both the user manual and strategy guide, it will enhance the sale of your game. Doing so increases the user's enjoyment of your game; when users enjoy a game, they tell other users who in turn buy the game, creating the buzz that is so important for games that sale.

Additionally, strategy guides and well-done user manuals give the game an aura of quality. Quality games have strong user manuals. Quality games have quality strategy guides. You want your game associated with quality because quality games are games that sell.

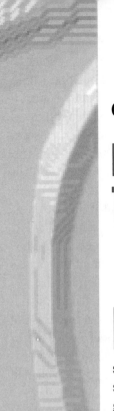

Chapter 8

Playing the Game— The Fun Factor

P eople play games for a variety of reasons. Some claim that simulations teach them, others say that strategy games stretch their minds, and still other role-players claim that they enjoy the story. Whatever the reason people say they play games, you can be sure that a significant reason is *fun*. People play games because they are fun. Although things like well-written user manuals and drop-jaw graphics contribute to gamers' enjoyment, what makes or breaks the fun is the play within the game. If the act of playing isn't fun, no one is going to do it.

Although everyone knows fun when they see it, it's a tough term to define. So I thought I'd ask professionals within the industry to help nail it down, but first let's do a little nailing ourselves.

When Is Fun, Fun?

What makes fun, fun? Ask a hundred gamers and you'll get—if not a hundred—at least quite a few different answers. But in my research, I found that there are two things that all gamers seem to agree on: challenge and immersion.

No one likes a game that is either too easy or too hard. A game that is too easy will bore most people, and one that is too hard will frustrate them. Either way, they'll quit playing. But a game that hits the sweet spot between easy and hard is going to get some serious playtime. I'll never forget playing the first boss mission in MissionForce: CyberStorm or the climactic battle in Parasite Eve. Both were thrilling because while they were challenging, they were also eventually beatable.

Games that are too hard have often fallen victim to their own play testers—men and women who spend months with the game and master every nuance. To the play testers *everything* has become easy, so their feedback is often inaccurate, and they claim that a mission is easy when in fact it would be quite a challenge for the average gamer. In a similar manner, games that are too easy show a lack of vision, a failure to understand and appreciate the audience. One of the best ways to balance a game is blind play testing at the end of the development cycle. This places a fresh group of play testers in front of the game and lets them decide what is wrong and what is right.

No one likes to take out the garbage, cut the grass, or sweep the garage. These are the mundane chores we must do to survive. We want a game that takes us away from all that—a game that creates a fantastic world and then immerses us in it. Creating immersion, however, is easier said than done. To immerse, a game must make the gamer believe he is inside the game's environment.

To do this, the game must be exciting, believable, and realistic.

Excitement may be generated through action, challenge, or association with the character—or all three and more. Believable games are true to themselves and, even more importantly, play out well-written stories. For example, a radical twist in plot that was not foreshadowed will jerk the gamer out of the game's reality and throw him back in his. Realistic games are, well... realistic. They are not realistic in the sense of adhering to our laws of reality but rather remaining true to the laws of reality that the game has established. Above all else, an immersive game doesn't remind the gamer that she is playing a game by routinely crashing.

Those are my thoughts on the matter. Let's hear what some gaming insiders have to say.

Steve Bauman
Executive Editor of *Computer Games* **Magazine**
Fun is kind of like pornography: You know it when you see it (or in the case of games, when you're playing). Trying to articulate "fun factor" is difficult, but it generally results from doing something interesting and seeing and/or receiving an interesting result. It's about the mechanics of play (i.e., "what you're doing" and the feedback from the game itself). This really isn't any different than any "fun" thing in the real world. You

do something and receive something in return.

Jim Werbaneth
Publisher, Line of Departure,
Game Designer
A fun game has to hold my interest and keep on presenting challenges that bring me back again and again. It can't give up its secrets very easily. At the same time, there has to be a level of consistency in the way it plays so that it doesn't appear that the programmers put in random gimmicks just to break the pattern. Having a subject that I enjoy doesn't hurt either.

Randy Sluganski
Owner of Just Adventure
(www.justadventure.com)
What makes a game fun? I think that depends on the individual. What I think is fun may be considered boring to someone next to me. I think shooting aliens who then drop weapons packs is the apex of stupidity and laziness, while combining inventory items to create a new object that can then be used to solve a puzzle is my idea of a fun game.

Personally, I know many developers, so when I am playing a game that a friend of mine wrote or programmed, it helps me to appreciate all the more the hard work and dedication that goes into game development. This adds greatly to my enjoyment, rather than viewing the game as a generic product developed by a bunch of faceless individuals.

Steve Grammont
Co-owner of Battlefront.com
(www.battlefront.com)
Fun depends on my mood sometimes. Generally, a game that can successfully transport me into another "world" gets my attention. Sometimes that means cool graphics and action, sometimes story, often role playing something realistic, and best of all assuming a role of responsibility. But in all cases, games need to challenge me in a fair and fulfilling way. Mario Brothers puzzle games bore me to tears because the challenge is simply reflexes. This is no doubt why I do not own game boxes (Xbox, etc.). There are too few of the games made for these boxes, which aren't also made for PCs, that I find interesting.

I like being challenged in ways that real life doesn't directly require of me. For example, being a fighter pilot is an experience I enjoy while playing a great flight sim, but it is something I will never do in real life. I don't ever want to go into combat, yet teaming up with some other guys to accomplish a "dangerous" mission is quite exciting and fulfilling.

However, not being yanked out of the experience because of flaws, bugs, shortcomings of the design, etc., is very important to me. I hold different standards for different types of games, and some bugs/flaws can be overlooked, but an otherwise good game can be ruined if I am reminded that it is just some code and graphics running on my PC. If that happens, I might as well be "playing" Photoshop or FileMaker Pro, or more seriously...reading a book or watching a good movie.

Howard Jones
Author
A fun game has a good, logical interface that isn't too difficult to learn but that allows flexibility; well-written plot, dialogue; a plotline that's not rigid; the unanticipated; freedom to move through the world; humor.

I also like a game that evokes a sense of wonder, both through its imagination and graphics, and all of the above. Attention to detail.

Figure 8-1: Silver—expect the unexpected

Tom Ham
Journalist (*USA Today, Newsweek, Maxim***), E3 Judge**

What makes a game fun? It's a number of things actually. Where in the past wickedly cool graphics were enough to sell a game, without question gamers have become savvier. As the saying goes, looks can only get you so far. For me, a game that manages to draw me in in the first five minutes has something going for it. Does it make me laugh? Does it make me cringe in fear? Do I get giddy when playing it? Those are the qualities I look for when playing games now. Time is too important nowadays to waste playing something that isn't up to par. I feel that developers are aware of this and thus are creating experiences that are truly compelling, not just filler. What's great for the industry is that games are just going to get better and better.

My favorite game? It would have to be Half-Life. From a storytelling perspective, it was and still is revolutionary. Valve took a dated engine (Quake II) and created a game and story that could be a Hollywood motion picture. From their brilliant use of scripted scenes to their great use of sound and suspense, Half-Life truly epitomized what it means to play a great game.

John Keefer
Managing Editor of GameSpy Network

Fun to me is when a game immerses me in the story and game play so much that I can't rest until I get through a particular mission or scenario. Fun is when I have to play "just one more turn" or complete "just one more mission" (several times) before I go to bed. And finally, fun is when I am excited about telling someone I completed the game or killed that ultimate boss...

Tiffany Spencer
Senior Public Relations Manager of Ubi Soft

What makes a game fun? It's interesting that you didn't ask what makes a great game because I probably would have described a combination of great game play, good graphics, and a compelling story line. But the fun factor is something totally different. For me a fun game is something that triggers a reaction. I really like getting stressed out when I play. I like fighting and shooter games that get my heart racing and trigger that "Oh no!" feeling. I like games with timed challenges that make me panic. I like mentally challenging games that frustrate me to no end—something that leaves me thinking about game strategies even when I am not playing any more. Anything that really makes me tense and freaked out. I think I am just a glutton for punishment!

Scott Osborne
Journalist (GameSpot, GameSpy, IGN)

What makes a game fun? Sometimes it's easier to say what doesn't make a game fun: flashy but empty graphics that don't serve the game as a whole, a sequel that plays it safe, a retread of a successful design (does the world need yet another uninspired copy of great games like Diablo or Age of Empires II?), a rushed tie-in for a popular movie or TV series created by developers who don't genuinely love the property, an interface that makes the gamer work instead of play, strictly linear game play, cheap "gotcha" attacks, unconvincing AI, lack of a clear manual and/or tutorials, an immature mindset that makes it seem like the game was designed by and for perpetual adolescents…. The list could go on, sadly.

Looking at things positively, the most enjoyable games generally engage both your mind and your reflexes. They engage your emotions, too, through captivating and *original* stories, characters, themes, and/or settings. (No more rip-offs of *Aliens* and Tolkien, please!) They do something fresh by inventing a new genre or hybrid, or they move an existing genre in a new direction. They feature not merely great graphics and sound on a technical level, but more importantly, they feature real artistry behind the art. The interface is as intuitive, clear, clean, attractive, and transparent as possible. Characters aren't cardboard clichés but seem to have real motivations and histories and emotions. Stories are written by and for mature adults. (A bunch of gratuitous violence and profanity and sexual innuendo doesn't at all equal "mature"—quite the opposite.) Plots don't merely provide a framework for the action but actively draw you into the action. They fill you with wonder and make you really care.

Most importantly, really fun games feature their own unique and unforgettable worlds, worlds created with meticulous attention to detail and brought to life with high production values. These worlds deeply immerse you in an alternate reality or a recreation of some fascinating part of our real world. These worlds grant you the freedom to act and react and explore and discover—not merely to jump through a set of hoops set up by a designer. The beauty of gaming as an art form is that games put you in control, letting you create novel solutions to unexpected problems. The best ones let you, in essence, write the story. They certainly shouldn't drag you around on a leash, as so many lesser games do!

If I were forced to pick just one, my favorite game would be Doom, one of the first and best games to show the true potential of the medium in a remarkably vivid way. Right up there at the top of my list would be Combat Mission: Beyond Overlord and Tony Hawk's Pro Skater 2 (Dreamcast version). A few others, including some favorites from long ago: Deus Ex, Tribes 2, Team Fortress Classic (Half-Life mod), Shadowgate (Mac), Dark Castle (Mac), Miner 2049'er (Atari 400/800), Gauntlet (arcade), and Zork I.

Bill Roper
Executive Producer of Blizzard
Entertainment
What makes a game fun is one of those questions along the lines of, "What makes jokes funny?" or "Why does chocolate taste so good?" Although there are some guidelines we follow as developers, not everyone has the same idea of what makes for a fun experience. Identifying the key elements to what is entertaining and captivating about your game

design and then embellishing those areas is a good way to keep the game fun for the people who are looking for that play experience. For example, Diablo II is an action-oriented RPG, so all of our design decisions needed to support that style of game play. People who find the pace of a Diablo-style game entertaining are probably not looking for a lengthy and time-consuming crafting system, for example. Randomness is another element that keeps Diablo II fresh and entertaining, so we made sure to use this element whenever it made sense, such as with item generation, tile set construction, monster spawning, and so forth. It is our job as developers to define a play experience and then stay true to that vision. If we do a good job of that, the game will remain fun throughout for players who are excited and entertained by that experience.

Fun Is as Fun Does

Bottom line: What is fun to one gamer may not be to another. So, in the long run designers and development teams have to decide what they like, listen to their fans' input, and adapt the game to the best of their ability.

Part Three

Marketing and Public Relations

Some of the greatest games of all time sold piti-
fully. Whether it was poor topic choice, poor public
relations, or poor marketing, the word either
didn't get out or when it got out no one cared.
This part describes how to avoid those mistakes
and generate the type of buzz that sells games.

Chapter 9

Public Relations—A Primer

As I have said before, making a game that sells takes a plethora of ingredients. Make no mistake, the foremost of those ingredients is quality. To sell a game greatly, it must be a good game. But only slightly behind the quality of the game is the quality of the public relations effort with the game. To sell a game well, you must get news of the game out to gamers, create a buzz about the game, and try to generate favorable press. That is what this chapter is about: public relations and getting press. Let's get started.

Building a Theme

It is a fast-paced world that we live in. Voters vote on candidates based on 10- to 15-second sound bytes, one-liners are most people's favorite jokes, and people cannot get from their home to the grocery store without making a quick call on their cell phone. It only makes sense that such pacing would affect the computer game industry.

If you hope to sell a computer game, you need to get the idea behind the game across to the public. If you cannot get this idea, this theme, across in a sentence, you are not going to sell the game. So, simply put, you need to develop a theme, hook, slogan, whatever you want to call it. Good themes have a couple of things in common. Number one, good themes are catchy. A great example is the theme for Max Payne. Max Payne's theme was simple: "When it's ready." Those words meant that Remedy was going to make a quality game, and Remedy was only going to release the game when it was ready to be released. "When it's ready" said all of that, but it said it in three words. That created a theme that stuck in gamers' minds.

So themes must be catchy, and themes must be simple. The best themes are no more than a sentence—ideally no more than five or six words. The themes that people remember are the short themes—the short, powerful themes.

Finally, you have to hammer the theme home. Every mention of the game must mention the theme. Every advertisement for the game must mention the theme. Every interview that the developer and publisher gives must mention the theme. Every telephone conversation must mention the theme. The theme must be hammered home. The theme must be on the front of the box. The theme must be on the back of the box. You need to get out to the public what the game is about: the theme. Get it out constantly. Keep it simple, and make it catchy.

Creating a Buzz

Creating a buzz is one of the hardest things in the gaming industry to define, yet it is one of the most important. In writing this book, I talked with dozens of gaming journalists and PR managers, but none of them knew exactly how to define it. Nevertheless, once a buzz is created, a game takes on a life of its own. A buzz is when gaming people (be they gamers, journalists, the press, or buyers for Wal-Mart) start talking about the game. It is when the game becomes the topic of numerous previews and interviews, becomes a hot topic on discussion forums, and perhaps even gets some press in mainstream media.

Creating a buzz takes three things. Number one: You must be fan friendly. That means that the developers and producers must be accessible or have representatives who are accessible. They must be willing to talk with the fans in chat rooms, and they must seem amenable to fan suggestions and fan input. This does two things: First, it lets the fans feel that they are part of the game. When people become part of something, they identify with it. Also, talking with fans creates the impression that the developers and producers are nice guys, game guys, guys just like the people who are buying the game. When fans identify with the developers and producers, they are more likely to plunk down their hard-earned bucks to buy the game.

The second way to create a buzz is through web sites. Of course, every game should have an official web site. That web site should smack of professionalism and have everything that people want to know about the game. It should have an FAQ, downloadable trailers, screen shots, wallpaper, the game's background story, conception art, and above all else a forum where gamers can meet and discuss the game. But as important as a snazzy professional site is, it must also load quickly. Not everyone in the world has a T1 connection; many people still use a dial-up. They won't wait three or four minutes for your page to boot. Bottom line, make it look professional, make it look clean, make it look smart, but make it load quickly.

Not only do games need official web sites, but for games to take on a life of their own they need fan sites. The developers and producers should actively promote fan sites. Make the tools to create fan sites available on the official web site, make it easy for gamers to create professional-looking sites, support the sites, release news clips to the sites before you release them to other media, and make the people running the sites feel important. They generate the fan base that you need to actively promote a game.

Release a demo. Release a demo early. Release a demo again. If you have a game whose strongest selling point is quality, and if you have a game that is so much fun to play you are sure that whoever plays it will buy it, get that demo out there. Make the demo look polished. Rather than create a big demo, create a small but well-made demo. If you get the demo out well in advance of the game, release a second demo to update the original demo and, once again, create buzz.

Involve the Press

Public relations people can't make the press write about a game. Public relations folks can't make gamers get interested in a game. Public relations people can't generate the favorable press they would like a game to have. There are, however, ways to involve the press and increase your chances of getting favorable press. Let's talk about a few.

Freelancers can be a company's best friend. In fact, freelancers can be a small company's lifeblood. This is a fact commonly overlooked by newcomers to the public relations industry. These newbies often spend their time and money wowing the editors at gaming magazines and web portals. Make no mistake, editors are important. Editors can influence what their writers write about. But make no mistake either that the full-time freelancing core in the electronic entertainment industry, although small, has significantly more stability than the editor core. Editors come and go. In one year alone, I saw *Computer Gaming World* go through three editors, but the freelancers, the full-time freelancers, are here to stay. Many times, establishing relationships with freelancers exposes your games to more sites than just sending your games to nameless editors. Freelancers want the money earned by selling an article about your game. So professional freelancers will actively seek to place an article if the information is given to them. Use that professional freelancing core. Send them preview discs, and keep them in your press release loop. You will find it pays big dividends.

Public relations folks must put a personal touch on all their work. Do the research. Find out which freelancers, which editors, which staff writers have been around the longest and what their preferences are. Take a minute to meet them at E3. Learn something about their families, and jot it down; it will pay off later. To a new public relations person, the number of journalists can seem overwhelming, but many of the journalists are just casual writers. The actual number of staff writers, editors, and full-time freelancers is no

greater than in any other industry. Take a minute to learn them. When a freelance writer queries for a product, take a moment to do a search on the web. You will find out if they are a serious freelancer or not. If they are not, don't waste your product on them. If they are, treat them with the same courtesy as an editor or a staff writer. Editors are the least numerous journalists of the group. The public relations people should know each, know their preferences, and keep them informed of upcoming releases. Use the personal touch, use research, and make them feel special.

Bribe them. Of course, I am not saying to do anything dishonest here, but a T-shirt, coffee mug, or other promotional material goes a long way in generating goodwill toward your company. Don't be afraid to use those. Don't be afraid to use other promotional material as well. At the Electronic Entertainment Expo, a show that rivals the glitz and glamor of Hollywood, the displays have often been a source of much controversy. Some journalists feel the scantily clad "booth babes" are an insult, while others live for the weekend to scope out the babes. In reality, the "booth babes" are neither scandalous nor should they be the center of attraction. Let's face it, we are all visual people. An attractive face, an attractive body is something we all enjoy looking at, but even more, a serious journalist wants to talk to someone who knows the game inside and out. They don't want their time wasted by someone who can merely refer them to a producer who has to ask a designer who then asks one of his coders for the answer to a relatively obvious question concerning the game. Bottom line, when deciding whether to go for glitz or substance at your E3 booth, substance will always win out, but if you can get substance with glitz, then you will really have something special.

The Last Review

So, in this chapter we discussed what works and doesn't work with the gaming press. In short, it is important to build a theme. Keep it simple and hammer it home. You want to create a buzz by being fan friendly, having excellent web sites (both official and fan sponsored), and releasing a demo. Involve the press. Remember that freelancers can be a small company's best friend. The personal touch works with editors, staff writers, and freelancers. Do your research first, and find out who likes what and why they like that. Cater to those needs, and you will get better press. Bribe the hell out of the writers on your contact list. Finally, when debating whether to invest money in beautiful "booth babes" or knowledgeable demonstrators at E3, go with both if you can afford it. If you can't, go with the knowledgeable demonstrators.

Chapter 10

Marketing the Product

I t would be a better world if all games sold on merit alone, but such is not the case. Not only must a game be outstanding, but it also must have an outstanding public relations and marketing team behind it. As Blizzard's Bill Roper says, "…you absolutely *must* have the best possible PR and marketing you can get on your game because they are the ones that present your game to the world."

Furthermore, developers—even when they aren't doing PR for their game—must know how to not only handle the press but their own public relations and marketing people as well. Yet the first step in handling them well is to understand their job. I hope that the following information lays the groundwork for that understanding.

Public Relations

Erica Kohnke at Kohnke Public Relations once told me that the difference in public relations and marketing is simple. "PR *prays* for press; marketing *pays* for press." Although the marketing and public relations people normally work as one team, their jobs are different. The public relations folks' job is to interact with the trade magazines, web sites, television, radio, and even the gamers themselves. The success of their efforts is measured in the number of previews, interviews, and screen shots that appear in their targeted medium. In short, how much buzz do they create? This success can be maximized by using the following strategies. Take it from me; I've been writing for gaming magazines for over ten years. I know what I like and dislike about what public relations folks do.

Know the Game

More often than not, the gaming press is made up of gamers. They are enthusiastic about their profession and the games that they cover. Nothing excites them more than talking about games. A public relations representative who knows the game she represents and can talk about it catches the magazine editor's interest. Conversely, those same editors can spot a "poser" after a couple of sentences, and it turns them off.

PR reps must take the time to learn their game. What are its strong and weak points? What is the game's technological innovation, and how much demand does that innovation place on a computer? How does your game differ from the competition's? If it's an RPG, what type of combat system does it use? If it's a first-person shooter, what type of damage model (realistic or not) does it employ?

The folks representing the game should spend some time with the game. Nothing gives a better feel for the game than playing it. Three hours with a game teaches much more than a day of briefings with the development team will.

Know Your Public Relations Representative

Just as the PR reps must know a game, so must the development team know their PR rep and his job. To do their work, the public relations folks must have access to the team and their materials. For the team to finish its project, it must be left alone. These seemly irreconcilable differences can be reconciled. The most efficient way to include PR rep time in the development process is to schedule it at the beginning of the cycle. Three to five percent of the total development time should be allowed for public relations interface and development. It's also best to have two to three members of the team that deal with the PR reps and one person through whom all PR requests are channeled. Don't look at public relations as a burden but rather as an opportunity to share your vision with the consumer.

Inviting the press to your studios is a great way to show off a game—especially before the code is exportable to unfriendly computers. Make sure, however, that all concerned are briefed and that you practice the press tour before the big day. You may even want to tell the artists to shave (that's a joke).

Know Your Editor

PR reps must build a trusting relationship with the editors they work with. It's important to know what the editors like and dislike, who covers which beats, and who the significant freelancers are. All this needs to be done without harassing the editors or overexposing the product.

Give editors a call when the game reaches milestones and offer screen shots. Drop them a holiday card, and make it a point to meet them at the trade shows. Keep the relationship positive, but keep it professional.

Above all else, be honest. Some game issues must be kept secret. Tell the editors so. If the game doesn't do something as well as a competitor, admit it. You need not advertise that fact, but denying it will only ruin your credibility.

Screen Shots

Screen shots sell the game. Most gamers can tell as much about the game from a handful of screens as they can from a handful of previews —and in less time to boot! Feed your preferred web sites a steady stream of exclusive screen shots; don't get your kid brother to capture them—at least, not unless he is very good at it. You want screen shots that display your game in the best possible light. Choose screens that are colorful, vibrant, and packed with action. It's best to have one person on the team who is the screen shot expert. Have him or her take all the screens.

Demonstrate the Game

The best way to demonstrate your game is with a demo (makes sense, doesn't it?). Of course, all developers know that game demos are a pain in the, well… you can fill in the word. They may be a pain, but demo time needs to be built into the development cycle. Early in the cycle, PR reps and the marketing department need something (usually non-interactive) to show editors and buyers. It needs to stress the game's strong points, so don't forget the vision. Select something within the game that shows the vision and what is unique. Barring a visionary demo, something with stunning eye candy works well too.

Later in the cycle, gamers need something that they can play. There is no better advertisement for a game than the game itself. Whenever you release a demo, be it interactive or looping (non-interactive), remember that anything you release will make it to the public. So, don't just "whip up something quick" for marketing to show a buyer. Chances are you'll see that demo on the Internet within a few days.

Marketing

The marketing people on the publishing team also help you sell your game. In many ways they are even more directly responsible for the sale of the game than public relations representatives.

Marketing is responsible for assembling and studying gaming demographics. These are the people who know the average age of someone willing to buy a Spider-Man game and if that person is a man or a woman. These are the folks who can study the public's interest in a license, such as Spider-Man, and determine if it will not only help sell a game, but whether it would sell more copies of a first-person shooter or a turn-based strategy game.

Marketing also studies what feature sets, interface, and genre appeal to which demographic. Part of making a game that sells is fitting your vision of the game within a set of parameters that marketing claims will sell the game. This doesn't mean

Figure 10-1: Activision's Spider-Man

selling out. It just means making the game that you have always wanted to make in a way that it is likely to sell.

Marketing also decides how to market the game. To do this, they must create an image for the game, and to create an image for the game, they need the developer's help. The developer must convey the coolness of the game to marketing. Basically, in a couple of sentences, tell marketing why gamers should buy the game.

Marketing takes this image of the game and tries to sell it. They sell it to the public through advertisements, and they sell it to the buyers (the people who buy for an entire chain of stores) through face-to-face meetings, demos, special incentives, and even groundswell support for the game. Make no mistake, if there is an obvious, vocal, and large fan base for the game before it is released, it will be much easier to sell the game in large store chains.

There is a bit of a fine line here between public relations, marketing, and sales. In a simple world, PR and marketing create a demand for the game that the publisher's sellers cash in on.

The cashing in takes several forms. Sellers sell to the buyers for chain stores, such as Wal-Mart, or wholesalers. Either buyer has one goal—to move the product off their shelves. If the customer isn't moving it (i.e., buying it), the store will move

it themselves by returning it to the publisher. This is the difference between sell-in and sell-through. Games that are sold to the chain stores or wholesalers are sold in. Rarely does the publisher receive any "up front" money for these sales. Games are sold through when someone buys it off the shelf. This money will eventually make its way back to the publisher's hands, and a percentage of it will get back to the developer (royalties). Unfortunately for the publisher/developer, unpurchased games that are "sold in" may be returned and no one gets any money.

Nevertheless, the first step in selling a game is making your publisher's seller believe in the game. There is no better way to get the seller to push the game with a chain store buyer than to get the seller personally interested in the game.

Take the time to meet the seller, and take the time to demo the game for him (or her). Find out what makes him tick and share your vision of the game with him. Explain how the game can make the company money. Sell the seller, and he will sell your game.

Original Equipment Manufacturers (OEM)

Original equipment manufacturers are companies that make hardware. That hardware can be computers, graphics cards, joysticks, game pads, or any other computer equipment. Frequently, OEMs want to bundle software with their equipment. Although the price per unit is not high, the money is paid up front, and the exposure can enhance a publisher's or developer's reputation.

The Final Advertisement

Although public relations representatives, marketers, and sellers can help put a game into a gamer's hands, it is up to the development team and publisher to keep it there. If the development team wants to breed the sales that come from an extended life game, they must make a great game that gamers want to play. Public relations can help the initial sales of a game, but only a good game will keep on selling.

Part Four

Range of Appeal and Cool Factor

Establishing a broad range of appeal is important to large volume sales. Just as important is inserting the hard-to-define "cool factor" that gamers love. This part will explain how to do both.

Chapter 11

Range of Appeal

The broader the appeal of a game, the more units that game will sell. It only makes sense. After all, gamers are going to buy games that they enjoy. For example, strategy game sales historically make up 24 to 27 percent of all PC game sales. Mercenary publishers wishing to cash in on those strategy game sales might push their development studios to develop strategy games. Unfortunately, the discount bins are littered with failed attempts based on that train of thought.

Those titles failed not because of their genre but rather because of other shortcomings. At the heart of a good game is a development team that is driven to make the game, not a development team that is assigned to the game.

Games need more than a popular genre to succeed. They must also have an interesting topic, high-quality production values, strong marketing and public relations, and a strong cool factor. But coupled with those four facets is a broad range of appeal. All things being equal, the quality game with the broadest range of appeal will sell the most units. There are a couple of ways to do this—scalability and cross breeding. Let's look at each in turn.

Scalability

A friend of mine once remarked, "I won't play a game if I can't have fun without the user manual." I agree. We are, after all, playing on some of the most sophisticated machines ever known to man. If the computer can't handle enough of the game to let a newbie play right away, the game may frustrate the beginning player enough for him to turn off the computer or move on to another game.

Clearly, a game that attracts beginners and hard-core gamers alike will have a broader range of appeal than a game only accessible by expert flight simulation players or hard-core first-person shooter players. The ability of a game to flex in order to meet the needs of the player is what is called scalability.

Scalability means to grow or shrink easily (my definition, not Webster's). The term first found widespread use in the non-gaming technology world, where it was most often used to define the ability of Internet servers to grow with the demand put on them. The term, however, is no less relevant in the world of gaming. But in this context, it means the ability of a game—both technologically and difficulty of play —to meet the needs of a diverse range of gamers and gaming systems.

Technology

In 1964 semiconductor engineer Gordon Moore came up with what has come to be known as Moore's Law. His law states that the logic density of silicon integrated circuits has closely followed the curve *(bits per square inch)* $= 2^{(t-1962)}$, where t is time in years; that is, the amount of information storable on a given amount of silicon has roughly doubled every year since the technology was invented. Although that doubling of capacity has slowed to 18 months, the basic precept remains true and may be simply stated as, "Computers are fast, and they are going to get a lot faster."

It's a huge temptation for developers to use that speed. Increases in processing power, especially graphical processing power, make almost lifelike images possible on today's computer screens. Breathtaking graphics are an important element in computer games that sell.

Unfortunately, the mainstream public doesn't have the same high-end machines as those on the desks of development studios' graphic engineers. A game that needs a

Figure 11-1: Operation Flashpoint

high-end computer to run will seriously limit its range of appeal. The solution is to use a scalability of technology to allow a gamer to configure the game to suit his needs.

Codemaster's Operation Flashpoint is an excellent example of this type of scalability. Released in August of 2001, the game required what was then a fast computer—a 600 megahertz Pentium III—to run all of its bells and whistles. In the options menu, however, the game presented multiple means to lower the graphical load on the computer so that gamers with slower computers could still enjoy the game. It wasn't that these options alone made Operation Flashpoint a success, but rather the combination of a clever game blended with a desire to let gamers—with or without top-end equipment—enjoy the title that helped boost the game's sales.

But technical scalability is not the only important variable contributing to a broad range of appeal. A game's ease of play and degree of complexity are also important factors. Games must have scalable difficulty if they are to succeed. At a minimum, gamers must be able to set their own level of difficulty. Even better are games that set the difficulty level to match the player's skills. Max Payne does this. The code measures how well you are doing against the antagonists, and the artificial intelligence adjusts accordingly. This technique is not limited to first-person shooters or action-adventure games. The excellent Gran Turismo 3 racing simulation does the same thing. If the opponents are beating you too badly, it slows them down. Such scalability is critical to the gamer's immersion. Everyone loves a challenge, but no one enjoys beating

their head against a wall. We get enough of that in the real world; who needs it in a game?

A facet of play related to—yet different from—ease of play is complexity. In other words, how difficult is a game to comprehend? By nature, some games are complex. For example, war games, flight simulations, and Sid Meier's Civilization series are complex because they cover complex subjects. The challenge for a designer, development team, and publisher is to make such complex

479 km/h
3600 m

Figure 11-2: IL-2 Sturmovik

games readily accessible to all gamers. If you want to sell well, you have to sell to a broad market, and to sell to a broad market you must develop a game that is readily accessible to the masses. Unfortunately, "dumbing down" the game isn't an option for detailed flight simulations, such as 1C: Maddox's IL-2 Sturmovik. The solution is to create a game that has the complexity that gamers expect but options, such as a simplified flight model in flight simulations or traction control in racing simulations, that allow beginning gamers to enjoy the experience and learn at their own pace. Again, it is important to challenge a gamer, not frustrate him (or her).

Switch Hitting and Cross Breeding

A batter who can hit well from both sides of the plate has a better chance of getting a hit than one who only bats from one side. The same is true in the realm of electronic entertainment. A game that does well in one genre probably won't sell as well as one that pleases gamers from two (or even three) genres.

The late '90s and early 21st century have seen a huge increase in these multi-genre games. Activision's Battlezone and Battlezone 2 mated real-time strategy with action, and Nival Entertainment's Etherlords crossed the adventure and exploration made famous in New World Computing's Heroes of Might and Magic with the challenge of card-based combat first introduced in Magic the Gathering. Blizzard's successful Warcraft III blended elements of role-playing with immersive real-time strategy.

Multiple genres cannot, however, appear to be bolted together. They must form an integrated whole, and the whole must support the developer's vision. Bill Roper, the executive producer for Diablo II, states, "Identifying the key elements to what is entertaining and captivating about your game design and then embellishing those areas is a good way to keep the game fun for the people who are looking for that play experience. For example, Diablo II is an action-oriented RPG, so all of our design decisions needed to support that style of game play. People who find the pace of a Diablo-style game entertaining are probably not looking for a lengthy and time-consuming crafting system, for example."

Role playing is a non-intrusive addition to any genre. All role playing supports character development, and characters can develop whether they are in an action adventure or a real-time strategy game. Yet, it's important to mold the role playing—or anything for that matter—to fit

Figure 11-3: Warcraft III. ©2002 Blizzard Entertainment, All Rights Reserved.

your vision. For example, extensive character creation would seem out of place in an action adventure.

Even so, there are no rigid dos and don'ts in the world of genre mixing. It's important for developers to follow their initial vision, make an early working model of their game,

decide what is fun, and stick with it. Do that and go the extra mile to make both the game's technology and complexity scalable, and the game will have a much better chance of having a broad range of appeal than its non-scalable, single-genre competitors.

Part Five

Been There and Back—A Few Games That Have Sold and Some That Haven't

Part Five takes several of the best-selling games from the past two years and analyzes why they have sold well. It is here that the previously discussed points will be used to figure out why these games have sold. Also included in this section is a chapter on a handful of great games that haven't sold well and why they haven't.

Chapter 12

Empire Earth: Put One Up for PR

E mpire Earth is not a great game. If that statement
stuns you, perhaps you have not been reading
this book closely. I'm discussing what makes
games sell greatly, not what makes great games. As
I've said before, the two are not one and the same.
Empire Earth is a perfect case in point.

Make no mistake; this is not a bad game. In fact, Empire
Earth, which was designed by Rick Goodman—a key player on
Microsoft's Age of Empires team—is quite good. But it does
not grab gamers as The Sims does, thrill them like Max Payne,
or creatively stun them as Etherlords does. None of that, however, is necessary to sell a game, and Empire Earth proves that.

What Sierra did exceptionally well with Empire Earth was
market, publicize, and sell the game. What Stainless Steel Studios (the game's designers) did not do well is design a great
game; they did, however, design a solid game. Luckily for
Sierra, few noticed Empire Earth's transparent robes, and the
game garnered several "best of 2001" nominations and awards.
That dichotomy makes this discussion critical to this book. This
chapter does not analyze a great game but rather a game that
sold greatly. In other words, it is about the essence of what
makes games sell. Let's take a look at each of the attributes that
make games sell and see how they apply to Empire Earth.

Quality

Empire Earth is a high-quality game. That is no surprise; games that made this book's cut understand that quality (to paraphrase an older commercial) "is job one." But what specifically does it take to make that quality? What is it that gamers and journalists are looking for in a game?

Simply enough, I believe gamers and journalists both want to feel that they are getting their money's worth. Cheap games come across cheaply. The first thing to enter my mind, and most other people's minds, when playing a surprisingly cheap game is, "Hey, these guys are asking for top dollar but weren't willing to put top effort into their project."

I recently wrote a strategy guide for a mediocre real-time strategy game. Producing a mediocre game is not damning in itself. Although mediocre games rarely sell well, they are frequently the best a producer can manage. Either because of monetary problems, lack of experience, development team ego, or a myriad of other problems, many development/production teams are doomed to mediocrity before they begin. In this case, mediocrity was not the best the company could manage. The producer knew the game had significant design flaws but did not take the steps to eliminate them. That is taking advantage of the gamer, and

journalists can smell that from a mile away.

The result of that olfactory analysis is often scathing reviews and plummeting sales. Bottom line: The game doesn't earn its potential, and producers and development teams lose their jobs.

So, quality is often as simple as the design and production team doing everything within their power to deliver the best product possible. Blizzard, and their games, is a perfect example of this. They release no gaming wine before its time.

A brief aside: I can't tell you how many producers I've talked with who bemoan Blizzard's money and market power. "Sure," they say, "if I had that kind of money, I could turn out that kind of quality."

Maybe, maybe not.

Proper time and resource management cost nothing. If producers and developers with sufficient experience plan their work and then work their plan, many games' quality shortfalls (not to mention crunch-time pitfalls) could be overcome.

Empire Earth has obviously avoided these pitfalls. The game has hit all the quality wickets. The software is bug free. I read ten reviews of the game, and none of the ten mentioned bugs. Neither could I make the game crash on any of the five machines in my office. If quality is job one, bug-free software is the first step in accomplishing the job. Simply put, if the software doesn't run well, all the time, on all but the most esoteric computers, you are going to lose sales. Developers, don't kid yourself; don't say that it is impossible to code for all possible configurations. The editors, journalists, and gamers don't care about that. They consider it your problem. If you want to sell your game, it must run, first time, every time, right out of the box. Empire Earth did that.

Empire Earth is a complex game. That's the way Stainless Steel Studios planned it. But complex games can frequently lose favor with time-challenged gamers. There are two ways to retain that favor, and both weigh heavily in the overall quality impression that a game makes. Way one: Write a tutorial. Way two: Give players a high-quality user's manual. *Empire Earth succeeded on both counts.*

Not just any tutorial will please demanding consumers. Tutorials must be easily accessible and interesting, give the gamer a sense of accomplishment, and move quickly. Empire Earth's was all that, *and* it let

Figure 12-1: Empire Earth is a quality game.

gamers skip to any part of the tutorial. To their credit, the development team stepped out of their shoes and looked at Empire Earth through the eyes of the gamer. That is a small piece of good game design that showed Stainless Steel's commitment to the gamer. Why make those familiar with Age of Empires and real-time strategy games in general (with which the Sierra marketing and public relations team strongly linked Empire Earth) play through the baby-step beginning tutorials if they don't want to?

Additionally, the tutorials are narrated. Certainly, gamers interested in playing Empire Earth would have no trouble reading tutorial text, but well-narrated tutorials give a game a sense of polish, a sense of quality, and quality sells games.

Two hundred and thirty-eight pages. That's the length of Empire Earth's user manual. In the age of CD-ROM case-sized manuals, 32-page PlayStation 2 manuals, and skimpy 96-page simulation manuals, 238 pages says one thing—quality. Actually, 238 pages says several things, not the least of which is, "We are proud of our game, and we want you to know all about it."

No doubt manual size is a balancing act. The more pages in the manual, the higher the production costs for the game. The production budget can be compared to a pie. If the manual gets a larger slice, some other part of the game's production costs must be reduced. While that is true, make no mistake that a good manual is a strong indicator to the gaming public that the production and development team cares not only about the game but also about the public's enjoyment of the game.

As I mentioned in Chapter 7, some games don't require thick manuals. There isn't much to learn when playing Crash Bandicoot. On the other hand, strategy and role-playing games, and simulations need that manual. Don't confuse the issue. Without a good manual, the game seems somewhat second rate, and its sales will suffer.

I once wrote a succession of manuals for a successful racing simulation developer. I was given free rein for the first manual and wrote a 120-page book that covered in great detail every facet of the game. The manual garnered praise in several of the game's reviews. The company's subsequent title was published by a new company, which chose to limit its manuals to 50-some pages. The manual content suffered and was never mentioned in the reviews. The moral is simple: Reviewers notice manual quality, and whatever reviewers notice can affect your game sales.

Many games release with campaigns or stories that end abruptly, without editors, or with buggy multiplayer. Empire Earth had none of those problems, and the completeness of the package created a quality of atmosphere that enhanced review scores and sales alike.

Confuse not, however, a complete campaign with a long campaign. Too many products, in an effort to compete with the competitor's game, stuff redundant, simplistic, or boring campaigns/levels in order to pump up the time needed to complete their game and establish longevity bragging rights. That's a dangerous practice. Gamers grow older every year. Although many new young gamers come on board the gaming boat, many others grow older, marry, have children, and develop a life outside of games. Their gaming passion may not have waned, but the disposable time to feed that passion has. Hence, making needlessly long, repetitive games will alienate these gamers. Don't forget, these older gamers are often the audience that has the disposable income to purchase numerous games each year.

Table 12-1

Gamers by Age (from Business Communications Report G-260)							
Gender	2000	2001	2002	2003	2004	2005	2006
17 and Younger	28%	28%	28%	25%	23%	20%	20%
18-35	30%	31%	31%	32%	33%	34%	34%
36 and Older	40%	41%	41%	43%	44%	46%	46%

No doubt, completeness was the final feather in Empire Earth's quality cap. With four campaigns, a strong multiplayer suite, and a useful level editor, the game felt like the whole enchilada and impressed fans and journalists alike. As Dave Kosak, one of the founding employees and creative director at GameSpy, says, "The completeness of the package, and the amount of polish that went into it [made the game successful]. It's a great game concept (real-time warfare through every epoch of history and into the future) that's executed well on every level. The single-player game is deep, challenging, and lengthy. The multiplayer game is thorough and extremely well-balanced, even including tournament modes for the hard-core players. And an editor is included, fully featured, polished, and integrated into the product for future expansion. Many games shirk on one or more of these elements or drop them—not Empire Earth. They executed on everything."

The game reviews speak for the quality themselves. Or, as we discuss in the "Marketing and Public Relations" section, perhaps they don't.

Topic

Topic is one of Empire Earth's strong points and one that the Sierra marketing and public relations department ably exploited. This is a game that covers human history from the dawn of the human race until 200 years in the future. A game with such an epic scope no doubt fired the imagination of gamers across the globe.

Empire Earth is not an innovative game, but its topic is. That fact, and the exploitation of that fact, sold the game as nothing else did. If the game had solely depicted real-time battles during the medieval, colonial, modern, or science-fiction eras, it would have faced stiff competition. Choosing its ambitious topic not only avoided direct confrontation with

Figure 12-2: Empire Earth modeled a wide range of military units.

other games but injected a unique-ness that the game would have otherwise lacked.

Notice that the word I chose was *uniqueness*, not innovation. Much is said in journalistic circles about gaming innovation. Yet at the end of the day, innovation is *not necessary* to sell games. Yes, it may garner a developer award or a place at the Academy of Interactive Sciences, but it does not in and of itself sell games. Yet Empire Earth's unique topic signifi-cantly aided its sales.

Genre

Discussing topic leads to genre. Also enhancing Empire Earth's appeal is its genre. Real-time strategy sells well. It has broad appeal, attracting strategy and action gamers alike. Additionally, gamers are familiar with the genre and understand what to expect when they pick up the box. As Kosak comments, "They benefit from being part of an established genre—PC gamers can pick up the box, look it over, and they know what kind of game they're going to get."

Civilization III, a turn-based game, covers the same topic. Yet going

head to head with that Sid Meier classic would be foolhardy. Pro-ducing a real-time game sidestepped comparisons and competition between the two. Better still, the real-time strategy offers more options within the genre. Real-time strategy is a broad category that encompasses production-based strat-egy such as Age of Empires, fixed unit games (like the Myth franchise), and tactical games (like Com-mandos). Sierra chose production-based strategy. After all, Rick Good-man was on the design team for Age of Empires, a fact that Sierra would exploit when marketing Empire Earth. Choosing to link Empire Earth to Age of Empires but developing an entirely different type of real-time experience (such as a fixed unit game) would have misled gamers.

"There was never a major debate what the design team would build from the beginning," says Rich Rob-inson, the game's producer at Sierra. "We wanted an open-ended game with a massive scope. Something that let the gamers do what they wanted."

Game Play

Strange as it may seem, playing the game is somewhat of a letdown. Although that is strange, it is not surprising. The play didn't sell

Empire Earth; the topic, outstanding public relations, and marketing job did.

Make no mistake, Empire Earth plays well. "We wanted to give gamers an 'out of the box' experience," says Robinson. "Something that was easy to get into. But hard to master." That it no doubt does, but it also plays like dozens of real-time strategy games released before it and dozens that will come after. The gamer collects resources, builds an economic infrastructure, produces an army, and overwhelms his enemies. There is also research, technology advancements, and cool new units, but the play is essentially the same as 1992's Dune 2, the game that many credit with breaking open the real-time strategy genre.

Stainless Steel Studios might argue the case that this game is in fact different from other real-time strategy titles. After all, what other real-time strategy game allows the player to cloak his units, fight the Battle of the Bulge, and maneuver Napoleonic armies? The answer is none, but then again, those are facets of topic as much as game play. If the studios wanted to strongly establish the linkage with Age of Empires, they did a good job. The game's tutorial starts at the beginning of time. The little citizens hunt food, chop wood, and mine gold just like those in Goodman's earlier game. To compound the problem or strengthen the linkage, depending on your view, the Empire Earth Internet demo also plops players into the heart of an Age of Empires-like game.

Not even the 3D graphics engine strongly differentiates Empire Earth from the 2D real-time strategy games that have come before. Again, this may have been intentional. Linking to one of the best-selling real-time strategy games of all time is not a bad idea. Yet, injecting Empire Earth with a bit more of its own "in-game" personality probably would have further enhanced sales.

Tom Chick, writing for Computer Games Online, said, "…ultimately Empire Earth is yet another game about gathering resources. The winner is almost invariably the guy who cranks out enough peasants (called citizens here) to gather the most resources and who most efficiently converts them into military units. There's something profoundly disappointing when such a vast game ultimately comes down to herding peasants."

Greg Kasavin at GameSpot adds, "Empire Earth is clearly designed to appeal to those who enjoy Age of Empires II: The Age of Kings." Such comments are certainly not damning, but neither do they enhance sales.

Of course, Empire Earth did some things well. The 3D game engine, although not visually cutting edge, easily handled immense battles with hundreds of units. Also well handled was combat through the ages. It is amazing that a game engine that can render Napoleonic battles can also depict tank warfare. Of course, none of this was truly accurate. In fact, gamers play with the United States' M1A1 Abrams tank in the modern scenarios no matter which side they choose. It would have been nice if the Russians used a tank that looked like their T-80. It's a small point, but those are the small points that contribute to a coolness factor that contributes to better sales.

So, although the game was fun to play, its play wasn't the earth-shattering experience of Max Payne or Diablo II.

Cool Factor

Outside of the immense span of time covered, there was no bigger than life "cool factor" in Empire Earth. The idea of Civilization Points, which allow you to customize your civilization, is neat but not cool enough to

Figure 12-3: Pretty cool

merit mention in many reviews. Neither were the cloaked units, heroes, priests, and prophets universally acclaimed.

For a "cool factor" to generate sales, it must first generate buzz. Perhaps the classic example of a "cool factor" is Max Payne's "Bullet Time." That single feature is mentioned whenever gamers discuss the game. It is a prime example of one feature selling a game. Epic scope aside, Empire Earth had no such feature (at least, not in the press and in the public perception).

Rich Robinson said, "There was no single cool factor such as Max Payne's Bullet Time. The game's scope, its 14 epochs, were its cool factor. After all, there are 300 units. In a sentence, there is lots to do, and lots to manipulate."

Marketing and Public Relations

Marketing and public relations was where Empire Earth truly made its money. A focused, aggressive public relations plan turned a solid product into a game that sold strongly (well over 350K units worldwide in the first quarter of sales). Focusing on one or two selling points was the critical element of Sierra's public relations and marketing campaign.

"It's hard for gamers to completely understand what a game is about by looking at the box," says Adam Kahn, Sierra's point man for Empire Earth's public relations. "We wanted to keep it simple." Keep it simple they did. Sierra focused their add campaign on two fronts: Empire Earth's epic nature and linkage to Age of Empires.

Empire Earth covered the entire breadth of human history. Obviously, that was the game's strong point, and Sierra used it as the sales hook. They never stopped hammering it

into journalists', buyers', and consumers' minds. Their ads used phrases like "Epic is too small a word," and the box claimed Empire Earth was an "Epic Conquest, Spanning 500,000 Years." Calendars were sent to the press with each month depicting a different epoch. The advertising was relentless, and all of it focused on the grand scale of the game. Almost.

Sierra also linked Rick Goodman, the game's designer and member of the Age of Empires design team, with the game. Above Empire Earth's title on the box and in ads were the words "From Rick Goodman, Lead Designer of the Age of Empires." Hence, gamers—and there were well over a million of them—who bought and loved Age of Empires were told that they might also like Empire Earth. To further the strong link between the two games, Sierra centered a mounted warrior, similar to a soldier that might be found in Age of Empires, on the box cover and many magazine and Internet advertisements. Although Sierra representatives denied that this was an attempt to link to Microsoft's famous game, the coincidence was too strong to ignore.

The focused ad campaign and linkage not only got the Empire Earth message across to gamers across the world, but it had a subtler—although no less important—effect on the gaming press. To understand the effect, it is important to understand the press.

The gaming press is an underpaid, harried lot. Staff writers are constantly bombarded with a never-ending stream of games they must evaluate, meetings, trips to game companies, calls, and emails. Freelance writers are in no better shape. To earn a living they must generate an incredible volume of work.

Accordingly, both staff and freelance writers are looking for ways to work more efficiently, cut through the fat, and get to the meat of any game or news story. If a public relations agent does the fat cutting for them, the press will often accept what is being promoted at face value.

So, by hooking the epic nature and linkage to Age of Empires, Sierra public relations was in essence telling the newsies what to write. The newsies bought it. PC Gamer said that Empire Earth was "...the true successor to Age of Empires," and few (if any) reviews failed to mention that Rick Goodman was on the Age of Empires design team—a fact that not many journalists would have researched if the data had not been given to them.

Additionally, the game was named "Game of the Year" by some of the press and lauded by most of the rest (again, not because the game was

Table 12-2

Representative Review Scores for Empire Earth	
Publication	Score
Computer Games Online	3/5
GameSpot	79/100
Electric Playground	85/100
Gameover	88/100
Game On	84/100
GameRaider	89/100
GameSpy	94/100
Gamezilla	91/100
Media & Games Online	90/100

necessarily game of the year material, but because Sierra did a good job of convincing everyone that it was).

Of course, the game had to back up the public relations claims. You can't claim that Crash Bandicoot is a role-playing game and expect anyone to buy it. Nor can you claim that a poor quality game is anything but. However, once Sierra's public relations department found a suitable focus and dedicated themselves to centering their campaign on that focus, the battle to sell Empire Earth was halfway home.

Of course, all the ads in the world won't sell the game if it doesn't have strong distribution. Empire Earth had that distribution. The game was sold in to all the major retail outlets and guaranteed end caps (prominent displays on the aisle's end). This major sell-in not only assured that the game's distribution could meet the pre-release hype but further branded the game as a "triple-A" title.

Of course, there was a strategy guide. In today's market, a strategy guide is as important to the game as are the gamers who use it. It's simple; if your title doesn't warrant a strategy guide, it's not a top line product. If it isn't a top line product —or at least, if it isn't perceived as a top line product—the game won't sell.

Summary

The Sierra public relations and marketing team and the development team and producer settled on a winning strategy early in Empire Earth's development. They stuck with their "epic" hook and Age of Empires linkage, and it paid off at the cash register. Through the first three months, Empire Earth amassed close to a half-million units sold.

Bottom line: Empire Earth played well enough to back up the excellent public relations and marketing of Sierra. Better than average game play coupled with an excellent strategic vision of topic and marketing made Empire Earth a game that sold.

Chapter 13

Max Payne: Cool Cash

ax Payne was one of the most anticipated titles of 2001. In fact, it was one of the most anticipated titles of the past few years. You see, the game's developer (Remedy Entertainment, LTD.) took so long to develop the game that they actually made the delay a game slogan. Any gamer familiar with Max Payne is familiar with its famous slogan: "When it's ready," meaning the game would be released when it was ready, and not a moment before.

No one can debate that when Max Payne was released, it was well and truly ready. Highly rated by every gaming magazine and web site that reviewed it, the game was an instant critical success. Furthermore, it sold over 222,000 copies in the year 2001, making it a commercial success as well. What was the key to this success? What made Max Payne sell? That's a tough question to answer, but answer it I do in the next few pages.

Perhaps the sales could be attributed to a crafty public relations campaign. No doubt, the game's three-year development cycle and high visibility at the Electronic Entertainment Exposition (E3) heightened fans' awareness. Also, no doubt, the "When it's ready" ad campaign provided a hook that caught gamers' attention.

"I would say that our marketing was successful," says Petri Jarvilehto, Max Payne's lead designer. "Really, the results speak for themselves. The game was #1 in all major territories when it came out and has remained on the charts for a long time. Max Payne had a solid PR and marketing campaign as the sales and marketing efforts managed to effectively communicate what sets Max Payne apart. The message was well received, and Max Payne was successfully positioned as the first truly cinematic action game."

The folks at SquareSoft might argue that point, as they believe their Parasite Eve was the first cinematic action game. Similarly, there are other publishers that might lay claim to that honor. First or not, Max Payne made a splash. Yet some think the marketing and public relations could have been better.

George Jones, former executive editor of *Computer Gaming World*, stated, "I think that Take 2 and Gathering of Developers' (the game's publisher and subsidiary) feud totally left this title out in the dark. I also think that G.O.D.'s need to over-hype all their titles (every one of their games was the 'greatest

ever!') undermined their efforts with Max Payne, because the press didn't really pick up on the title like they should have."

Who is correct is unimportant. The point is simple: It's as important to stroke the press as it is to develop your game. Whether busy, inexperienced, or immature, the gaming press rarely picks up on a game unless the game's public relations' people spoon-feed it to them. Hence, if you want your game to sell, break out the spoon.

So, unlike Empire Earth, Max Payne's public relations and marketing campaign were not the game's linchpin. Beyond a doubt, the critical feature in Max Payne, the one thing that gamers talk about when discussing the game, is the Bullet Time. First-person action games have been around since Id made Castle Wolfenstein. Unfortunately, most first-person shooters are similar to that aboriginal. Bullet Time was the first genre-specific innovation in many years. That, as much as good press, a quality game, strong story, and the film noir ambience, sold Max Payne.

Figure 13-1: Bullet Time is so cool.

Quality

There is no mistaking that Max Payne is a high-quality game. From the gorgeous graphics to the well-written story, the game exudes a sense of perfection. It is a perfection born of enthusiasm and love. I met the design team at E3, and it was immediately obvious that the developers were in love with their project and would do everything in their power to make this the best game possible.

This is not a unique emotion among game developers. In 11 years of writing about games, the men and women who make them, and the gaming industry, the common thread that I have found in development teams that produce high-quality games is a love of gaming and a love of the game that they are making. Frequently, I'll interview developers who spend their days designing their own games and their nights playing other people's designs. Some call it crazy; I call it passion. That passion is evident in Max Payne.

The game comes with an excellent tutorial. Again, as all tutorials should, it engages the player and moves him through the steps necessary to learn the game. The pacing is perfect, and pacing is critical to a tutorial's success. If a tutorial is too simple, if the baby steps are too small, it loses the gamer's interest. If a tutorial moves too quickly it will frustrate gamers, causing them to turn off the game. When a gamer turns off the game, he tells his buddies, and they buy something else.

Oftentimes, a tutorial is a gamer's first impression of a game; Max Payne creates an excellent first impression.

Unlike the user manual provided in Empire Earth, Max Payne's manual is not a 200-page missive. That isn't, however, indicative of low quality. Max Payne's user manual covers everything needed to play Max Payne. A large manual isn't warranted. The manual given was detailed, humorous, and insightful —in other words, a quality work. That quality was indicative of the care put into the entire project.

Topic

You have to love Max Payne's topic. Playing the game was like watching *The Matrix*. The film noir ambience had been attempted—albeit without much success—in many games before, but in Max Payne the ambience pervaded the game and made it more than it would have been without it.

Story is the key element to any entertainment medium and especially so to games. Max Payne's graphic novel, rich story, and tight scripting helped propel the gamer to the next level. Max is a character that gamers care about, a man with emotions with which gamers can identify. That identification is part of what kept gamers coming back. That identification is part of what sold the game. That identification is part of what created the buzz.

Figure 13-2: Payne's graphic novel Look was an interesting way to spin Max's story.

That's no surprise. The sooner developers learn to hire a scriptwriter to pen the story of their game, the sooner they will sell more games. When looking for a graphic artist, a programmer, or an artificial intelligence specialist, development studios look for the best their dollars can buy. By contrast, the writer of the script, story, or in-game text is a producer or someone within the development staff that has extra time. That lack of talent does not lead to an engaging story, nor does it produce a story that pulls gamers back to their monitors. Max Payne's writing does.

Genre

As always, genre is a subset of topic. First-person shooters or action games have long been a popular genre. Interestingly, that popularity hasn't recently translated into big hit sales. Of the ten top-selling games in 2001, none are action games. Nevertheless, the potential baseline sales of an action game will often exceed the baseline sales for a strategy game.

So, part of Max Payne's success was due to intelligently choosing the genre. It was, however, a small part of its success. This genre was chosen because the folks at Remedy wanted to make this story, not because they were looking to sell a game. Always critical in selling games is developing a game that you love, one that you would play yourself.

Game Play

Playing Max Payne is a strange endeavor. Once you've worked through the tutorial and begin using the famed Bullet Time, most gamers think, "Man, this is the coolest game I've ever played."

And it is.

Slowing down bullets so they can be seen (á là *The Matrix*) mated with the dodge-shoot technique gives the game a cinematic quality never before seen in a PC action game. It's an exciting quality and one that immediately sucks the gamer into the play. After 45 minutes of playing, gamers often say it's the best game they've ever played.

Interestingly enough, after two hours, that same gamer will say, "It's no big deal." The point is that although the play is good, the Bullet Time innovative, and the story enthralling, making it through the levels is frequently no different than blasting through Quake, No One Lives Forever, Unreal Tournament, or any other shooter.

In other words, strip away the coolness of the Bullet Time and the engaging story and beautiful graphics, and Max Payne is just typical first-person fare. That may be the reason the game didn't crack America's top ten games for cumulative 2001 sales. Coupling the game's strong features with innovative levels might have been the difference in a game that sold well and a game that sold *fantastically* well.

Table 13-1

Representative Review Scores for Max Payne	
Publication	**Score**
GameSpot	9.2/10
PC IGN	9.3/10
Gameover	90/100
Game On	91/100
GameRaider	89/100
GameSpy	90/100

Cool Factor

Well, this one is obvious. The defining Max Payne feature is Bullet Time. In fact, it may be said that one cool factor (i.e., Bullet Time) was responsible for much of Max Payne's sales.

It's a perfect example of how an innovation could define—and sell—a game. Bullet Time is not cutting-edge technology. In fact, the technology has existed for years, but no one had thought of using it. Bullet Time is a perfect example of how innovation adroitly woven into the fabric of a game can sell a title.

I once had a famous designer share a curious insight. "You don't want to be the first person to innovate," he said, "but rather, the second." Sometimes innovation, although critically acclaimed, does not resonate with gamers. Hence, a game that brings along a new innovation, whether in game play or technology, may garner rave reviews but mediocre sales. Activision's Battlezone is a perfect example. A game that adroitly blended action and real-time strategy, Battlezone was critically acclaimed but didn't sell as well as Activision had hoped.

Max Payne, however, is a game that innovated but so adeptly wove innovation into the game that it sold better than hotcakes at a fat man's festival. It's a perfect example of cool factor driving sales.

Marketing and Public Relations

Max Payne's marketing and public relations were a mixed bag. In Finland, which is where Remedy Entertainment is based, gamers I interviewed claimed that Max Payne was well publicized. They claimed the public relations campaign created a heightened sense of awareness and great anticipation before the game's release. Conversely, on this side of the Atlantic, there were those, including George Jones (who was quoted earlier in the chapter), who felt that the feud between Take 2, G.O.D., and Remedy hampered public relations efforts in the United States. Furthermore, the hype constantly associated with the Gathering of Developers' games, through which Max Payne was released, tends to deaden journalists' perceptions of the quality of Gathering of Developers' games. Remedy's Petri Jarvilehto doesn't agree.

"From the very start of development George Broussard and Scott Miller at 3D Realms thought of positioning Max Payne, as a character and as a game," says Jarvilehto. "This was then followed through with professionalism and dedication by our publisher, mainly Terry

105

Donovan and Sam Houser at Rockstar. We worked really well with Rockstar and 3D Realms and enjoyed the process, and I think that it shows in the quality and sharpness and focus of the product that manifested itself in marketing."

This raises a good point. Certainly public relations and marketing's job is to heighten public awareness and sell games, but to heighten that awareness takes a well-focused plan. Getting across what sets Max Payne apart (i.e., its Bullet Time, film noir ambience, and story) is critical to selling the game.

"When we talk about marketing, people often understand it in the narrow meaning of the word—really meaning PR and advertising," says Jarvilehto. "It is important to go deeper than that and to think of marketing as a way of designing the game and defining it in relation to others and how it fulfills needs and wants. When people think of slow motion, Hong Kong style action, and gun ballet in games, they think of Max Payne. Naturally, the plot and strong film noir themes spring to

mind, but Max Payne is first and foremost a cinematic action game."

Jarvilehto continues, "When reading through the reviews, 90 percent of them mention the key elements of the game (John Woo, *The Matrix*, Bullet Time, and strong character) in the first chapters of the review. The strength of character, deep action with motivation and meaning, and the coolness of Bullet Time were communicated successfully to the players. In the end of the day, the game has to deliver, but an essential part of any success is communicating what the game does to the gaming public."

In other words, publishers must stress the game's focus in the review package sent to the industry's journalists and then hope that journalists can get that focus across to the gamers who buy the game. Many good games fail to get their point across to the gaming public. Like Age of Empires, Max Payne's publicist did convey the difference in the game, perhaps not as well as the public relations department as Sierra, but well enough to sell their game.

Summary

Without a doubt, Max Payne is a quality game. Its public relations and marketing campaign were well executed. Those certainly contributed to the game (so did the story and the film noir ambience). But what made Max Payne sell was its "cool factor," Bullet Time.

Chapter 14

Diablo II: Quality Counts

There are other things in life that are just as certain as death and taxes: Stephen King's books shoot right to the best-seller list. George Lucas' *Star Wars* movies are box office legends. Any computer game produced by Blizzard Interactive is bound to make the competition green with envy.

Diablo II and its expansion, Lord of Destruction, are among the latest success stories for this bona fide hit factory. While the seminal title of the series, 1997's Diablo, sold around 2.5 million units, Diablo II shipped in 2000 with an initial production run of two million units. To date, Diablo II has sold in excess of four million copies, and Lord of Destruction reached one million in sales faster than any game expansion in history.

Quality

Many developers claim that their products will not ship before they are ready. In reality, many are under the gun to ship by deadlines that are not entirely related to the game's readiness, either to meet publisher commitments, perhaps get the game on the shelves for the holidays, or meet marketing agreements related to the game's franchising (for example, movie deals or buyer commitments). Blizzard, however, has the economic clout to remain true to their word and has gained a reputation for shipping well-balanced, well-tested, and, above all, fun games. When asked at 2001's Electronic Entertainment Expo when the company's latest development project, Warcraft III: Reign of Chaos, would ship, then-public relations coordinator Beau Yarbrough merely shrugged his shoulders and commented, "Maybe early next year, maybe not. It really doesn't matter to us." In fact, the game shipped on July 3 of 2002, and when it hit the streets it was a highly polished piece of work.

Quality is a term that can mean different things to different people. Many developers assume this means aesthetic characteristics and focus on gee-whiz graphics and spectacular surround sound, often at the expense of game play. Blizzard's games won't necessarily showcase your latest hardware. They will, however, keep players up late and account for more than their share of lost jobs and failed classes, and they will, above all else, sell.

"Blizzard and Ensemble [Studios, developers of the successful Age of Empires series of games] are unique," says *Computer Games Magazine*'s Robert Mayer. "They are polishers. Their forte is doing solid,

Figure 14-1: Warcraft III is a beautiful game. ©2002 Blizzard Entertainment, All Rights Reserved.

well-conceived, and basically standard games with a superb level of finish and testing. They leave the blindingly fantastic innovation to others and focus on what's truly hard—implementation. It's not a good model for others because you have to have the ability, the inclination, and the financial wherewithal to pull this off."

While Blizzard's "Midas touch" grants them nearly unlimited resources to throw at a particular title, money alone can never turn bad concepts or poor practices into winning products. Of course, they could afford the latest in graphics wizardry; that they choose not to makes a statement that indeed some sacrifices must be made to ensure that quality is consistent and pervasive throughout the product. Older technology is not only refined and stable but will also work (and work well) on a broader range of computers and components. Steve Bauman, editor in chief of *Computer Games Magazine,* suggests, "I do think their lack of 'state-of-the-art-ness' helps them with their mass appeal, as it keeps their system requirements lower. But it's really a combination of polished game play (which is a result of the extra time) and a sterling reputation that makes a game like Diablo II such a smash."

Let's look at the various specifications and how they relate to an expanded market:

- **Video:** Diablo II runs in 640x480 resolution, while Lord of Destruction bumps this up to 800x600. Graphics are 2D, and the only requirement made on video hardware is DirectX compliance. Virtually every video card and monitor sold in the past five years meets these requirements, including most laptop computers. Keeping the requirements low broadens the consumer base. Also, by writing to long-perfected video standards, Blizzard avoids the bane of many games: graphic driver inconsistencies and incompatibilities. This cuts down significantly on support costs and adds to the bottom line, which in turn makes more development funds available for the next project so it doesn't have to be rushed… well, you get the idea. Keep in mind too that every customer who experiences technical difficulties is one customer who will almost assuredly be wary when the next title comes around; these customers talk and make others gun-shy as well.

For best results, however, Diablo II does make use of 3D acceleration if present. Additional lighting and transparency effects as well as faster frame rates reward players with newer equipment. In keeping with its quest for compatibility, Diablo II supports both DirectX and Glide technology. The game's compatibility with older technology does not mean those with modern equipment have to suffer, and vice versa.

- **CPU**: The minimum recommended CPU is a modest Pentium 233. Intel's Pentium line debuted in 1993, reaching its apex with the 233 just as the Pentium II was rolled out in 1997. By 2000, the number of PCs in use was approximately 530 million, with an increase of about 300 million from 1995 to 2000 (source: Computer Industry Almanac Inc.). While most people who consider themselves gamers ride the crest (if not the leading edge) of the technology curve, Blizzard is casting a broad net, hoping to catch more casual or heretofore non-gamers.

- **Memory**: The game requires 32MB—a trivial amount by today's standards—but a laptop or older desktop sporting a Pentium processor and low-end video card is also likely to be rather anemic when it comes to system RAM.

- **Drive Space**: Here is where Diablo II may strain older systems that have not seen a recent hard drive upgrade. 650MB (950 for multiplayer) is not particularly large by any modern measure, but a vintage Pentium 233 box may have only contained a 2GB drive in the first place.

- **Modem**: Broadband access is not necessary; the game is playable on Blizzard's own Battle.net service with as little as a 28.8KB modem. Once again, the specifications show sympathy toward laptop users who may have no better options from their hotel rooms or those owning older equipment.

With technical concerns kept to a minimum, Blizzard is able to concentrate on offering polished, exciting play. The Diablo II world is huge, and Lord of Destruction is just as massive. Many developers consider their jobs complete once the customer shells out their money, so what does it matter if they play the game five minutes or 500 hours? Blizzard seems to realize the value in keeping players glued to their PCs for extended sessions; many hours spent in delightful game play translates into indelible affinity for future releases. Expanded business provides a nice bonus, but it is repeat business that you can take to the bank.

Topic

Diablo II is typically characterized as a fantasy role-playing game (FRPG), a popular genre as Table 14-1 indicates. While the game system doesn't neatly fit into RPG conventions (see "Game Play" below), the high fantasy backdrop is most common and popular among role-playing games. This can generally be attributed to role-playing's roots in the venerable Dungeons and Dragons pen-and-paper system, which was created in the mid-'70s by a pair of Wisconsin gamers, Gary Gygax and Dave Arneson. High fantasy (also known as medieval fantasy) is popular in pulp fiction and during Diablo II's tenure has been the topic in several popular movies, including 2000's *Dungeons and Dragons: The Movie* and 2001's *Lord of the Rings: The Fellowship of the Ring.*

Where many traditional FRPGs rely on mythological lore from various historical cultures, Blizzard allows their designers to exercise their imaginations to come up with ideas that feel both familiar and unique. In an interview published at RPG Vault, designer Bill Roper comments, "We really let the whole team go wild with their concepts. Some

ideas are from mythology, ancient writings, bad dreams, caffeine-enhanced hallucinations, and jam sessions. The setting for each monster is also important in that the

environment and monsters must make sense—no squid beasts in the desert, no monkey demons in the plains, that kind of thing. Basically, we let our imagination run wild."

Table 14-1

Select 2001 Fantasy Role-Playing Games	
Game	Publisher
Legends of Might and Magic	3DO
Wizardry 8	Sir-Tech Software
Gothic	Xicat
Throne of Darkness	Sierra Entertainment
Balder's Gate II—Throne of Bhaal	Interplay
Arcanum—Of Steamworks & Magick Obscura	Sierra Entertainment
Blade of Darkness	Codemasters
Dark Age of Camelot	Vivendi/Sierra
Pool of Radiance	SSI/Ubi Soft

Genre

Diablo II also falls into a subclass of the FRPG genre known as the "dungeon hack." These games are usually combat intensive, often at the expense of characterization and plot. Diablo II, like Diablo, revels in its shameless pursuit of the dungeon

hack paradigm. Indeed, Blizzard has embraced the concept and made it its own to the extent that other dungeon hacks are often labeled "Diablo clones" and judged to the standard set by this series.

Table 14-2

Sampling of Notable Diablo Clones	
Game	Publisher
Darkstone	Gathering of Developers
Nox	Electronic Arts
Revenant	Eidos Interactive
Throne of Darkness	Sierra Entertainment
Dungeon Siege	Microsoft

Game Play

Game play in Diablo II is streamlined and easy to master. The 90-page manual contains ample information for playing the game solo and online. Diablo II isn't a traditional role-playing game in the sense of a rich story line laden with interaction between the player character(s) and non-player characters (NPCs), a variety of puzzles to solve, and deep mysteries to uncover. Sure, Diablo II includes these elements but it does not focus on them. Instead, players spend much of their time embroiled in combat. Opponents become tougher and more numerous as the game wears on, and the art of the slaughter becomes almost a catharsis of clicking and killing gigantic bugs and slugs, wretched undead, and horrific demons.

Diablo II uses Pavlovian tactics to keep the player engaged. Whack something until it's dead, and some prize often pops out: weapons, potions, and gold, for example. Leveling up is frequent early in the game, and even well into the game a player will be rewarded with another level for every couple of hours of time spent. The game's story line is advanced through a series of quests, which coincidentally also takes roughly the same amount of time needed to level up. When gaining new levels, points can be allocated to learn new skills (or improve those

known) and increase personal attributes.

David Brevik, president of Blizzard North (the development studio responsible for the Diablo franchise), commented on the game play attraction in an interview published by TechTV: "Timing, and the idea is really good—a progression with a character where you go through and defeat enemies and get rewarded. There's overriding goals as well as lots of sub-goals. There's many things to do, yet it's very simple. It's very straightforward. There's no, 'What am I supposed to be doing now?' It's pretty much in your face as to what you're supposed to be doing. It's very easy to click, and it does things automatically.

"The things that make it successful are things like [the fact that] the interface is really easy to use and intuitive, the addictiveness, and the feedback to actually controlling the guy, the progression and completion of goals through the game—[it] makes you feel good about yourself and makes you feel good about the game. Combine that with the sleekness and the polish and the time that we put into it, as well as the Internet. All that together with what was kind of a dead RPG market contributed to the success. You can't really put your finger on one thing. It was a lot of things."

Frustration is also kept to a minimum. Death is not a permanent condition (unless playing in "hardcore" mode), but this is hardly unique to fantasy role-playing games. However, in single-player Diablo II, players have two viable options when their character is killed. The character is automatically resurrected back in town but without any of the weapons or armor with which it was equipped when the reaper came calling. The player may choose to reequip the character with resources available and seek out his or her own corpse where it had fallen. Alternatively, exiting the game and reentering will find the fully equipped cadaver at the feet of the rejuvenated avatar. Which path the player chooses depends on the progress made toward the end goal; restarting the game also resurrects slain monsters. To further reduce common aggravation, many regions of the game contain teleportation waypoints, which, when discovered, allow easy access to an operational area without the need for exhausting replay.

Multiplayer is generally a cooperative effort, although it is possible for characters to become hostile toward each other. Character development takes on a different meaning in multiplayer games. Rather than focusing on general skills that assist with surviving a variety of encounters, players may specialize, with the collective talents of the group outshining the capabilities of an individual. Playing with others is fun, and the sense of camaraderie adds a quality to the game that can't be packaged in a box or burned to a disk.

Cool Factor

The Blizzard mystique and vast multiplayer community sets Diablo II apart from its legion of clones. Games such as Dungeon Siege add full 3D and much better graphics, but the game's complexity doesn't sell well to the masses. Darkstone did a good job integrating quests into the main story line of the game, but it also came up a little short on game play. Revenant did a great job with character development, but it also …well, you get the idea. Come to think of it, game play in Diablo II doesn't hold up well to intense scrutiny, a fact many solo players in particular are quick to point out. But it's a Blizzard game, and with every Blizzard game comes membership in the always-active community known as Battle.net. Players themselves add that bit of *je ne sais quoi* missing in those also-rans. No doubt, someone could build a better Diablo, but it takes a trusted powerhouse like Blizzard to sell it to the masses.

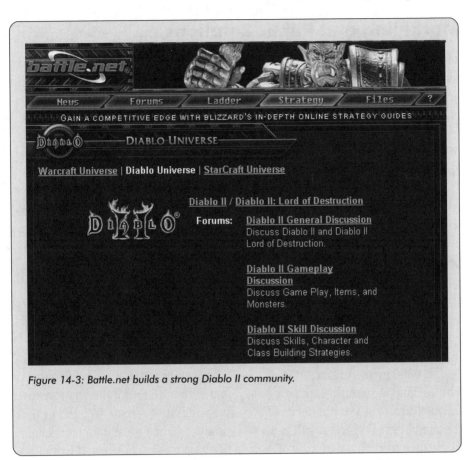

Figure 14-3: Battle.net builds a strong Diablo II community.

Battle.net represents the evolution of online play. The original Diablo gained a legion of fans but also became the target of cheaters and hackers who spoiled the experience for many. Blizzard's response with Diablo II is separate protected and unprotected gaming areas, with the latter containing no guarantees of fair play. Diablo players, however, were not content to wait more than three years for the sequel and took matters into their own hands, creating "guilds" of players with like-minded playing preferences. Many of these guilds grew to be quite extravagant, with their own naming conventions on Battle.net and even their own web sites.

Marketing and Public Relations

The marketing wizards at Blizzard took the "guild" solution to their programmers' shortcomings and embraced it fully in Diablo II. Guilds were no longer to be secret societies baffling the newbies but an integral component of Battle.net and the Diablo II game world instead. Guilds could be formed within the game world itself with players banding together and investing their in-game booty in the construction of a guild hall. Once established, guild identity could be managed from the Battle.net system. Players could even engage in political upheaval and overthrow unpopular guildmasters. As the guild grows in size, more gaming gold is spent in expanding the facilities to serve the needs of the members. The end result is a formerly external community of players brought inside and tied down to the gaming system; with each subsequent Diablo product release, this membership can be counted upon to light up the cash registers *en masse*.

The external support provided by the guilds or by user communities as a whole cannot be underestimated. Yahoo lists 47 Diablo series guilds; these each have their own web site. Additionally, 23 fan sites are provided. A common feature of fan sites is the forums, where players from around the world can share their common interest. When a company churns out four million units of a game, the personal touch can be lacking from a corporate perspective. Experienced forum manager Jason "Kornkob" Robinson (general gaming site, The Wargamer, and Rainbow 6 fan site www.piestactics.com) comments:

"Online communities also provide several services to the membership. One service that most certainly provides a direct benefit to the publisher is the provision of free technical and end user support. Online communities, almost without exception, provide members with a venue through which they can have technical answers provided free of charge and without limiting the support to merely issues directly related to the product. While most companies will not help a user choose and install a new video card or more RAM to solve a problem with a game, most communities will. Not a single game publisher provides support for people 'tweaking' or optimizing their systems to play a game—but almost every community does that very thing. These services help new fans get started and keep people playing the games longer."

Some developers are hesitant to comment on works in progress until the game is far enough along to show working code or pretty graphics. Sometimes they don't want the distraction of unwanted input early in the design process. Other times, features are trimmed as testing proves which concepts work and which cause problems. Potential customers anticipating a certain feature might be disappointed upon hearing of its removal, leaving them negatively predisposed toward the title. Some developers fancy themselves as "friends of the people," revealing design intentions early and soliciting input from the general public.

On the other hand, Blizzard's public relations machine kicks into action the moment a title enters development. With development cycles lasting three years or more, this adds up to one long campaign. Diablo II was shown at trade shows more than two years before its release; Warcraft III, with its new engine, had a three-year run. When playable alpha or beta code was not available, movie trailers were created to give players and press an early look.

Blizzard maintains frequent contact with the press and parcels out new information to whet the appetites of their fans throughout a game's development. Fans are even welcome to participate in the development process come beta time, when large numbers of applicants are signed on (not so much to test the single-player balance but to stress-test the product on Battle.net). The beta period is always an exciting time for fans, and fan sites and message boards explode with early reviews and after-action reports by excited players.

Again, Blizzard's sterling reputation for delivering the goods in the end avoids the pitfalls of full disclosure. Sure, there is always some griping and complaining when a feature is cut or altered, or the game is delayed another six months, a year, maybe two. These folks aren't dyed-in-the-wool malcontents; as they know full well, Blizzard will come through with a winner. Developers with a more checkered past would find such sentiments genuine in Blizzard's case; it's a matter of anticipation bursting at the seams.

The press has been a willing accomplice to Blizzard's success. It helps that Blizzard is a trendsetter and not a follower. Diablo II might get a little tedious after 20 to 30 hours of game play, but many reviewers spend far less time at the game than a typical player.

Table 14-3

Representative Review Scores for Diablo II (LoD)	
Publication	Score
Computer Games Online	4(5)/5
GameSpot	85(82)/100
Electric Playground	90(90)/100
Gameover	91(92)/100
WomenGamers	90(74)/100
GameRaider	92/100
GameSpy	86(85)/100
Gamezilla	89(93)/100
Media & Games Online	90/100

All in all, Blizzard's web site lists 23 awards for Diablo II and another 20 for Lord of Destruction. Twelve of these awards were "Game of the Year" honors.

Blizzard's Diablo II web site is informative and contains numerous enticements for the prospective customer. Game features, system requirements, and optional recommendations are clearly enumerated. Links to download a playable demo, MP3 sound bites, cinematic trailers, and wallpaper images, as well as game patches are prominently displayed. Novels and ebooks based on the Diablo world are available for purchase—a somewhat unusual but not unique cross-merchandising opportunity as far as a computer game franchise is concerned (Sid Meier's Alpha Centauri spawned a series of novels, and a number of games such as Tomb Raider and Wing Commander have made the jump to the silver screen).

Summary

With three wildly successful franchises (Diablo, Warcraft, and StarCraft), brand marketing and community development are an ongoing process at Blizzard. Expectations are carefully managed so the final product does not exceed the capacity to provide adequate support for a vast customer base. Scaling operations to meet multimillion sales demands often call for different techniques, but Blizzard maintains a grassroots approach, never losing touch with their player community.

Blizzard games are addictively easy to play. They provide a high level of rewards and actively minimize unpleasant or dull tasks or unduly repetitive play. Players do not have to be gaming experts to play a Blizzard campaign to completion, but skill levels and added features, such as permanent death, offer scalable challenges to meet the needs of all players. When targeting a massive audience, it is important to identify the broad concepts—in this case, number of seats (system requirements), demographics (FRPG fans), and objectives (what do the players want to do and what is their range of capabilities?). Where these concepts intersect lie the parameters for the final design; the tricky part is creating a focused product that still manages to snag the largest percentage of individuals within this set. Blizzard consistently manages to turn that trick. The company creates polished, addictive games that are equally enjoyable for hard-core and casual gamers alike. This creation, coupled with a sterling reputation and an active fan community, makes Blizzard titles games that sell.

Chapter 15

Harry Potter: The Movie Sells the Game

O nce in a while, a product comes along that becomes a cultural phenomenon. It happens with movies: *Star Wars* becoming a veritable license to print money for George Lucas and his various production companies. It happens with toys: Who will forget the Cabbage Patch Kids craze or Tickle Me Elmo? Half the planet is still infested with Beanie Babies. Even games have generated their own hot commodities with the likes of Trivial Pursuit and the whole "collectible card game" trend started by Magic the Gathering and blossoming with Pokémon. In the late '90s, lightning struck the normally quiet world of children's literature with the explosive popularity of the Harry Potter series of books by British author J.K. Rowling.

The Harry Potter saga is a tale that combines fantasy and real-life problems. The first book, *Harry Potter and the Sorcerer's Stone*, develops a sympathetic character: Harry Potter. Harry's parents are killed, and the bookish youngster is forced to live with an unpleasant aunt and uncle, along with a spoiled brat of a cousin. He is rescued from this lugubrious existence when he discovers he is the son of a witch and wizard and is thereafter enrolled in the Hogwarts School of Witchcraft and Wizardry.

Harry finds friendship among his peers and eventually must confront the evil forces responsible for his parents' deaths. Moving from the harsh realities of life to the escapist realm of fantasy was a perfect segue for the target audience—adolescents who, no matter how good they may have things, always seem to want to be anywhere but in their current shoes. The timeless message of triumph over adversity and good over evil is popular from the parents' perspective; Harry Potter is a rare youthful fad that also enjoys the consent and support of adults. Indeed, the stories are so intriguing that many parents become Harry Potter fans in their own right.

Against this background, Electronic Arts released Harry Potter and the Sorcerer's Stone. No one nominated the game for adventure or role-playing game of the year, nor did it addict serious gamers, but that was not the design focus of Electronic Arts. Presumably, EA paid big bucks for the Harry Potter license. They made good on their investment by targeting the prime Harry Potter audience, 9- to 14-year-olds, while also making it enjoyable for the kids' parents. Hence the game reached the broadest base of consumers the license could net.

Figure 15-1: Harry Potter is a blockbuster franchise.

Quality

It is not unusual for hot franchises to spawn uninspired efforts when it comes to licensed merchandise. Part of this has to do with the franchise owner's lid on creativity. "Property holders generally need to approve everything and exert some level of control that may negatively impact a game's development," suggests *Computer Game Magazine*'s Steve Bauman.

A prime example lies in Paramount Picture's Star Trek universe, where scriptwriters and book authors are not permitted to kill off or alter the characterization of individuals popularized by the series of TV shows and movies. Such constraints usually stunt the growth of any design. In the worst cases, developers fail to allow the material the game is supposed to be based on to dictate sensible design choices and instead shoehorn the unfortunate license into the type of game the developers actually want to make. One notable example is Interplay's Star Trek: New Worlds, a real-time strategy game of ground combat—a bizarre choice of genre given the nearly complete lack of such battles anywhere in the Star Trek franchise.

Although Harry Potter and the Sorcerer's Stone isn't a brilliantly designed or implemented game, it is well coded, beautiful, and bug free—factors that go a long way toward pleasing the casual gamer. Whether Electronic Arts was not given the rights to or didn't wish to pay for the rights for composer John William's excellent compositions or the voices of the original actors, they used neither in their game—a use that would have enhanced the game's overall quality. On the other hand, if the movie production can be called first-rate, EA's efforts can hardly be considered cut-rate. Graphics, music, and voice are all well done and truly evoke the Harry Potter experience. A game with similar production standards but without the sizzling franchise would be a tougher sell, but not a failure.

Figure 15-2: Harry Potter makes for a pretty game.

Investing heavily into better graphics and production values would have reduced the game's return, a return that was guaranteed by the popularity of the subject. "It's a cynical way of doing business," comments Bauman. "But I suspect publishers spend less time and money on licensed properties knowing that the game will sell itself if it comes out with the license regardless of its quality." Conversely, a minimum standard of quality is necessary to not only sell this game but sell sequels also.

Topic

Considering the success of the Harry Potter franchise, how could EA go wrong? By last summer, according to BBC News, more than 100 million *Harry Potter* books had been sold. When the game appeared last fall, the movie had broken several box office records and was on its way to grossing nearly $1 billion, the second most successful movie ever behind *Titanic*. Such monstrous popularity has made author J.K. Rowling the wealthiest woman in the U.K.

The Harry Potter franchise enjoys popularity across all demographic groups. The game likewise has an appeal that transcends the usual gaming market. Nevertheless, a beloved subject matter goes a long way toward enhancing sales. Hardcore gamers, conditioned by years of tepid efforts on licensed material, likely passed on this game, but they weren't EA's target.

Could Electronic Arts have failed with the game? Probably not, but poor design and presentation of Harry Potter's world would have reduced the number of units sold. Prior to the release of the movie, *Business Week* predicted, "The celluloid Harry could backfire, too. Kids, already steeped in everything Potter, may rebel against a drab movie that doesn't convey the magic of the wizard school Hogwarts or the soccer-on-broomsticks game Quidditch."

The movie was a smash hit, however, and Harry Potter fever had never been higher. In short, topic was the prime factor that sold Harry Potter and the Sorcerer's Stone. Purchasing a license such as this ensures the publisher a huge base of receptive fans. Product recognition is an important factor at the cash register. With Harry Potter, Electronic Arts had access to the most popular license on the planet.

Game Play

Harry Potter and the Sorcerer's Stone was developed simultaneously for the PC and several console game systems, including the Sony PlayStation2, Game Boy Color, and Game Boy Advance. It was a smart move on EA's part. They had an established product with wide-ranging name recognition. It only makes

common sense to leverage recognition across the widest market.

Console ports have a generally good record for stability on PC platforms. Harry Potter and the Sorcerer's Stone is no exception; aside from some graphic anomalies involving transparencies, the game is remarkably bug-free. This is an important issue when considering a market of non-savvy gamers; many are unaccustomed to the routine of updating drivers or downloading patches. Each satisfied customer of The Sorcerer's Stone is a potential buyer of possibly six sequels, whereas an unhappy camper will shy away from investing in even a single follow-on. Some may take EA to task over the length and depth of the game, but remember, the goal here was not to create a gaming classic but to deliver a gaming experience in a timely manner. Complexity, length,

and depth all add to the development time, as well as expanding the opportunity for insidious bugs to infest the product—all counterproductive to the objective EA set to accomplish.

Harry Potter only partially benefits from a simplified interface. Magic spells are learned by tracing a figure with the mouse, hardly the right tool for the task (or a particular good task given the tools). While the game performs smoothly on a fixed platform such as the PlayStation, it scales poorly to the PC. Owners of machines on the low end of the

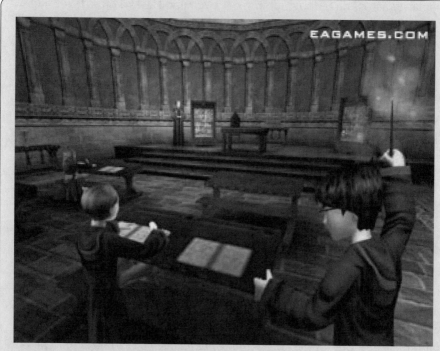

Figure 15-3: The game plays well.

system requirements report sluggish game play, while those with fast CPUs and high-end graphic cards find elements of the game too quick and difficult to manage. The customers who report the most favorable feedback seem to have mid-range machines that provide an optimal playing experience. The machine type seems to heavily impact the difficulty level of the game as well; some users are reporting the game is too easy (older machines), and others complain that it is too difficult. Nevertheless, Electronic Arts balanced the play well enough to attract hundreds of thousands of players, and that is what mattered.

Harry Potter and the Sorcerer's Stone is a hybrid game. The game tells the story in the same manner as an adventure game. On the other hand, Harry learns new spells and becomes more powerful as the game progresses, just like a role-playing game. Harry also spends a lot of time hopping around, collecting various power-ups, just like a platform action game. There is even a measure of sports, with a Quidditch game that can be unlocked during play.

Yes, this isn't a long game, but although average-length games may draw journalists' criticism, they very seldom hurt sales. Casual gamers rarely invest the time needed to complete long games. In fact, as the average age of gamers increases, the length of games will become less of an issue.

Young Harry Potter fans and casual gamers seem to be having the most fun with the game. A fan from Guilford, Connecticut, wrote in a review on Amazon.com: "I am an adult who loves the Harry Potter books and bought this to see how the story was manipulated into a game. I was extremely pleased and had a great time playing! This game is not just for kids. The game play is designed like a school where lessons are learned and expanded on until the big showdown with You-Know-Who [Lord Voldemort]."

The previous poster, hailing from Los Angeles, appears to be a far more discriminating gamer and concludes, "Overall it's a mixed bag— almost like a demo for the actual game. It's interesting enough for fans of the books and movie, but severely lacking in terms of what some truly thorough, professional design could have made it. Hopefully the game's producers will dedicate some serious time to any subsequent Harry Potter games. Rowling's world is perfectly suited to a great PC gaming experience, but this debut falls far short."

That may be true, but those thumbing noses at Harry Potter and the Sorcerer's Stone miss a key point. Electronic Arts bought the license because they saw a tremendous potential for sales. The youngish book audience matched perfectly with the gaming audience that they targeted with the game. They created a well-paced, pretty game that was enjoyable for children and their parents. Hence, the game sold.

Cool Factor

Obviously, all things Harry Potter are immensely popular, and this has a "cool factor" all its own. If you have kids, bringing home a game such as Harry Potter and the Sorcerer's Stone will make you a hero. But of course, the game has its own level of cool. It's a cool directly related to immersion. Gamers buy licensed games to immerse themselves in the world. Harry Potter and the Sorcerer's Stone does a good job with the immersion, placing gamers in Harry's shoes as he wanders through his world.

Timing is everything when cashing in on a popular franchise. What is in or cool today can be lame tomorrow. "To capitalize on a property, you need to time it with a significant event (the release of a movie, for example)," says Bauman. "So you may be forced to make concessions to get that simultaneous release."

Fads are fickle, and while a good game might sell well at any time, the marketing bonanza afforded by hot property fades quickly, and expensive licenses can become liabilities on the books. The 1995 James Bond thriller, *Goldeneye*, spawned a well-received video game two years after the fact, an accomplishment owing more to terrific game design than residual popularity of the movie. Conversely, Microprose's 2000 release of Starship Troopers completely missed out on the brief celebration of the Robert Heinlein masterpiece that coincided with the big-budget Hollywood epic released in 1997. Gamers and press were both largely ambivalent toward the game, which quickly found its way to the bargain bins.

Marketing and Public Relations

Harry Potter and the Sorcerer's Stone sold an incredible 771,000 units in two short months to become the third largest-selling PC game of 2001. For the cost of the licensing fee, Electronic Arts bought into a vast marketing powerhouse, including upwards of 500 products spanning the gamut from T-shirts to action figures to expensive collectibles.

"J.K. Rowling's great successes in terms of writing Harry Potter was she tapped into mainstream thinking and mainstream culture," Chris Nurko, managing director of

FutureBrand in London told CNN. "If you look at the book, she's actually integrated branding and marketing into her characters and her story line. For example, the Nimbus 2000, it's not just an everyday ordinary flying broom, it's a Nimbus 2000. And organizations are willing to spend a small fortune to be part of the Potter phenomenon."

Coca Cola is estimated to have spent $150 million for exclusive marketing rights in the beverage industry, while Warner Brothers invested $140 million just for the rights to make the first two movies.

Business Week reports that Rowling condemns excessive marketing practices. "They can say all that stuff about not wanting to over-commercialize their movie," says DreamWorks SKG marketing chief Terry Press, "but this is about keeping their author happy."

In a CNN story, Bruce McMillian, a senior vice president at EA, added, "A lot of licensed properties get overexploited to the point where the public just has enough of it. And I think Miss Rowling has been very careful to not allow that to happen."

Table 15-1

Merchandising Harry Potter and the Sorcerer's Stone (selected items)		
Item	Publisher/Manufacturer	Year
Book	Scholastics	1998
Movie	Warner Brothers	2001
Video Game (PC, PlayStation, Game Boy)	Electronic Arts	2001
DVD/VHS	Warner Brothers	2002
Board Game	University Games	2000
Puzzle	University Games	2001
Collectible Card Game	Wizards of the Coast	2001
Board Game	Mattel	2002
Soundtrack (John Williams)	Warner Sunset Records	2001
Action Figures	Mattel	2001

Source: Amazon.com

Media treatment of the Harry Potter and the Sorcerer's Stone computer game was somewhat dismissive. This is neither surprising nor a cause for concern. Electronic Arts made little attempt to curry the favor of the gaming press. By and large, media reviewers are "professionals" with thousands of gaming hours logged over the years. Compared with serious RPG or adventure games, Harry Potter and the Sorcerer's Stone is a horse of a different color. That doesn't make it a bad color, just a color that Electronic Arts knew would be hard to sell to the gaming media. Keep in mind, however, that most professional PC game reviewers are writing for an adult audience of experienced gamers, rather than the casual crowd that purchased Harry Potter. Hence, the lukewarm press didn't adversely affect the game's sales.

Table 15-2

Representative Review Scores for Harry Potter	
Publication	Score
IGN	48/100
GameSpot	55/100
Electric Playground	70/100
GameZone	72/100
PC Game Review	3.7/5
Gaming Source Network	77/100
GameSpy	68/100
EdutainingKids	A-
TechTV	3/5

Table 15-3

Representative Player Review Scores for Harry Potter	
Publication	Score
Gamerankings.com	69/100
GameSpot	71/100
PC Game Review	3.77/5
GameZone	72/100
Gamers.com	56/100

This too can be expected. After all, if the gamer-oriented media was under-whelmed, it goes to follow that their constituents would also be. Harry Potter fan sites and web sites discussing family-oriented fare are almost universally in support of The Sorcerer's Stone. User ratings at Amazon.com average 4/5 with a large sample base.

The official web site is a well-done advertisement. The cursor becomes an animated magic wand, but there really isn't much substance. Basic game features and video trailers are available, as well as a special offer for purchasing the game directly from Electronic Arts. User support is covered by no-nonsense EA Support; there are no message boards or other evidence of community development. Also absent are any links to reviews or other press. There is, however, a link to the excellent Warner Brothers web site, which does cater to community involvement and brand development, offering a gathering point for fans of all Harry Potter products and even a forum targeted toward fansites. On the opposite extreme, developer Know Wonder's web site scarcely mentions the product; it is neither a source of support, information, or community development.

Summary

The popularity of the Harry Potter franchise, particularly at the time surrounding the release of *The Sorcerer's Stone* movie, can be considered a bona fide mania. Electronic Arts was faced with a challenge to put out an engaging product based on immensely popular literature. Secondary goals involved creating a sufficiently immersive, memorable, and trouble-free experience in order to sustain the almost certain success of *The Sorcerer's Stone* to subsequent titles in the series.

Overall, Electronic Arts' use of the license illustrates intelligent use of the property. They knew their audience and targeted it perfectly. Casual gamers, children, and heretofore non-gamers are simply looking for some interaction with familiar and beloved characters. Virtually all of them have read the book or seen the movie and are playing the game because they can't get enough of a good thing. The overriding mandate for Electronic Arts was to give them more but, most importantly, not blow this good feeling by introducing too much frustration or unpleasant technical issues. Electronic Arts and developer Know Wonder displayed expert judgment in setting attainable goals and competent execution in their implementation; hence they produced a game that not only sold but sold well.

Chapter 16

Sim Theme Park: An Amusement Park in Your Home

Two "virtual amusement park" simulators grace the top-ten list of best-selling games of 2001. This is hardly surprising; after all, what is more wholesome and family-oriented than a day at the amusement park? Some of my most vivid childhood memories are of such trips, but I have to admit, these days, I find the shorter lines and the absence of vertigo on the PC almost as appealing as a day at Six Flags. What is unusual, however, is that the flagship title in both franchises was released in 1999.

While Infogrames' RollerCoaster Tycoon is credited with igniting the explosion of "Tycoon" titles, Electronic Arts and Bullfrog were first on the scene in the waning days of DOS with Theme Park. Bullfrog had been long known for their "god games," with their 1989 Populous refuting the notion that computer games had to be win/lose propositions. In Populous, designer Peter Molyneaux granted players the power of creation; land could be moved, buildings created or destroyed on a whim, and other environmental settings tweaked to the discomfort (or not) of the digital congregation. What the player could not do was directly interfere with the lives and actions of the individuals, making them lab rats of sorts to be observed. That same year, another software toy, Maxis' SimCity, confirmed that there was a permanent market for computer entertainment that did not necessarily resemble competitive games in the traditional sense.

Fast-forward ten years; now both Bullfrog and Maxis are under the enormous umbrella of Electronic Arts. Bullfrog had used the "god game" paradigm with a variety of subjects, ranging from Theme Hospital to Dungeon Keeper. Maxis, meanwhile, had been building a brand of "Sim"-everything, from SimCity 2000 to SimPark to the disastrous SimCopter. The two largest developers of software toys were now assets to be deployed by the largest publisher in the business. The success of Sim Theme Park would prove to be a combination of leveraging the popularity of a topic made hot by a competitor, a widely recognized moniker borrowed from another property, and a prior release

known for pushing technological limits.

But what gave the game its long-term salability? No doubt the RollerCoaster Tycoon tie-in helped, as did the "Sim" prefix. In other words, franchise tie-ins help sales enormously. Franchise games sell what is a "known" product, overcoming gamers' fears of the unknown. Gamers are less likely to buy products with which they have no experience. Sim Theme Park overcame this reluctance by positioning itself with both the "Sim" and Roller Coaster franchises.

Of course, Electronic Arts delivered a quality product—a product that was not only a challenge, but one that was viscerally exciting as well. Who could resist the offer to ride a roller coaster right in their own home?

Quality

When judging the quality of Sim Theme Park, a trip in the time machine is in order. A big year for strategy was 1999. Releases included Microsoft's Age of Empires II: Age of Kings, Electronic Arts' Sid Meier's Alpha Centauri, Sierra's Homeworld, Hasbro Interactive's RollerCoaster Tycoon, and TalonSoft's Jagged Alliance 2. Considering 1999 brought us three of 2001's top-selling titles, it was a good year indeed.

In the graphics world, 3D play in strategy games was beginning to take hold, although two-dimensional graphics were still common. Indeed, the art of creating 2D sprites likely was hitting its apex around this time. Sim Theme Park uses the same graphic engine created for Dungeon Keeper 2, a real-time strategy game released earlier in 1999. Since EA was looking to cast a wide net with Sim Theme Park, the game had to look reasonably good and run well on the budget computers that were flying off the shelves in computer and electronics stores. The result is less than cutting edge but one that nevertheless evokes a proper feel for the game. Bob Mandel, reviewer for Adrenaline Vault, was decidedly unimpressed by Bullfrog's effort:

Table 16-1

Minimum Specifications for Sim Theme Park World
Pentium 200
32MB RAM
4MB graphics card
Optional Direct3D graphics card w/8MB RAM

"Sim Theme Park uses 3D graphics hardware acceleration, and while the net result is decent, the visuals are in many ways poorer in quality than many construction simulations lacking this feature. At its maximum resolution of 800x600, the graphics still are somewhat grainy, contain a low polygon count, and lack detailed textures. The ground in particular is downright ugly. Oddly enough, there are numerous options for improving the graphics that are not supported by Bullfrog and are only available by manually editing one of the configuration files; you may, for example, activate triple buffering, bump mapping, and 32-bit rendering, but even with these operational, I am not overwhelmed with the visual quality."

The review is telling. It's not because Mandel identified a problem in Sim Theme Park but rather because it demonstrates how hyper-critical reviewing is out of sync with the general gaming populace. As I said, the visuals were not cutting edge but neither did they need to be. Cutting-edge visuals take cutting-edge computers to run; the number of gamers with cutting-edge computers is much less than the number of families with mid-range computers capable of running Sim Theme Park. Hence, quality yet mid-range graphics not only immerses the player but makes the game accessible to a greater number of players. That in turn increases the game's sales.

Furthermore, the game ran without flaw on a wide range of machines —an important factor when designing a game for the masses. The game doesn't run well on Windows XP or 2000. But how could EA have foreseen the longevity of the title, let alone incompatibility problems with later editions of Windows?

Figure 16-1: A crowded amusement park

Unfortunately, graphics did affect what was perhaps the game's coolest feature. While playing, gamers may drop from their overhead view into a first-person "camcorder" view. While in this mode, players may walk around the park and actually ride the attractions. Conceptually, this is way cool and a major selling factor (see "Cool Factor" below), but technically, there are problems with object resolution. Again, however, this is a design choice that Electronic Arts had to deal with. Better object resolution would have meant lower frame rates, something that would have detracted from the experience. After all, gamers used this view to ride the roller coasters and little else.

Topic

Sim Theme Park combines a number of popular concepts into a winning topic. The most apparent is the amusement park setting. A trip to the amusement park is a family event; this translates to Sim Theme Park being a family game. Boys and girls and mothers and fathers can sit down to an enjoyable evening without fear of violence, sex, foul language, or complex game mechanics encroaching on the experience. More importantly, the ESRB rating of E guarantees that retailers such as Wal-Mart and Target will have no qualms selling it. These outlets are the largest distributors of computer games in the country. Discover Learning.com, in a review by Brock Anderson, suggests, "Young teenagers, in particular, are sure to love this game. This is one of the few quality games that isn't violent in any way whatsoever, so it's sure to be a hit with parents as well."

Figure 16-2: View from the grounds

The second component of the game is the "Sim" portion. Certain keywords in game titles have come to signify certain features in a game, particularly "sim" and "tycoon."

"I think the Sim name helps consumers know the kind of game to expect, which actually helps consumers," said *Computer Game Magazine*'s Steve Bauman. "Obviously, it gave a sales boost to the game 'Theme Park,' which wasn't much of a hit here in the U.S. in the past."

While those interested in the visceral portion of the game might be content with placing and riding the attractions, more experienced gamers, particularly those with a background in Maxis' various Sim games, will spend hours tweaking countless settings in order to maximize profits and build a bigger and better park. As is common with all Sim games, parameter changes are often two-edged swords. Raising the level of fat in burgers, for example, might lower the cost of goods sold and generate more profit, but patrons will be less happy purchasing inferior-quality food.

Figure 16-3: Building a coaster

Nearly every discussion of Sim Theme Park will quickly elicit a comparison with its rival for public affection, Chris Sawyer's Roller-Coaster Tycoon. Both games obviously share a common subject matter, but RollerCoaster Tycoon has a greater focus on being a simulation. Sim Theme Park is a less challenging game, but one with fun features absent from Infogrames' popular hit.

"Unlike [RollerCoaster Tycoon], which had an ultra-realistic approach to coaster building, Sim Theme Park lets your imagination run wild," writes Scott Meyers of Maximum3D. "Instead of placing each segment of track one by one, you simply click where you want the track to go, adjust the height and angle of the pylons, and that's it. You don't have to worry about intensity ratings that scare away guests here; it's all about building a cool-looking ride, not a realistic one."

Game Play

Sim Theme Park has two modes of game play. "Instant action mode" immediately puts the player in charge of a staffed and operational facility, albeit a sparsely equipped one. "Full simulation" is a complete sandbox, challenging players to create an all-new park from the ground up. Instant action mode is more suitable for children and those looking for a light, easy game. Full simulation requires more management skill; research and development, previously automated, is now the responsibility of the player to monitor.

To further reduce the learning curve, an advisor will pop in on occasion and audibly alert the player to notable events or make helpful comments. This can range from notification that a ride has broken down and that not enough mechanics are employed to keep the rides in working order to comments from the people suggesting that ticket prices be raised or lowered. As the park becomes larger, the constant interruption of the advisor will become a nuisance, and thankfully it can be shut off. At this point, it is time to start making use of the charts and graphs to evaluate performance and make any necessary adjustments.

Figure 16-4: Configuring the sideshows

A single click brings up a box where new rides, sideshows, vending booths, or miscellaneous objects can be purchased. Placement is made anywhere with sufficient open space, but the attraction will not open for business until foot paths are constructed to and from the object. Many rides will become popular, and just like the local Six Flags park, the virtual park should also contain sufficient queues for storing waiting visitors.

Clicking on a placed object brings up a properties window. Here is where the "Sim" portion of the game comes into its own. The properties that can be changed will depend on the object; one may increase the number of cars in a roller coaster, for example, or reduce the ride duration of a spinning ride. Carnival sideshows can be tweaked to determine quality of prizes as well as the odds of winning. Food stalls can also be manipulated in terms of price and quality; you might increase the amount of salt on the fries, for example, and then jack up the price of drinks as parched customers flock to quench their thirst.

The variety and degree of ride customization found in RollerCoaster Tycoon is lacking in Sim Theme Park, but that's an intelligent design choice on EA's part. The game appeals to a wider audience. The company never lost sight of that and strove to make a game with a broad experience. Better still, they added a cool factor and hook, which no doubt dragged players into the game.

Cool Factor

Having spent hundreds of hours prowling the grounds of various amusement parks over the years, one of my more memorable experiences occurred indoors, at the IMAX theater. This particular film was recorded in conjunction with the opening of the theater, years ago when the technology was new. Cameramen went to some of the park's

Figure 16-5: Riding the coaster

most popular attractions, filming the experience in first-person view from the front seat of various roller coasters and other rides. The huge IMAX screen completely covers one's field of vision, and the resulting illusion slips the brain into a roller coaster seat (vertigo and all!).

Now, Sim Theme Park may not make your gut rise to your eyeballs, but riding the rides can be pretty cool. The animated ride sequences are not canned video but actually generated by the game at the time of the ride. In addition to cruising on the coasters or rushing down the rapids on a water ride, the player can enter "camcorder" mode and stroll around the park, viewing it from a first-person perspective. While building a park is a single-player activity, it is possible to connect via the Internet to other players' creations and stroll about, admiring their work. This first-person view was obviously the cool factor. That factor, coupled with solid gaming quality and sound PR and marketing, sold this game.

Marketing and Public Relations

Sim Theme Park enjoys several organic benefits that help set up the title for big returns. Theme Park enjoyed a measure of success, and RollerCoaster Tycoon had already been a mainstay on the charts, making the subject matter hotter than it might normally have been. The "Sim" prefix, as mentioned earlier, suggests a powerful brand well-built by Maxis over the years.

"In some ways, I think it might have even bigger brand recognition with the "Sim" slapped on there, most likely misleading many to think it's a Maxis product," claims Tim Jordan, co-owner of Gek's Game Grotto, a game store in Eugene, Oregon.

The press was very receptive of Sim Theme Park. The reviews proclaimed the game as a worthy addition to the collections of fans of the original game or RollerCoaster Tycoon. Their conclusions, however, seem to vary widely, as some laud the game for ease of play while others berate the game's micromanagement.

"People who thought [Roller-Coaster] Tycoon was too realistic may find this game just their speed," said Meyers. "What you do get are some cute graphics and a simple game that is easy to play. If you don't like the miniscule details of Roller-Coaster Tycoon, this is your game."

Figure 16-6: Charts and graphs

Meanwhile, TechTV writes, "Despite its amusing setting and visual appeal, Sim Theme Park is really just a business simulation. There's too much micromanagement required. Between keeping an eye constantly on the condition of your rides, hiring enough employees, setting their patrol routes, and building fun rides, players will also be spending a lot of time organizing their park and not enough time enjoying it.

"Sim Theme Park's major flaw is that once your park is large and successful, there are too many details to manage. So if you're planning on running a major theme park, here's a nice reality check for you. Gamers, however, might want a game that seems less like work."

In his review for Game Revolution, Ben Silverman writes, "I also have an issue with the difficulty or lack thereof. It's just a bit too easy to do well. It doesn't seem to matter much how ergonomically pleasing your park feels to the guests—the game is far too forgiving."

Table 16-2

Representative Review Scores for Sim Theme Park	
Publication	**Score**
Adrenaline Vault	3/5
Computer Games Online	4/5
Electric Playground	90/100
Gameover	86/100
GameSpot	80/100
Happy Puppy	90/100
IGN	84/100
PC Gameworld	93/100
Strategy Gaming Online	80/100

Yet, despite the reviews, Electronic Arts did a good job of getting the essence of the game into gamers' brains: "Build the coaster of your dreams, and then ride it" was the line, and it did what good ads should do—deliver the essence of the game in one sentence. On the other hand, unlike RollerCoaster Tycoon, Electronic Arts has not fed the popularity of the series with add-ins or expansion packs. A new product, Sim Coaster, was released early in 2001 and was more of a knockoff on the competing product than a sequel to their own.

User community was promoted through the use of an innovative online feature. While the game itself is a single-player exercise, it was possible to connect via the Internet to other players' virtual parks and take their own tour. Parks could also be uploaded to the official web site and made available for others to play.

Electronic Arts did a great job managing price points to keep Sim Theme Park hovering among the most popular titles. The 457,000 sold in 2001 came in at an average price-point of $19, down from the $35 average unit price posted when the game first arrived on the best-selling list late in 1999. Throughout 2000, prices fell slowly, and the title played hide-and-seek with the top ten lists, dropping out one week at $29 and reappearing the next at $27. By 2002, however, Electronic Arts had dropped the title from their catalog and closed the official web site (both measures in, perhaps, anticipation of the sequel).

Finally, Electronic Arts also released a version for the Sony PlayStation. Popular console versions can contribute some to the success of the PC version, particularly if parents like what they see on their kids' machines and want one for their own system. Console games also tend to linger at higher price points; a console version selling at $40 might make the $20 PC version seem like a more attractive option.

Summary

Sim Theme Park is an excellent example of leveraging available resources and capitalizing on a popular theme. Having the fortune to own the rights to use the popular keyword "Sim" in the title lends a certain credibility that attracts core gamers familiar with the line of Maxis products. Subject-wise, the phenomenal popularity of Chris Sawyer's RollerCoaster Tycoon, as well as the continued active promotion by Infogrames, has had a collateral effect on maintaining interest in Sim Theme Park. Ease of play and the family theme also ensures a long life in a sometimes underserved market. Few topics can elicit the interest of adults and children alike; but amusement parks are near the top of this short list.

Sim Theme Park is exactly the type of game that fuels the popular fires but does not quench it. The game was marketed well, selling tons in both Wal-Mart and Kmart.

Sim Theme Park is an excellent example of how to make a game that sells. Choose an interesting topic, add an intriguing cool factor, identify your audience, and both design and market the game to them. Finally, wrap it all in a high-quality, technologically simple package that scares no one but entertains all.

Chapter 17

RollerCoaster Tycoon: Hey, Mikey Likes It!

Chris Sawyer's RollerCoaster Tycoon is quite the phenomenon. First published by Hasbro Interactive under their newly acquired Microprose brand, by 2001 the property was firmly in the grasp of French giant Infogrames. All this time, popularity had never wavered, and the business/roller coaster simulation was the second best-selling game of the year with sales approaching 850,000 units.

A number of stars aligned perfectly to account for the success of the game. Production values are good, but not too good as to limit the audience to the technological elite (indeed, minimum specs call for a low-end Pentium machine). The topic is also quite popular, appealing to adults and children alike. Advanced features like roller coaster design using realistic physics models appeal to core gamers, while the spectacle of it all ropes in the casual set. Finally, we have the great intangible—Chris Sawyer's (the designer) passion for the subject (a passion that infuses all who play the game).

"After spending over two years working on Transport Tycoon and its sequels, I wanted to do something a bit more lighthearted, something which would be fun to research," Sawyer told Guide to the Point, a web site devoted to Cedar Point Amusement Park in Sandusky, Ohio. "Roller coasters seemed like the ideal candidate. I've always been interested in them from an engineering and design point of view, and I was also beginning to enjoy riding them."

Quality

RollerCoaster Tycoon is a quality undertaking that excels in the details. No doubt there is enough game to show those interested in the visceral experience a good time without delving deeper into the business models. But make no mistake, the complex business models are there. Neither is roller coaster design a mandatory play element, but for those with unused physics degrees lying around, coaster design is far more realistic than in Sim Theme Park. The 2D graphics are easy on system requirements and do not add unnecessary overhead to the design (there is no first-person experience as in Sim Theme Park).

Indeed, the lack of 3D graphics led Sawyer to believe that he needed a finished game to sell itself. "Right from the beginning I knew it would be an impossible concept to sell, so I developed the game virtually to completion before even approaching publishers. Trying to 'sell' a concept to a publisher is much easier if you can sit them down in front of a 90 percent complete game and get them playing and enjoying it."

Figure 17-1: Who needs three dimensions when two look this good?

Sawyer's comments reflect a growing trend among publishers to require game designs to be largely complete before signing a publishing contract. While his is the only title among the top ten developed independently, providing a largely completed product is becoming a common burden for developers not already owned by a major publishing house.

"The main reason is lack of risk for the publisher," suggests Richard Arnesen, director of marketing for Internet-based publisher Shrapnel Games. "By getting a game that is close to completion, you don't have to worry about missed milestones or funding. The advantage for the developer is that the royalty agreement will probably be a great deal friendlier with a finished product."

Another benefit enjoyed by developers is the ability to follow through on their vision without needless distraction. Had a publisher been involved earlier in development, the result could have been something similar to Sim Theme Park, a fine game in its own right, but also a game that sacrifices some game play in exchange for putting the 3D buzzword on the box. When concessions are made and the developer isn't allowed to create the game as originally intended, players often notice the incongruity in game play.

Topic

A full 20 percent of the top sellers feature an amusement park setting. Coincidence? Adults love amusement parks. Children love amusement parks. Men and women alike love amusement parks. Perhaps the only market segment wary of such places are the "B-movie" fans who know that the more innocuous the park, the more hideous the crime that is about to be committed therein. No worries; everyone knows this kind of thing only happens in closed or abandoned parks, and parks in RollerCoaster Tycoon are always open.

Figure 17-2: A thriving amusement park

"It's a thoroughly appealing premise that delivers amazing visual and audio feedback—it really just makes you happy to play," comments Steve Bauman, editor in chief of *Computer Games Magazine*. "And it's relatively easy, in the literal sense. So in a sense, it stands out because it pushes a lot of buttons for players; it's easy to play, it gives great feedback, it's simple and a topic we can all relate to, but there's also a lot of depth for those interested in digging below the surface."

A good salesman always believes in the product he or she sells.

"RollerCoaster Tycoon only came about because of my growing interest in roller coasters," Sawyer told the Coaster News Network, "and I'm sure that even long after I've moved on to other gaming subjects, I'll still be craving my next ride on a coaster."

While core gamers will quickly pick up on the challenging business simulation, parents are quick to see the value as an educational tool for their children.

"I think there is something timeless and familiar about it," suggests Tim Jordan of Gek's Gaming Grotto in Eugene, Oregon. "Everybody loves an amusement park and the idea of being able to create your own has such a broad appeal. Mothers could get it for their kids since it's non-violent; kids might grab it because they like the idea of making their own rides; and adult strategists [core gamers] might get it for the challenge of making a viable economy in their park. A game like this doesn't have to have the latest 3D graphic engine to still keep the public's attention."

"I'm not terribly interested in the Sim City series, but I love Roller-Coaster Tycoon," writes Jacquie, a contributor to Epinions.com, a web site that solicits consumer feedback on a variety of products. "Unfortunately, so does my son, husband, and daughter. This makes for some evil eyes waiting for you to finish so they can have a turn. I was particularly happy that my 9-year-old daughter has taken such an interest in this game because it really is educational because it involves math, budgeting, and critical thinking skills."

Such testimonials are evocative of the Quaker Oats Life Cereal commercials, where young Mikey unwittingly consumes a product that is "good for him" because it also tastes great.

Figure 17-3: Select a coaster.

"As children do loop-de-loops in their computer chairs, they learn about the economics of running a business," writes Jinny Gudmundsen in her five-star review for Computing with Kids. "The simulation allows children to have complete control over their park: They set ticket prices, build rides and attractions, hire maintenance and security, and even determine the hamburger prices. This simulation will appeal to a large age-span of children (and even adults) because it comes with individual scenarios that vary in difficulty. Younger children can tackle the easy ones, whereas teens and adults will enjoy the challenge of the more difficult scenarios where land is scarce and time is short."

RollerCoaster Tycoon is one of those rare games that succeeds in trying to be all things to all players. Not every design can or should aspire to this; a first-person shooter destined for an "M" rating need not consider a child's skill or powers of deduction. A family style game is normally more open to this treatment, however. A game that only targets the lowest common denominator (young children, in this case) might bore the parents. These parents might allow the PC to "baby-sit" the child playing the game but are less likely to participate themselves. Sales via word of mouth to other parents are lost. Conversely, if the game is too difficult (geared toward parents at the expense of content compelling or accessibility to youngsters), then it has to compete head-to-head with titles targeted solely toward adults. The top three games of 2001 (The Sims, RollerCoaster Tycoon, and Harry Potter and the Sorcerer's Stone) are all family games that are well balanced between adult and children fare.

In short, choosing a topic with universal appeal is a certain way to enhance sales. But it is certain only if the developer believes in and is passionate about the topic.

Game Play

If the word "addictive" ever applied to a computer game, this was it. Each park in RollerCoaster Tycoon comes with a specific victory condition, which must be met in the specified time period. Often, this is as simple as maintaining a certain park rating and attracting a minimum number of visitors. Parks will often have some attractions in place, and terrain issues are a primary concern in many scenarios. Early parks available to play are easy in terms of victory conditions and terrain challenges; successful play unlocks more difficult parks.

Since RollerCoaster Tycoon must be accessible to young players or non-core adult gamers, you need not play perfectly to win the initial scenarios. Hence, the game makes gamers not only feel good about the game but about themselves as well. At no point is it ever required that players take on the daunting task of designing their own rides; the game comes with an ample supply of prebuilt coasters and other designable rides, and others may be downloaded off the Internet or incorporated through the two expansion packs.

Players who want the maximum challenge can try their own hand at design. RollerCoaster Tycoon uses a realistic physics model, and it is therefore quite easy to design rides that are too intense (increasing nausea, making for unhappy patrons) or downright dangerous (killing customers is bad for public relations).

Elements in the game often have multiple purposes, increasing the depth and immersion in the game. Innocuous footpaths are a good example. Visitors to the park use these footpaths as primary transport to various rides and attractions. If the

Figure 17-4: Victory conditions

system becomes too confusing, or if a portion of the park inadvertently becomes isolated due to poor placement, visitors will complain that they can't find the exit when they want to leave. Complaining customers lower the park's rating and thus the player's score. Footpaths may also impart fatigue upon the visitors (particularly if they go uphill) and are a source of complaints when litter accumulates to unacceptable levels. As a result, players must think before they pave.

Cool Factor

RollerCoaster Tycoon allows players to indulge in their own creativity, and that combined with the amusement park theme is its cool factor. While Sawyer presents a great set of tools and options, no two parks will ever really develop the same way twice. Players not only enjoy a sense of accomplishment from completing the goals set forth by the scenario, but they are left with a creation that they can call their own. Again, this is something that not only allows players to feel good about the game but also feel good about themselves. This is especially true if players go the extra mile and design their own rides. While anyone can level the terrain and plop an existing coaster on some wide open space, it is possible to design rides that dive underground or intertwine with neighboring structures to create a truly unique visual. Once more, this rises from the designer's personal involvement with the subject.

"One thing I noticed in the U.S. is that most parks have vast amounts of land available to them and very few restrictions on what they can build," Sawyer told the Coaster News Network. "Here in the U.K. most parks have crippling restrictions on how high they can build or what type of ride they can build, and they very rarely have much spare land available to them to expand the park. However, I think that restrictions like this have actually produced some of the most creative ride designs ever built, like Nemesis diving through the rock cuttings, half-buried to keep its height below tree level."

Figure 17-5: A partially underground coaster

Other little details in the game increase the personalization of the simulation. Color schemes can be changed on many rides and attractions. Electronic signs can be placed containing whatever text the player wishes to display. Rides can be renamed. Even the balloons sold at concession stands can be changed to different colors. Clever use of color schemes allows the player to evaluate at a glance the most popular areas of the park on the basis of colored balloons alone. When all is said and done, the park created is *my* park, not the designer's park and certainly not the publisher's park.

While RollerCoaster Tycoon may have sparked the current infatuation with amusement park-themed games, it certainly wasn't the first. Bullfrog's Theme Park was considered an innovative concept when it was released in 1995. Now owned by publisher Electronic Arts, their 1999 hit, Sim Theme Park is a kindred spirit of RollerCoaster Tycoon and enjoys a place in 2001's top ten list as well. Electronic Arts has a second entry in the field with SimCoaster, released in early 2001. The presence of multiple titles on a narrow subject is not necessarily cannibalistic, and the interest generated by any of these titles can result in sales for the other players.

Marketing and Public Relations

When RollerCoaster Tycoon was released in 1999, it carried an average price tag of $25. This pricing strategy is significant and contributed greatly not only to its commercial success among casual gamers but its quick acceptance by core gamers. By 1999, the "$19.99" price point was a favorite with the Wal-Mart crowd and resulted in successful rollouts of titles such as Deer Hunter and Who Wants to be a Millionaire?. Core gamers were generally unimpressed by such games and have come to be leery of the quality of a game that debuts at such a bargain price. But core gamers do not push large sales. At a slightly higher price, Hasbro indicated to core gamers that RollerCoaster Tycoon was not another commodity aimed at folks who quite possibly bought the cheapest computer that Best Buy or CompUSA had to offer. Yet the price difference wasn't so high as to deter this massive consumer base, and early advertising specials quickly had the price down to $19.99 at retailers such as Wal-Mart and Target.

The pricing methodology worked wonderfully. Budget-minded core gamers were the first to discover RollerCoaster Tycoon, finding a new title at a price they were willing to pay. The addictive game play took hold immediately, and as soon as they could spare a moment, they were on web sites and message boards shouting the praises of the game for all to hear. Curiosity piqued, others discovered the game, and they too gushed in response. There was virtually no criticism at first—even on Usenet where such behavior is almost unheard of.

Professional critics fell in love with the game as well. "RollerCoaster Tycoon is the most purely entertaining strategy game in ages, one that's virtually guaranteed to put a smile on the face of even the most jaded gamer," concludes Bauman in his published review of the game. "It's a wildly exuberant game that reminds us that fun is an honorable goal for any entertainment medium, even one as 'serious' as a strategy game."

Table 17-1

Representative Review Scores for RollerCoaster Tycoon	
Publication	**Score**
Computer Games Online	4.5/5
GameSpot	86/100
Electric Playground	90/100
Gameover	89/100
Happy Puppy	80/100
PC Gamer	91/100
Adrenaline Vault	4.5/5
Strategy Gaming Online	90/100
PC Strategy Gamer	5/5

In contrast to methods used by Blizzard and many other developers and publishers, pre-release hype was kept to a minimum—something I wouldn't recommend if you hope to sell a game. Much of this had to do with Sawyer developing the game on his own, as marketing generally falls under the contractual duties of the publisher.

"It's been my opinion that there's entirely too much pre-release hype about games nowadays," writes Strategy Gaming Online's Ed Sherman. "I can't stand it when we get article after article about a game before it's released, and it turns out to be total junk. We know everything about the game even before we open the box, so nothing is a surprise anymore. That's why I was surprised to hear about RollerCoaster Tycoon from Microprose. I hadn't seen anything about this game until it actually came out."

Pre-market advertising can be a two-edged sword, and there is no definitive rule of thumb governing its use. Hyping a decidedly bad game, however, can increase the damage done to one's reputation, as does promising features that fail to make the final cut (3DO and Infogrames were recently taken to task by fans for omitting multiplayer in the initial release versions of Heroes of Might and Magic IV and Sid Meier's Civilization III, respectively). In the case of RollerCoaster Tycoon, the absence of advance marketing meant more funds were available post-release. The meteoric popularity of the game made further advertising dollars available as well.

Many titles burn through their entire advertising budgets months before the game is actually available, leaving little to fuel interest beyond its initial splash in the marketplace. Long life spans do not happen by accident, and titles that manage to retain popularity over several years are usually guided by timely and persistent advertising campaigns. During the 2001 holiday season, many RollerCoaster Tycoon fans took notice of the television ad campaign launched by Infogrames. PC games generally get little TV time as it is, and rarely does a title with core appeal receive such treatment. The campaign kept RollerCoaster Tycoon from being lost among the surge of new holiday releases, and the game remained on the best-seller list well into 2002.

The official web site for the game is static and has changed little since the critical early days following the game's release. Visitors are encouraged to register for a mailing list. New rides, scenarios, and the latest patch can be downloaded, as well as a demo. While there are no message boards to sustain a community of players, the Gone Gold Guide lists 33 active fan sites, so there is no shortage of destinations for fans seeking the company of like-minded individuals. The strict single-player aspect of the game, usually an obstacle in the development of a player community, is offset by the pride players take in the parks they develop, which they then offer as a download for all to see.

The franchise was further supported by the release of two expansion packs, Corkscrew Follies in late 1999 and Loopy Landscapes in 2000. Each of these products was priced similar to the game at around $20. There has even been some repackaging combining the original game with either of the expansions, and a single product combining them all was released in 2002.

RollerCoaster Tycoon

Publisher:	Hasbro Interactive
Developer:	MicroProse Software, Inc.
ESRB:	E
Media:	Release Date
CD-ROM	03/22/1999

Figure 17-6: The RollerCoaster Tycoon product line

Summary

RollerCoaster Tycoon proves that it doesn't take a big budget or massive hype to make a best-selling game. Just like a good novel transports the reader into the author's world, good game designs show off the designer's passion for the subject matter while at the same time rewarding the player with a decidedly personal experience.

"I think it touches on two of the most fundamental elements of our human nature," Sawyer told Computer Games Online. "We all like doing something constructive, where we can see that we are creating something from virtually nothing, and we all have a desire to nurture or look after things. This is what the game is all about. You spend hours painstakingly building your park and roller coasters up piece by piece, and then it becomes your own baby, which you want to look after and keep running smoothly, watching it grow in popularity and delighted by the little guests who are enjoying all your hard work. Of course the subject matter, roller coasters and theme parks, helps a lot as well. What could be more fun in a game than to build and run a park which is full of little people also having fun?"

Chapter 18

The Sims: Everyone's Favorite Game

Maxis Software has long been known for developing innovative entertainment software. Sometimes described as "software toys," their games often have no absolute objectives or winning conditions. Instead, focus is on the game play itself, not as a means to an end.

Designer and co-founder Will Wright had an epiphany one day while designing the scenery for a helicopter attack game. "I found out that I had a lot more fun building the islands than I did flying around in the helicopter," Wright recalls in a GameSpot feature. "From that point onward, the seed was planted."

The result was SimCity, published on the PC platform in 1989. The object was simply to grow a thriving city from a barren patch of land. The concept was innovative, and it took Maxis several years to convince publisher Broderbund to take a risk. As more and more players discovered this unique product, word spread until one day *Time* did a full-page article on the game, and overnight SimCity became a sensation.

Subsequent "Sim" releases followed, scaling up to SimEarth and down to SimAnt. SimCity 2000 was another giant hit for the developer, after which they made the fateful decision to go public. Driven by investor demands for immediate returns, the studio cranked out four questionable releases in 1996. Careening headlong into disaster, the company was pulled out at the eleventh hour by publishing giant Electronic Arts, which acquired Maxis in the summer of 1997.

Figure 18-1: Building the city

As part of the bailout plan, Maxis was allowed to once again focus on their strengths. In 1999, they released their biggest hit yet with the year's best-selling PC game, SimCity 3000. Later that year, they began to show off their next project at trade shows, a virtual people simulator known as The Sims.

The idea for The Sims was one that had been simmering in Wright's mind for quite some time, and was initially conceived as an architecture simulation. In 1994, the developer

discussed this idea with *Wired Magazine*, "I have a game in mind called Dollhouse. It gives grown-ups some tools to design what is basically a dollhouse."

Within two months after its February 2000 release, The Sims had already become Maxis' fastest selling title ever. It would finish the year as the best-selling PC game, with approximately 1.3 million units sold, a number that would be duplicated in 2001 when it once again led the PC gaming market. With no signs of slowing, The Sims is proving to be a phenomenon that threatens to expand beyond the confines of the gaming world.

Quality

Maxis takes a fairly minimalist approach to the outward appearance of The Sims. Shooting for a broad audience, system specs are low by 2000 standards—a Pentium 233 with 32MB RAM. Maxis eschewed the 3D buzzword in favor of an isometric approach familiar to anyone who has played the company's previous offerings. Graphic detail is present in an almost impressionist sort of way.

"What inspires me is how much people were able to read into that little rectangle," Wright tells the web magazine Salon. "You only have to give people the briefest, most tentative scaffolding to hang something on, and they'll build an elaborate narrative and fill in the gaps with their imagination. We humans are so good at that. And that was one of the things we were really trying to leverage in The Sims. We were trying to present everything at a certain level of abstraction so that anybody could come in and personalize the story just through interpretation. We can do a lot of really cool stuff with graphics and sound, but that's not where the magic happens."

By keeping the graphics standards rather basic, The Sims provides a platform for a greater number of "modders," fans who take it upon themselves to create new objects or modify existing portions of the game. Wright admired the community participation in sustaining games like Id Software's Doom and Quake series and determined that modability would be a feature of The Sims.

The result is a groundswell of community participation on a level heretofore unseen in gaming. More than 200 web sites feature objects and artwork for the series, ranging from furniture and fashion to the inevitable adults-only fare. Even the official web site has plenty of freebies that can be downloaded at no additional charge. "What we shipped is probably going to end up being about 30 percent of what the game is by the end of the year," Wright told Salon in 2000. "There's so much we wanted to do, but we knew we just couldn't manage it all in a reasonable time frame. So whenever we came across something like that, we made sure that our underlying engine could be expanded in that direction."

Figure 18-2: Various objects available for download

Maxis also proved that expandability could be greatly profitable as well. The three expansion packs that were available in 2001 (The Sims: House Party, The Sims: Livin' Large, and The Sims: Hot Date) all placed in the top ten by themselves, each selling an average of 730,000 units. A fourth expansion, The Sims: Vacation, was released early in 2002 and has been a mainstay in the top five since.

Topic

A unique product, The Sims blazes a trail, treading where no computer game has gone before. That's not to say The Sims doesn't have an analog to be found elsewhere. A successful concept in one medium can transfer to another if it is done properly. In the case of The Sims, we have a modernized version of the old dollhouse. Unlike the Malibu Barbie and accessories of yore, this new dollhouse connects with a wide demographic range (adult women of course, but surprisingly, men as well).

"Real men don't play with dollhouses? Well, I suppose not," suggests Cindy Yans, features editor of *Computer Games Magazine*. "The Sims is an unusual phenomenon in several ways. First, its design is almost completely non-gender-specific, a sure bet if you are looking for widespread appeal. Next, designer Will Wright has a real knack—no, actually, a pretty

Figure 18-3: Going about their lives

scientific paradigm—for figuring out how players relate to success and failure, hence knowing just when activities take that crucial step from 'challenging' to 'just not fun.' Finally, it really took (and *continues* to take) simulation tools to another level. Earlier games simulated very specific systems (cities, aircraft, ant colonies, etc.), some with a lot of sophistication, but nothing prior to The Sims took anything as difficult to harness as human day-to-day behavior, giving the player a full-fledged 'anything goes' experience."

Wright agrees. When Gamasutra asked why the game was so popular with casual players, he replied, "The most obvious thing is that it's about an environment that they understand. It's not about magic, or purple dragons, or esoteric military hardware, or some hard-core sports thing; just about anybody can relate to this. Secondly, we designed this thing to be very projectable: It's really easy to project yourself into the game. There are a lot of things that we leave unstated or that we deal with in a fairly abstract manner, such as the way that the Sims speak or the way they look. You can't

actually see their faces that clearly, which makes it pretty easy to grab one that looks relatively like you and then imagine it's you. Whereas if you could zoom in very close, you could clearly see that it wasn't you, and it would be hard to maintain that illusion."

While The Sims might seemingly appear ideal for the female demographic, Wright disputes the notion that women gamers were a particular target for the design.

"I thought it would be popular with women, though I didn't think the game would be as popular as it has been, period," Wright told Gamasutra. "I always thought that the female attraction would be there because, in fact, something like 40 percent of our development team was female. I don't think that you can really target the female demographic the way a lot of people have tried. I think that what we really need to do is make better games. Females, in general, are more discriminating in their entertainment choices. So, as the quality of games goes up, I think that's one of the main ways that we're going to hit more of the female market."

Game Play

Without definable objectives, The Sims lives or dies on its ability to sustain open-ended game play. Considering the appeal the game has to non-core gamers, accessibility is important as well.

"The Sims is about process of just doing... stuff, with fantastic visual and audio feedback," says *Computer Games Magazine* Editor in Chief Steve Bauman. "You can set your own goals, but the game doesn't penalize you for 'failing' to achieve them. You get to create all of this cool stuff within the game, and you see all of the changes. And everything kind of makes sense—in a strange soap-opera-y kind of way. There's less of a learning curve as the game does mimic life to some extent."

While the virtual life of a "Sim" might appear light or even frivolous to players, the underlying principles behind them are anything but.

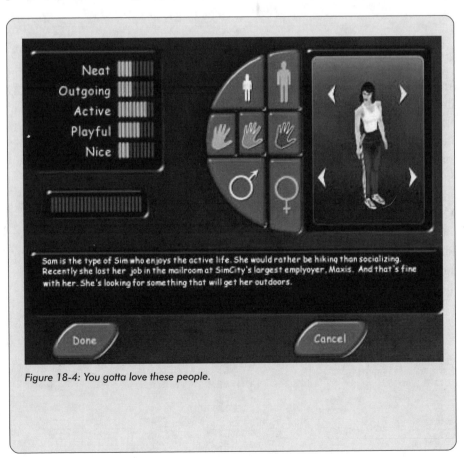

Sam is the type of Sim who enjoys the active life. She would rather be hiking than socializing. Recently she lost her job in the mailroom at SimCity's largest emplyoyer, Maxis. And that's fine with her. She's looking for something that will get her outdoors.

Figure 18-4: You gotta love these people.

"We were basically working roughly from Abraham Maslow's Pyramid of Needs," Wright recounts in his Gamasutra interview. "Ours is much simpler, but it's the same basic idea; you have these base needs like hunger, and shelter, and safety. Once you've met those base needs, then you can start working on your higher level needs, which have to do with things like socialization and/or family. Above that, the highest level needs are what he calls self-actualization— you know, self-improvement. Basically you're not going to be worried about self-improvement when you're about to starve to death or a tiger is running you down."

Ultimately, it's the pursuit of these higher-level needs that keep players coming back for more. They are living vicariously in the guise of their on-screen avatar; just as success in real life breeds happiness and contentment, achievement in the game can bestow a sense of fulfillment. It takes parents many years to rear a child and see it through to a productive life; a similar stimulus can be achieved in a few short hours with The Sims.

Cool Factor

An important part in the success of any "Sim"-type game is the ability of players to make it their own, to create with the game something unique that nobody else has or will experience. This aspect is evident in two other top ten games—Electronic Arts' own Sim Theme Park and Infogrames' RollerCoaster Tycoon. The Sims goes an order of magnitude beyond this, and it all relates to the customization abilities of the game.

Wright backs this up with his own comments in an IGN interview. "Anytime you allow people to take their own spin on something, it becomes more of an open-ended toy. The model the game is based on is more of a hobby than a movie. Most games are based on a movie model that has a clear beginning, middle, and end with a linear narrative. Our games are more like a train set or a doll's house, where each person comes to it with their own interest and picks their own goals."

ABOUT THE SIMS

EXPANSION PACKS

SUPERSTAR

UNLEASHED

VACATION

HOT DATE

HOUSE PARTY

LIVIN' LARGE

Figure 18-5: The Sims product line

"Whatever you want to see in this 'god game' is possible," confirms Yans. "If it's not there, you can find it. If you can't find it, you can make it. If you can't find *or* make it, there is certainly someone out there among the millions in this extraordinary gaming community that is just dying to try."

It isn't just finding what one is looking for but feeding the obsessive collector in all of us that adds to The Sims' appeal. "This game has become a hobby—not just a game," Wright tells TechTV. "Most games you play for ten hours and then put it on the shelf. This is something that people come back to and collect stuff for."

Marketing and Public Relations

The process of creating a bond between players and product began partway through the development cycle.

"We had been actively dealing with these webmasters for about a year before the game shipped," Wright told Gamasutra. "We actually started this thing where we got the 20 best SimCity webmasters, we asked if they wanted to be on this mailing list, and most of them said yes. Every week we would send an email to this mailgroup telling them what we were doing that week on the game and features we were thinking about adding or cutting, and they would write back and give their opinions of it. We got them very actively involved before the game was finished, you know, while we were still working on the game pretty heavily. At the same time, they were building web sites around the game very early on. Eventually, we started releasing tools for custom content that they started using, again, many months before the game shipped."

Wright himself was quite the tireless promoter as well, taking time to conduct interviews with a multitude of online and print media. Selling, say, a flight simulator is one thing; potential customers already have a reasonable assumption of what to expect. A completely innovative product such as The Sims requires much more effort, however. While the game concept needs to be adequately conveyed, promotion of the product has to include the creation of a market where none previously existed.

One primary focus was the online community. "[The online community is] absolutely vital," Wright continues. "The Sims is not a multiplayer game, but the online community is probably half the experience of The Sims because we designed it around this heavy customization, storytelling tools, and all these things. So, really one of the most entertaining parts about The Sims is sharing what you've done."

The official web site for the game contains a large number of downloadable objects for the game. Electronic Arts requires users to register before receiving downloads from the site, a process that helps cut down on piracy, as serial numbers for the game are tracked in the process. "We provide a lot of add-ons—these are objects you can download to the game such as new skins," says Wright. "If you register the game, you get more than a pirate would get."

The press adored The Sims. Virtually all published reviews rated the game in the top 20 percentile. Most reviewers would find themselves drawn in and addicted to the elegant charm of the game, much like consumers would and for all of the same reasons. Other common bullet points included praise for the unique experiences each playing has to offer, as well as the nearly infinite expansion possibilities. Some sample testimonials include:

"I didn't expect to like The Sims, but I did. I spent the larger part of a weekend entirely engrossed in the game," writes Christian Schock in his 4-star Intelligamer review.

"Between its incredibly unique game play and heartily realistic character response system, The Sims comes off as a highly entertaining and twisted mix of Tamagotchi and *The Truman Show*," concludes The Adrenaline Vault's Nick Stewart in his 4½-star review.

Finally, Gamers Pulse offers, "The Sims is a giant step forward in the software toy time-wasting genre. It is also a great cross-gender game. The only violence in the game is the havoc you create. My wife loves the game as much as I do, and that is amazing. Maxis and Will Wright have outdone themselves with this title."

Table 18-1

Representative Review Scores for The Sims	
Publication	**Score**
Ars Technica	5/5
Computer Games Online	4.5/5
Electric Playground	90/100
Gameover	88/100
GameSpot	91/100
GameSpy	86/100
Gamezilla	87/100
Gone Gold	92/100
PC Gamer	85/100

User reviews were no less stellar. On Epinions.com, the average ranking was 4.5/5 stars across nearly 600 reviews. Amazon.com averaged a similar rating over nearly 900 player reviews. Michael Reese, a player from Washington, D.C., writes this representative comment: "I love this game! My friend said it best, 'It's like a living dollhouse!' The game is great—the building and buying features are the most fun. Day-to-day game play can get annoying if you're not smart about time-management and strategy (who knew there was strategy in a dollhouse?), but if you play your cards right, it goes very smoothly."

Advertising for the game has been a combination of the ordinary, the unusual, and the fortuitous. Electronic Arts has always been active in securing prime placement on retail shelves, with large swaths of shelf space at chains like Best Buy and Wal-Mart. Window displays and massive display boxes were commonplace at smaller stores like Electronics Boutique.

As it became apparent that Electronic Arts had a hit on their hands, television ad campaigns were launched. The publisher maintained a focus on a younger demographic, and among the targeted shows was MTV's popular "Wanna' Be a VJ" contest. In 2001, The Sims was featured in the annual "April Fools" episode of ABC's hit sitcom, *The Drew Carey Show*. During a short sequence, characters from the show were represented as "Sims." Electronic Arts further leveraged the connection with the popular show by including a Sim Drew Carey in their The Sims: House Party expansion. In the expansion, parties hosted by the player's Sim may be crashed by

Figure 18-6: It's a House Party.

the comedian, who proceeds to entertain the virtual guests until the party is over.

Maxis has already followed up on the Sims' success with numerous expansion packs, The Sims Online, and the announcement of The Sims II. In a turnabout for computer games, The Sims Online is actively soliciting advertisers to put their branded products in the game world itself. Beth Larson, vice president of advertising sales for Electronic Arts,

told Ad Age.com, "Advertisers are looking to know where teens are spending their time," she said. "Gaming is their pastime and advertisers want to be among other cool brands."

Items targeted include cellular phones, computers, fast-food restaurants, snack foods, beverages, and apparel. "They're all tools in the game to help propel game play," Larson said.

Summary

Electronic Arts proves once again that casting a wide net catches a lot of fish. The Sims enjoys a broad base of market appeal, widespread availability, and a publisher with the resources to make the most of it. Developer Maxis came through to deliver on their part of the bargain, delivering on a number of key points:

- **First to market with a unique concept**: Risky to be sure, particularly if the execution is poor or the concept fails to catch on. The rewards, however, can be great; if and when the clones come, Maxis will still hold the hearts and minds of the consumers. Look at Blizzard's Diablo series for an example of how being first put them in a commanding position over similar and sometimes better quality titles.

- **Straddling the fat part of the technological bell curve**: There are two types of people with hotrod systems: core gamers, who make up a small portion of the potential market described by all home PC owners, and people in need of a new system who are accustomed to buying the best money can buy (again, a small number). High-tech games, therefore, have a rather limited, if dedicated, potential audience. Maxis enabled virtually anyone who bought a new PC in the past three years to play The Sims, removing a common obstacle to mass acceptance.

- **Appealing to the broadest possible market**: While not specifically targeted toward children, the material shipped with the game and its add-ons are non-objectionable. The game is quite popular among women gamers, an often underexploited market, yet doesn't do so at the expense of the male audience.

- **Endlessly expandable**: Not only has Maxis been successful selling their own expansion sets to the game, but by providing the means for the player community to generate their own, the game is allowed to expand its appeal to market segments that cannot be officially sanctioned by Maxis or Electronic Arts.

- **Players are in control**: Empowering players to play games however they see fit reduces backlash from those who might not care for predetermined game play or scripted story lines. Every player has his own concept of "the greatest story ever told."

- **Active community participation**: Just as politicians score points by kissing babies, Maxis gains popular support by participating in the gaming community. This includes soliciting and accepting ideas and suggestions from the gamers themselves. A game that relies solely on the path laid down by the designer is limited to the appeal of this singular vision.

Electronic Arts has given The Sims A+ product support. By channeling a portion of the profits back into marketing, the game has maintained an extraordinarily high level of visibility, allowing it to lead the PC market in sales for two years in a row. A common failing of many titles is their complete lack of after-market support; budgets are tapped out well before the first copy is sold, and titles are often left to sink or swim on the basis of interest drummed up before the title can actually be purchased.

In addition to its popular support, Maxis also garnered support from its peers, receiving the International Game Developers Association's (IGDA) Game of the Year award at the 2000 Game Developer's Conference.

"The fact that a game could be enjoyed by hard-core game developers and my mother and sister really gives me hope for this industry," Will Wright said while accepting the award.

Chapter 19

Age of Empires II: Good, Semi-Historical Fun

Microsoft has never done anything in a small way, nor did anyone expect their foray into the PC games market to be tentative. And it wasn't. Age of Empires was everybody's everything when it released in 1997, and Age of Empires II has been no less astounding. But what is it that makes those games sell? Quality, advertising, marketing? Or did Microsoft just find an untapped niche and exploit it?

Age of Empires II: Age of Kings and its highly regarded expansion pack, The Conquerors, is a prime example of a game built piece by piece with big sales numbers in mind. The strategy game by publishing giant Microsoft and Dallas-based Ensemble Studios leverages financial resources along with veteran industry talent and careful attention to details.

Ensemble Studios was founded in 1995 by Dallas IT entrepreneur Tony Goodman and game designer Bruce Shelley. With a talent for business development and recruiting, Goodman made use of his relationship with Microsoft to secure a publishing contract a year later. Shelley, a protégé of legendary game designer Sid Meier, has a long history of game design experience dating back to pen-and-paper games circa 1980. While working for Microprose, Shelley collaborated with Meier on two of his biggest hits: 1990's Railroad Tycoon and the 1991 blockbuster Civilization.

Ensemble's first effort was 1997's Age of Empires. Released in time for the holiday season, the game continued to sell well throughout 1998, finishing in the top ten in sales that year. Age of Empires was also recognized by its peers, gaining the coveted Best of Show Award and Annual Achievement Award for Game Design and Development at the 1998 Computer Game

Developer's Conference. It is a historically themed real-time strategy game; play took place from the late Stone Age to some of the early empires, such as Egypt, Assyria, and Persia.

"As we finished the original Age of Empires, we felt strongly that it was a very good game," Shelley told GameSpy. "We felt then that it was better than the best RTS games that had preceded it in many ways."

In 1998, Age of Empires was knocked off its perch as the king of

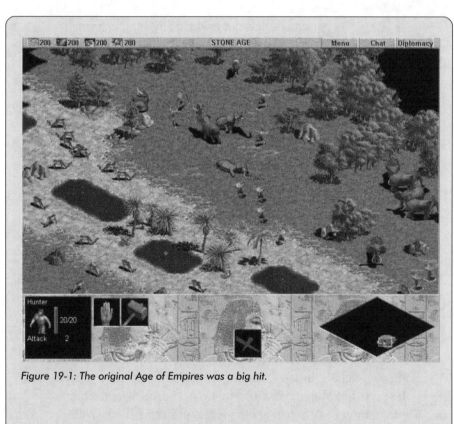

Figure 19-1: The original Age of Empires was a big hit.

real-time strategy by Blizzard's fabulously successful StarCraft. Still, the game had a strong fan base, and strong sales figures prompted an expansion pack, The Rise of Rome. In 1999, a Gold edition combining both products was released, but players were already anticipating the sequel. Age of Empires II: Age of Kings was released in September, and for more than two and half years afterward, it would occupy a spot in the top 20 sales lists. During 2001, Age of Empires II checked in with 425,000 units sold, and at an average selling price of $41 per unit, the game was still going strong at full price.

Quality

Ensemble Studios makes their games the best they can possibly be, and they did not define quality as technological one-upmanship. The Age of Empires games did not use 3D and didn't require the latest processor to run. Within these restrictions, however, Ensemble relentlessly pursued excellent production values.

"An extraordinary game that ships late makes its money in the long run and has positive effects on customer satisfaction, the franchise, and developer/publisher reputations," Shelley said in an article he wrote for Gamasutra, a web site targeting game developers. "A mediocre game that ships on time is a disaster (financial, brand, reputation)."

The timetable for Age of Empires II is a case in point. "We were planning originally to ship Age of Empires II in holiday 1998," Shelley told PC Game Review. "After we had been at it for a while, we decided there was too much to do in that short period. We elected to stretch out the work on Age of Empires II into a second year and do it right. In the meantime we shipped the Rise of Rome expansion pack in 1998. That decision worked out very well, turning a lose situation (big slip) into a win-win. Age of Empires II is a fantastic product, thanks to the extra work. Rise of Rome did extremely well. Age of Empires remained one of the best-selling games of 1998. In retrospect, bringing out Age of Empires II [in 1998] would have been a mistake."

Be careful, however, when digesting Shelley's words. Although such *is* true for Age of Empires, such is not true for all games. Pure and simple —if your game *is* mediocre, it is better to let the buying market dictate its release. Make no mistake, a mediocre game released in November will sell much better than a mediocre game released in July. To think otherwise is dreaming.

Developing and protecting a reputation can greatly enhance future sales. In 2002, Blizzard set a record shipping 4.5 million units of its highly anticipated strategy game Warcraft III. Selling at an extraordinarily high suggested retail price of $60, the game nevertheless sold very well from the start as customers were confident that Blizzard's reputation for excellence would not let them down. Ensemble also was surrounded with a similar buzz in anticipation of Age of Mythology, a game that was delayed until late 2002 to apply the final polish that has become the studio's hallmark.

Quality does breed sales. If you have the financial backing, public relations, design talent, and topic to make a blockbuster, it's best to take your time. If, on the other hand, your development studio has been assigned to develop Harley Davidson: Ride Across America, it's best to develop a bug-free product and release it in time for the Christmas rush (no amount of polishing is going to make it a blockbuster).

Topic

Before Age of Empires, most real-time strategy games had either a science-fiction or fantasy theme. Shelley, however, was an old wargamer and familiar with historical strategy games, both as a player and designer. Using history as a theme has some unique advantages over fictional settings. "Players already have some preconceived notions of what should be going on and thus have some ideas about how to play," Shelley said in an interview on Microsoft's web site. "They do not have to learn a pseudo-scientific rationale for what is going on. History gave us a framework upon which we could hang our game. We could pick and choose which interesting parts of history to include or discard."

Care must be taken not to overdo the history lesson. "We are in the entertainment business, not simulation or education," Shelley writes at Gamasutra. "Our priority is to create fun and engaging game play. Realism and historical information are resources or props we use to add interest, story, and character to the problems we are posing for the player."

Cindy Yans, editor at *Computer Games Magazine*, agrees. "What fans of history-flavored games realize, though, is that simulation of true reality is, in most cases, simply not fun. We realize that, while laboring over all of the minutiae might satisfy the diehard minority, it doesn't satisfy the masses. Making changes to alleviate a game's monotony, add excitement, pick up the pace, make tedious details transparent—all of these things will let the fun shine in."

Ensemble takes an innovative approach in assuring that their games don't slide into "fanatic historian diehard" territory. Rather than digging deep in scholarly tomes for archeological and sociological

minutiae, the team instead headed down to the local library.

"Extensive, detailed research is not necessary or even a good idea for most entertainment products," suggests Shelley. "The best reference materials are often found in the children's section because this is the level of historic interest for most of the gaming public."

Since Age of Empires arrived on the scene, history-based real-time strategy games have become something of a fad, particularly in Europe

Figure 19-2: Joan of Arc in Age of Empires II (real, but not too real)

Screen shot reprinted by permission from Microsoft Corporation.

where much recent development has taken place. Ukrainian developer GSC Gameworld had a world-wide hit with 2001's Cossacks – European Wars and German-based Sunflowers scored a year earlier with Anno 1602, just to name a few. The common element among these games is a focus on game play with "Hollywood history" providing flavor, context, and familiarity.

"History is just more popular here [in Europe], perhaps because we have so much of it," theorizes Friis Tappert, a producer for German publisher CDV. "We love history and we love RTS, so the combination is just natural for us."

The canonical real-time strategy game has changed little since Westwood Studios' defining title, Dune 2, made its appearance in 1992. Since then, hundreds of titles have presumed to put their face on the basic concept of gathering resources, building a base, and raising an army to vanquish one or more enemies. This paradigm has described some of the best-selling strategy game franchises ever: Westwood's Command & Conquer, Blizzard's Warcraft and StarCraft, and, of course, Ensemble's Age of Empires.

Ensemble firmly believes that to be successful, a game must innovate and give players a reason to choose it over a competitor. "We are all gamers and we find innovations by thinking as gamers," Shelley tells GameSpy. "Thinking about what we would like to be able to do in combination with an understanding of what is technically feasible creates our list of what is practical. We have worked like this from our start, and that has led to a continual stream of innovations in RTS like great random maps, levels of difficulty, recorded games, multiple paths to victory, etc. We think we are among the leaders already in the RTS genre, and we believe our process assures us that we will stay in the forefront. We are happy with where we are and where we are heading. I hope we don't ever change our philosophy."

Shelley further advises on the delicate nature of borrowing concepts versus innovation in his Gamasutra piece: "The majority of game play ideas in any game originate from other games. It is natural to be inspired by successful games and practical to borrow from them when creating games of your own. To be successful, however, new games must be clearly differentiated from the competition and innovative as well. Games that imitate without differentiation and innovation are considered clones. Clones are usually commercial failures."

Bottom line: Topic is a strong (if not the key) selling point to the Age of Empires series. The lesson to be learned is simple. Hunt for a topic that primarily interests you and then one that is not only unique but fills a gap in the current product lineup. Publishers should note that this only works if the developer/designer has the experience—both in games and in the retail side of the industry—to understand what gamers want and what sells. Bruce Shelley was a gamer foremost and a designer later.

Game Play

The amount of time that a player will spend playing the game is an important consideration for those designing top-selling games. A customer spending a lot of time playing a single game is more likely to participate in the player community and also becomes a testimonial, enticing others to buy over a long period of time—something that influences shelf life. That customer is also likely to buy future offerings by the developer without hesitation.

A compelling topic, whiz-bang graphics and sound, and challenging game play can be all for naught if the game is too difficult to play. As mentioned before, a game should make the gamer feel good about himself and the game. An author once told me, "A good book must grab the reader's attention in 500 words." So too must a game quickly and effortlessly snatch a gamer's attention.

"A confusing, difficult, and frustrating interface can ruin a game," Shelley suggests. "Players encountering these problems in their first play session may easily lose interest and give up."

A common feature among best-selling games is the flexibility that allows players to enjoy a game in a manner that he or she sees fit. Age of Empires II accomplishes this in several ways. Thirteen races each require a unique style of play. Five story-based campaigns and a random scenario generator will keep solo players occupied indefinitely. Multiplayer options include death match, cooperative play, and "king of the hill" games. The tutorial is well stepped, well-written, and well-acted. My 7-year-old daughter can work her way through it, and that's a testimony to great design. Additionally, in a feature borrowed from its turn-based brethren, combat is no longer the only path to victory; diplomacy and economics play a much bigger part, and one can win either by accumulating vast wealth or developing "wonders of the world."

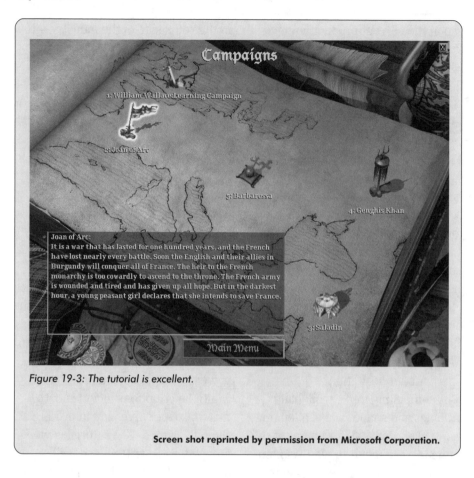

Figure 19-3: The tutorial is excellent.

Screen shot reprinted by permission from Microsoft Corporation.

Sid Meier's influence on Shelley is apparent in his insistence that all parts of the game experience be fun. "Making a game fun to play is the most difficult part of development," Shelley tells Microsoft. "Games fail to do so because they are not sufficiently fun. Games are a great success usually because they are a lot of fun. Graphics, sounds, and music enhance the experience but are all secondary to game play in importance. The key to fun is providing the player with a continual stream of interesting decisions that lead to a satisfying conclusion. When decisions are not interesting or lag, fun falters. Developing fun game play is primarily a function of testing and revising."

Cool Factor

The intention from the beginning was to adapt the essence of Sid Meier's classic Civilization, a turn-based game that could take days to play, into a real-time exercise that offers a similar experience in a far shorter period of time. The popularity of multiplayer Internet play was beginning to blossom about this time, a fortuitous opportunity seized by the Ensemble design team. While the numbers of multiplayer aficionados won't make or break a product by themselves, it is a growing and avid segment of the market and can help sustain interest in a game far after the single-player component has fallen off gamers' collective radar.

"A strong multiplayer component not only adds longevity to the product, giving it longer shelf life, but also adds the real proponents of multiplayer gaming to its audience," suggests Yans.

As with many other titles on the top ten list, Age of Empires II contains elements that allow players to adapt the game to their individual tastes. In the case of Age of Empires

II, a scenario editor is provided to allow players to create the environments they most want to play.

"They get a chance to be a game designer, create the add-on they want (but that does not exist), and see their own work running on-screen," Shelley comments in Gamasutra. "Players get a chance to be game designers. Consumer content lengthens the working life of a game and helps increase awareness of it in the marketplace."

The point is that the editor was very "cool" and some of the player-generated additions were better than the original campaign. It's this type of gamer input that keeps a game selling for years after its release and generates long-term buzz. Do you want a game to have legs? Make sure that you include an editor and a well-tested, accessible multiplayer. Remember, multiplayer means nothing if multiple players can't get together. Spend the time and money to develop your own multiplayer server system (like Battle.net Ubi Soft's) or piggyback onto someone else's (like GameSpy's).

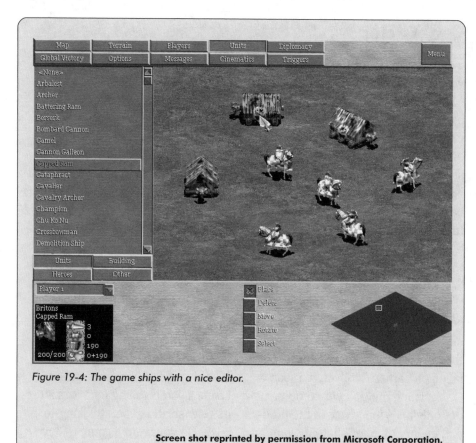

Figure 19-4: The game ships with a nice editor.

Screen shot reprinted by permission from Microsoft Corporation.

One of the facets of addictive games is the continued sense of accomplishment. Shelley terms this "player investments." Game elements are used by the player to shape and direct game play and also to provide a series of mini-objectives that sustain interest. The phrase "just one more turn" was coined in an earlier age to describe a player's attachment to a particular game.

"Examples of games requiring player investment include Sim City (city infrastructure), Diablo (character statistics), and Age of Kings (empire and technology)," describes Shelley. "Building, defending, and using in-game investments create a strong bond between the player and the game."

Marketing and Public Relations

With Microsoft as their publisher, Ensemble has access to the world's largest software distribution channel. Microsoft-labeled titles rarely fail to make it onto the best-seller lists. For their part, Ensemble designed a game that lends itself to extended popularity.

Selling the game all began with defining its target audience. "When you set out to develop a PC game, your potential market is basically everyone on Earth who owns a PC," says Shelley. "Once you begin making decisions about your game (gory, sci-fi, RTS, shooter), you begin losing potential customers who are not interested in your topic, genre, or style. Commercially successful games hold on to a significant share of the market because they choose a topic, genre, and style that connect with a broad audience base. The acceptance of the PC by more world communities, different age groups, and women requires that games not be targeted solely to the traditional gaming audience of young males."

Age of Empires II is successful in crossing the gender gap. "Actually, I think that Age of Kings is a game that will suit women, as time and resource management are classic areas women seem to excel in," claims reviewer Jay Tee at Women-Gamers.com. "Simply assemble an army of infantry, cavalry, archers, and siege weapons, and you're ready to rumble. Interestingly, one politically correct feature they incorporated within the game is that now there are female peons. [This] must be a request from female players."

Indeed, Ensemble does take all such request input seriously. Game-Spy comments on how even an Ensemble receptionist is solicited for input on design, and Shelley responds, "We want our games to reach out to a broad audience. To help get there, listening to as many people as possible during development is critical. Within our studio players run the spectrum from ultra-hardcore to very casual. Everyone's opinion is worth hearing. By designing by playing, listening to what a relatively broad audience tells us during development, we end up, hopefully, with a game that has wide appeal. We believe that is a large part of the reason the Age games have sold so well. We avoided the trap of designing for just a narrow audience. Keeping everyone involved has other advantages as well. Most importantly, people feel they are making a difference and being heard. This helps everyone take ownership and pride in our work. That leads to high motivation and a high standard of craftsmanship throughout the company."

40 | 200 | 100 | 200 | 4/5 | Dark Age

Builder

Goths
Q   Jessica

25/25
3

Figure 19-5: The female peon

Screen shot reprinted by permission from Microsoft Corporation.

I've been associated with numerous development teams, either through strategy guides, user manuals, developer interviews or contributing scenarios for the finished product. Inevitably, teams that accept input and act on it make good games; those that don't, rarely do (make good games, that is).

In the eyes of the media, Age of Empires II is an unqualified success. "Age of Empires II doesn't rely on neat 3D eye candy to grab the gamer," claims reviewer Christopher Hong at PC Accelerated. "Instead, it brings a number of smaller, evolutionary tweaks to the RTS game play that players have really yearned for. Don't get us wrong though. We're not saying Age of Empires II is great game play put in an ugly package. On the contrary, Age of Empires II sports arguably the most gorgeous visuals of any RTS game on the market!"

Computer Games Online's Xavori agrees. "Make no mistake, folks, Age of Empires II: Age of Kings is the current RTS monarch, reaching superlative heights of quality and fun. It accomplishes what almost every sequel sets out to do; it keeps the fun stuff from its predecessor while fixing any problems and adding new stuff that doesn't make the game too complicated. Not only that, but this is one sequel that is good enough to set the standard for all other RTS games that follow it. A pretty piece of work, indeed."

Table 19-1

Representative Review Scores for Age of Empires II	
Publication	**Score**
Adrenaline Vault	4/5
Computer Games Online	5/5
Happy Puppy	90/100
Gameover	87/100
GameSpot	91/100
GameSpy	89/100
Gamezilla	95/100
IGN	88/100
PC Gamer	91/100

During 2001, Microsoft sponsored a massive tournament requiring entrants to use the highly acclaimed Age of Empires II: The Conquerors expansion. Qualifying rounds were held in 15 countries spread out among all continents except Africa. Winners of the regional tournaments were then flown to Redmond, Washington, where they competed for a $50,000 grand prize (won by the South Korean finalist who defeated a challenger from Taiwan).

Many of the regional tournaments were held on Microsoft's multiplayer network, The Zone. The top online player communities are managed directly by the publisher or developer, with The Zone and Blizzard's Battle.net taking top honors. Here, company representatives actively attend to the requests and needs of the playing public. A community is fostered, and participation in the community can become just as fulfilling as playing the game itself.

Summary

The making of the Age of Empires series success story involves heeding the basics of good game design. A broad market is defined, and where mass appeal butts heads with core-gamer requirements, the majority usually wins. Like Civilization before it, legions of players laud the game's realism, although they are getting "Hollywood history" in return. This illusion works well at the box office for such movies as *The Gladiator, The Patriot*, and *Pearl Harbor*. Age of Empires proves this allure to be equally powerful in the gaming world.

When the first game in the series appeared, there was no real peer to Age of Empires. Seizing a theme that had not been done to death, such as the countless science-fiction and fantasy RTS games before and since, contributes much to the success of the series. Good, old-fashioned production values brought the customers back for more in Age of Empires II: Age of Kings and its add-on, The Conquerors expansion. Careful attention to the online community has contributed to the life span of the title far beyond the limits of most real-time strategy games.

The Age of Empires series of games proves that success is often not an accident and can be achieved through careful design and planning. Among all permutations, the series has sold more than ten million units, much to the delight of both Microsoft and Ensemble. Shelley fully expects that all future Ensemble projects will prove to be million-sellers as well. Why not? Ensemble need only ensure that their methods remain intact and their reputation untarnished. By delivering a string of highly polished and highly entertaining titles, they have earned the trust and respect of the marketplace.

> **Note:**
>
> Many of the quotes are from an article Shelley wrote for Gamasutra. If you haven't already seen it, it is probably worth reading and citing as a reference piece: http://www.gamasutra.com/features/20010815/shelley_01.htm.

Chapter 20

Games That Should Have Sold but Didn't

Massive Entertainment's Ground Control was an excellent game. Many of its real-time tactical strategy features presaged games that released years after Ground Control left retailer's shelves. Unfortunately, the game didn't sell. (Oh, it sold a few tens of thousands of copies to be sure, but it didn't sell the 100,000+ units most critics expected a triple-A title from a major publisher to sell.)

The truth is that not all great games sell greatly. It's saddening. We would all like to think that cream rises to the top, but such is not always the case. There are several reasons for this—poor public relations, lack of distribution, poor press, or just plain poor timing. Whatever the cause, the mall's discount bins are littered with good games selling badly. Let's look at some of the reasons for those poor sales and some of the games that should have sold but didn't.

Poor Public Relations

A game can't sell if no one has ever heard of it. This is the flaw in many of the games that should have sold but didn't. That doesn't necessarily mean that the PR department screwed up. There are several reasons for an inadequate public relations effort:

- **Poorly targeted effort**: In this case, the money is there, but it isn't used efficiently or pays for press/advertisements that never reach the audience that would enjoy the game. In part, this is actually a marketing failure; they do the market analysis. It is, however, also the failure of the developers. Analysis be damned, the developers must tell the public relations/marketing department who the target of their game is.

- **Underfunded effort**: If there are insufficient funds to advertise the game, it simply won't be advertised. A publisher's coffers are not bottomless; they must set priorities like any other business. There is never enough money to promote all the products. The games that appear to be winners will get the money, and the ones that appear mediocre won't.

Developers can influence the public relations effort. Keep in mind that a publisher's PR/marketing money supports the games that they feel will make them money. Developers must convince the publishers with looping demos, their own surveys, and swelling ground support that their game will be the one that sells.

Lack of Distribution

Even the best games can't sell if there is no one to buy them, and no one can buy them if they aren't in stores (at least not in stores with a significant distribution capability).

In order to sell, mainstream games must have mainstream distribution. Sometimes, however, that mainstream distribution either costs the publisher too much money or a game is pushed off the shelves by a larger publisher's product.

Publishers must pay chain stores a Market Development Fund (MDF). This money funds advertising in the store's flyer and shelf space in those elusive end caps (the end of the rows that are prominent selling positions). Some smaller independent publishers can't compete with the larger publishers' money. That, for example, is why Monolith's Shogo: Mobile Armored Division never sold as well as it should have. Monolith just couldn't get widespread distribution.

On the flip side of the ROM, some niche products can make their publishers significant money from Internet sales alone. Battlefront.com is an example of a publisher that makes good money over the Internet. Battlefront deals in one niche commodity—war games. From their semi-famous Combat Mission tactical combat series to the grand strategic treatment of the Second World War, titled Strategic Command: European Theater,

Battlefront.com has been able to make a profit on its offerings.

Another Internet-exclusive company, Shrapnel Games (www.shrapnelgames.com), has also managed to survive via the Internet. This company has made serious money on several of its titles (most notably Space Empires IV). Shrapnel Games published my game, Mark H. Walker's Lock 'n Load.

Niche sales aside, a game needs good distribution to make good money. If it doesn't have it, it won't sell. It makes no difference how good the game is.

Figure 20-1: Combat Mission: Barbarossa to Berlin

Poor Press

News flash: Gaming editors and journalists are not all experts nor are they impartial. What they are is human. Because of all the above traits, they may choose not to review a title that needs reviewing, delay a review, downplay a review, or play up the review of a rival product. Any of these actions can seriously hurt the press that a game is given, and without press there is little chance for game-selling buzz.

Both public relations folks and the game development team can mitigate these actions. Both should develop and nurture relationships with editors and the freelance journalist corps. Utilize the relationships to get a game noticed. Drop editors a line when the game reaches a milestone. Give them a call and discuss the game. The PR folks and developers should be persistent but not obnoxious. Once the game is released, they should follow up with the gaming sites, magazines, and freelancers and ask all of them if they plan to review the game. The work, however, doesn't stop there. The game team must track each review. If it's a good review, thank the reviewer and publicize the review; if it's a bad—but fair—review, ignore it. If it's an unfair review, PR should contact the editor and explain the problem with it. It may not change the review, but it will make the editor aware of the company's concern, and that may influence (for the good) future reviews.

Poor Timing

You can't release a football game in the middle of summer. Neither would it be a good idea to release a real-time strategy game in a fantasy setting one week after Blizzard drops Warcraft IV on the shelves. Poor timing is a monster that has gobbled up more than its fair share of game sales. Simply put:

- *Don't* release games…
  - In February—Christmas and the Christmas return season are long gone
  - July—everyone is playing outside
  - The week after your major, blockbuster competitor's title releases
  - If the shelves are already filled with games of the same genre
  - If the game isn't ready for release—first get it right. After all, Blizzard's Diablo released *after* Christmas in the middle of winter, and its sales weren't too shabby.

- *Do* release games…
  - ○ Just before Thanksgiving—you want them on the shelves for that *big* Friday after Thanksgiving
  - ○ Around the time of the Electronic Entertainment Exposition—it generates lots of press
  - ○ Right after school starts—the kids are looking for an escape
  - ○ When the game is well-tested and bug free

Good planning and an adequate budget can prevent most timing problems. The development team should develop a realistic schedule and then do their best to stick to it. The publishers should not push their schedule on the development team.

A Few That Should Have, But Didn't

Ground Control, Grand Prix Legends, Warhammer: Dark Omen, and System Shock 2 are just a few examples of top-notch games that should have sold well but didn't. Let's look at a few of them and what a couple of industry insiders have to say about games that should have sold but didn't.

Ground Control (Sierra)

Beautiful graphics, challenging play, innovative mechanics, solid PR effort—why didn't this game sell? As with all of the games mentioned above, it's hard to explain why. I'm not sure if Sierra realized how to sell this game to the press. Yes, it was real-time strategy, but a "thinking man's real-time strategy." Rather than making gobs of tanks to overwhelm their enemy, gamers were forced to use sound—almost turn-

based—tactics. It was a unique game, and I don't feel this uniqueness was ever conveyed to the gaming public.

101: The Airborne Invasion of Normandy (GT Interactive)

Mario Kroll, vice president of U.S. marketing and business development of The Wargamer Network on 101 Airborne, stated:

"As far as games that should have been commercially successful, there are many. Looking at war games, many are great games, from a play and conceptual approach, *if* you like war games. Unfortunately, most are low budget and lack the graphics and pizzazz that lead to mass-market appeal, which is where commercial success often begins. Games that transcend genres sell well. One of the most disappointing examples I can think of was 101st Airborne. The game was a solid game, offered something new, was painstakingly researched, had good graphics (for the type of game), and was fun to play. It also received plenty of positive press, including a review and endorsement in *The Wall Street Journal*. Unfortunately, copies of the game weren't available on the retail shelves over Christmas after the release, and shortly thereafter its developer went belly-up, completely abandoned by its publisher. Many of the smaller, independent developers have a hard time getting sufficient market penetration for commercial success, particularly with early or initial titles. The sad thing is that many consumers, relying only on retail stock and massively advertised games, miss out on some incredible gaming experiences since those smaller companies tend to focus on what used to be most important in games (the gaming experience), while so many others forsake that for eye and ear candy."

Grand Prix Legends (Sierra)

Grand Prix Legends is perhaps the greatest racing simulation ever coded. Everything from the Formula One car's clutch to its suspension is accurately modeled. It was hard, damn hard, to drive. But once mastered, Grand Prix Legends provided a driving experience like no other PC game. The problem is that there was no market for the game. Formula One racing has never been big in the United States, and the game sold only a few thousand copies. In Europe, where Formula One racing is much bigger, the game's steep learning curve kept many fans away. Hence, an absolute classic crashed and burned due to poor buyer targeting. Perhaps David Kaemer (the studio head at Papyrus, GPL's developers) was too close to the project, unable to see the lack of a fan base. Perhaps Sierra researched the market poorly. Whatever the cause, the game was a commercial flop.

The Final Sale

The bottom line is that it takes more than a great game to generate great sales. It takes a great game with good public relations, good distribution, and good press that is released at the right time. Of course, all of that doesn't guarantee success, but it does remove some of the roadblocks and keeps a game from becoming a game that should have sold but didn't.

Part Six

Speaking Out

This part of the book includes over 120 gamers,
editors, public relations specialists, journalists,
and designers speaking out on what makes games
sell. Divided into two chapters, here is a unique
perspective on what makes games that make
money.

Chapter 21

Insiders Speak Out

I spoke with many people while putting this book together—public relations representatives, corporate executives, and editors (to name but a few). I included some of what they had to say in the previous chapters, but I thought that you might like to see what I asked and all their answers. That's what this chapter is all about. Below are thoughts from some of the best minds in the industry.

Jason Bell, Senior Vice President of Creative Development, Infogrames, Inc.

In game sales, timing is all. The industry's history is rife with great games that didn't hit the numbers they could have if they had been launched at a different time or positioned differently in the marketplace. Outcast, Sacrifice, Asheron's Call, Splashdown, etc. There is, however, no such thing as "bad" if the game finds a market.

I think the developer is very important in the process, as the basic product has to be there for there to be any hope of success. But the publisher can help a developer improve a game and/or contribute hugely to its success through smart timing, marketing, and strong distribution.

On licenses...anything imprimatur that increases customers' perception of value or coolness in a title will enhance sales. Cross-medium identification is usually a benefit—unless the license has simply been slapped on a generic product—but that product probably wouldn't succeed anyway.

Bonnie James, Editor, Electric Playground (www.elecplay.com)

Great games only sell well if they're backed by great marketing. Both publishers and developers carry weight with their names. For example, people put their trust in EA Sports as a publisher and also in Sid Meier and Valve Software as developers. However, even if you have a kick-ass game, your success will be dictated by your publisher's ability to get your product out into the market. An established publisher can also give a developer lots of time to work on a game to be sure it's ready for release.

Licenses truly enhance game sales—especially for more casual buyers or those buying for others (e.g., Mom knows that her kid loves Harry Potter and she sees a Harry Potter game. You bet she picks it up.).

On franchises...They definitely do [help sales]. One of the toughest things about selling a product is developing name-share in the marketplace. Franchises have already established that name-share, and so their games are instantly recognizable.

Do journalists sell games?
I think journalists lead the consumer population with their interests. If journalists are interested in a game and make a point of playing a preview build and interviewing the developers and then disseminate their expectations and desire for that game through their work, consumers will be hyped up by that. But I don't think that reviews at release have as much of an impact on sales. I think for the most part, by the time a consumer reads a review, they've already made up their mind to purchase the game right away or not.

Ben Smith, Former Marketing Manager of CDV Software America

Briefly describe four things that make games sell. Note we are talking about items that make successful games—not necessarily great games.

Good product, good marketing/PR, trendy brand/license/style etc., luck

Which do you feel is more important to a game's success, the game's publisher or the game's developer (assuming that the two are different)? Why?

Assuming you rank success as how well a game sells, both parties are equally important. If the developer does not pull their weight, then you may never have a product to release (we all have many stories about that), and if the publisher doesn't do their job, then the manufacturing, sales, distribution, marketing, and PR are all at risk.

Do licenses, such as "Official NBA," Scooby-Doo, or Star Trek, enhance a game's sales? Why or why not?

Yes, definitely if they are marketed properly. However, the market is fussy and what is trendy one day can be gone the next, so you best be sure you are not holding a license that has just gone out of style or it may do more harm for the title than good. In addition, some licenses are just played out (i.e., there have been so many bad Star Trek games that putting a Star Trek label on it does not close the deal anymore).

Can they (public relations and marketing) make a bad game sell well? Can they make a good game sell greatly?

Yes. It is not guaranteed, and if they do make a bad game sell well, then trust can be lost and contribute to the detriment of the next game—even if it is good. Reversely, if the PR and marketing is affirmed by a good product, then the end user can gain confidence and help push future sales.

What is *the* most important thing that makes games sell?

Excellence. If everybody involved puts forth quality outputs in their respective fields, then the game will sell; everything outside of excellence is chance/luck.

Mark Barrett, Level and Scenario Design, Voice Acting and Directing, and Story

Briefly describe four things that make games sell.

In order of importance:

1. **Marketing** (including blitzes, licenses, and word of mouth): No game can be successful if the customer is unaware of the title or unable to locate it.

2. **Fun**: Whether mass-market or genre-specific, if a game isn't fun, you'll only be able to dupe a small number of customers before word gets out. Fun games have staying power beyond marketing alone and encourage positive word of mouth.

3. **Quality:** From solid code to good voice acting to a design that reinforces the player's suspension of disbelief, a qualitative effort will encourage play, encourage replay (if applicable), and encourage positive word of mouth.

4. **Interactivity:** Whether real or illusory, the computer game customer wants to feel as if the choices they make in a game affect the game's outcome. If you can provide that experience to the player, you will foster enjoyment in critics and customers alike, improving reviews and coverage and encouraging positive word of mouth.

Do you feel that great games sell greatly?

There's no guarantee that a great or good game will garner sales commensurate with its level of critical or entertainment accomplishment. A great game with no marketing, for example, will usually die on launch. However, it is not a coincidence that most of the non-license-based titles that have achieved great sales numbers over time have also been great games. Quality does count. On the other hand, bad games usually require a license in order to drive sales. That these licenses are often aimed at the mass-market audience, which is particularly unsophisticated

about computer games, is not an accident.

By the same token, a worthless publisher can kill a great game, and a worthless developer can kill a great development project or license. In either situation, you could have a potential windfall at your fingertips, but either party could blow it. If the goal is making money, both organizations need to be effective.

Do franchises, such as Resident Evil, Warcraft, Command & Conquer, and Tomb Raider, enhance sales? Why or why not?

A franchise is simply a self-sustaining license with subsequent products feeding off the success of the original. A good franchise can be even more successful than a good license because it doesn't need to go through the risky process of being translated into a computer game from another medium. The downside of a franchise is an elevation of player expectations, which can be very hard to satisfy.

What makes "buzz"?

Buzz is another word for word of mouth advertising that is often initially driven by insiders and in-the-know consumers. Buzz can be about how cool something is (how trendy or how advanced), but in the end it may say more about the people generating the buzz than it does about the product itself. Marketing types are always trying to create buzz, but no one has figured out how to do so with regular success.

Does public relations and marketing sell games?

Yes. Development makes games —PR and marketing sells games. Even a great game goes nowhere if marketing doesn't figure out how to get it onto store shelves or make it otherwise easily accessible.

Do journalists sell games?

People who read what the gaming press writes are generally more informed about the industry than the mass market. The most valuable service a journalist in the gaming biz can perform is to cut through the hype, buzz, and marketing spin to point out which games are really good and which are dogs. To the extent that an honest journalist, backed by a reputable editorial policy, can do this, it can influence sales with the hardcore audience. Nothing any gaming journalist has to say about mass-market titles will probably have any noticeable effect on overall sales.

Does distribution sell games?

Distribution is part and parcel of marketing; if you don't have the game on the shelf, you can't sell it through to the customer—no matter how good the game is or how good the license and the marketing. All things being equal, a game that cannot find retail shelf space is going to be seriously hurt.

Can they (public relations and marketing) make a bad game sell well? Can they make a good game sell greatly?

If the game is not tied to a license, there's a limit to how much a marketing team can do to move a bad title. Once word gets out, the customer base usually dries up quickly as people protect their wallets. A good marketing team can, however, be indispensable when trying to take a good game and make it into a runaway hit. At some point, it really is simply a question of how much visibility marketing can create for a game.

At what sell point (number of units sold through) is a PC game considered successful? Very successful? How about console games?

A successful game is one that makes its money back (assuming straight accounting with no cross-collateralization, etc.). A very successful game makes a profit. I see no difference between computer games and console games using this metric, particularly when the cost of the loss-leading console itself is rarely factored into the profits reported for console titles.

What is *the* most important thing that makes games sell?

Regardless of quality, marketing is the critical nexus between the customer and any available product. Even if a developer markets its own games, it is the developer's marketing effort that drives sales.

Kelly Ekins, Public Relations Associate, Strategy First

One thing that makes games sell in my opinion is reputation; either the reputation of the developer, publisher, or the game, meaning the game is part of a franchise. If a game has a big publisher behind it, then consumers are more likely to pick it up based on that fact. Once a publisher or developer has had a "breakout hit," they are pretty much solidified as a success in the business. This "success" means their games will sell well based solely on the fact that it is coming out of their studio. This fact translates into other businesses, like the music business for example. Once a band or solo artist has reached a plateau of success, their follow-up albums are more likely to sell better based solely on their reputation. This reputation is solidified by their "breakout hit," meaning one of their titles has been embraced by both consumers and the press. It is the combination of these two factors that creates a bona fide hit. A publisher/developer will need the gaming press as well as consumers behind them to claim success. Hmm, that's one thing…three

others…money, money, and more money.

Not all great games sell well. It's like the saying, "If a tree falls in the forest and no one is around to hear it, does it make a sound?" I use this analogy to emphasize the fact that a great game can go unnoticed if it lacks the proper PR and marketing to back it up. If no one knows about the game, then how will it sell well? Also, if the gaming press is not behind the game, then will it sell well? In the majority of cases, the answer is no. The exception would be if the game came from an already established reputation or franchise. For example, Warcraft III will sell well regardless of the quality of the title. It will sell *better* if it is a solid title, but it will sell *well* regardless.

I think bad games can sell well if the title comes from a successful publisher, developer, or franchise. A bad game can also be propelled to a certain level of success if it is backed by a well-timed and well-executed PR and marketing plan. If enough interest and buzz is generated, then I feel a bad game can sell relatively well (at least, better than without the aforementioned elements).

Which do you feel is more important to a game's success, the game's publisher or the game's developer (assuming that the two are different)? Why?

In my experience, I think the game's publisher is more important. It is the publisher's job to promote the title and, in essence, sell the game. Without a publisher, there wouldn't be a game to buy. This does not mean I think that the developer is unimportant (in fact, a game from a well-known developer is a big thing, but it is the publisher that will make sure consumers know who the developer is and why you should have their latest title).

Do licenses, such as "Official NBA," Scooby-Doo, or Star Trek, enhance a game's sales? Why or why not?

Yes, I definitely think such licenses can enhance a game's sales —again, the reason being reputation. This reputation will create the feeling for the consumer that they are in a way guaranteed quality if the game is based on a license. If not quality, they can assume that if they like the *Scooby-Doo* TV show, then they will most likely enjoy the game based on it. This is not true for other games. The risk for the consumer is brought down as soon as a license is attached to a game.

Do franchises, such as Resident Evil, Warcraft, Command & Conquer, and Tomb Raider, enhance sales? Why or why not?

Yes, and for the same reasons that I mentioned in the above question. It's that false sense of security for the consumer that will propel these franchise games to success (of course, only if the franchise is successful); but hey, it wouldn't be a franchise if it weren't.

Or, you could look at it from the other angle and say that a game being a part of a franchise could be a hindrance because consumers will assume that if they didn't like the first game, then they will automatically not enjoy the next installment, when in fact lots of features could have been changed.

But, I'm leaning more toward yes.

What makes "buzz"?

Buzz is made when consumers and journalists are excited about the release of a game. The feeling that everyone is talking about the same thing, the same game, usually creates this buzz. To make sure everyone is talking about the same thing usually requires the fact that everyone has seen the same game, meaning you've sent out hundreds of samples to the press and have secured features and demo disks, which costs money. Advertisements in popular magazines help too, and again that costs money. The illusion that your title is grandiose can be created by spending lots of money because the average consumer thinks that if the money is being spent, then the product is worth it, which is definitely not true.

Does public relations and marketing sell games?

To a degree, yes. Without any PR or marketing, it would be difficult for consumers to even know if a game exists. A well-executed PR and marketing plan can determine the success of a title.

Do journalists sell games?

Again, I agree that to a certain extent the reviews that journalists write definitely do help sell games. Many surveys prove that consumers look to reviews as the #1 deciding factor on whether or not to buy a title they are unsure of. Good distribution definitely helps sell games because if your game is not in the stores, how can consumers possibly pick it up? Surveys also show that consumers are still hesitant about putting their credit card numbers on the Internet, and a large majority of gamers are not an age where they would have their own credit card to use. So, yes, you need good distribution to sell games.

Can they (public relations and marketing) make a bad game sell well? Can they make a good game sell greatly?

In order to make a bad game sell well, you would need to effectively "trick" consumers into thinking it is a solid game. The best way to do this is to attach a license to the title like NBA or NHL. Another way to "trick" consumers would be if the title were an installment of a franchise. Hence, as I mentioned earlier, the reputation of this franchise would propel the game to a certain level of success, and the PR and marketing team would not have to work very hard. So, yes, effective PR and marketing can help a bad game sell well if the aforementioned attributes are present. All they would have to do is focus on the above qualities, ride the coattails of either the license of the franchise.

The one thing it seems PR people cannot do is make a journalist write a favorable review if they do not think the game deserves it. While advertising dollars and political viewpoints sway articles in newspapers and magazines, it seems those same rules do not apply as much in the game industry. Some may say we're lucky, while others will disagree. Reviews are the one thing PR and marketing do not seem to have any control over, and they are an integral part of the plan to sell a game. The only thing they can do is choose not to send out review code to journalists. This will result in the publisher being bashed on forums and maybe angering their journalists, but it might save them face in the long run.

Can we make a good game sell greatly? Well, if you've got a good game, it makes your life easy, and propelling it into the spotlight is much easier. So, yes, we can make it sell greatly by putting an effective marketing plan into action. Bottom line: Reputation sells games—the reputation of the franchise, license, publisher, or developer.

What excites you about a new game?

Innovation, the use of new technology, and when the innovation or new technology runs smoothly. That means someone took a risk and backed it up...I like that. They put their money where their mouths are, in a sense.

Jeff Vitous, Director of Partnership Development, The Wargamer (www.thewargamer.com)

Briefly describe four things that make games sell. Note we are talking about items that make successful games, not necessarily great games.

1. Lots of hype and marketing.
2. Ease of play.
3. Accessible and popular topic or theme.
4. Publisher/developer reputation.

Do you feel that great games sell greatly?

That's like asking if the smartest people get the most attractive spouses and the highest paying jobs. Sometimes it happens. Often, it does not.

Do you feel that bad games can sell well?

Of course! Marketing hype can make an instant best-seller out of total junk. Sometimes the public catches on before the game becomes a runaway hit, but when talking about computer games, it doesn't take a whole lot of units for a game to be considered successful.

Which do you feel is more important to a game's success, the game's publisher or the game's developer (assuming that the two are different)? Why?

The developer makes the difference between a good game and bad game. In most cases, the publisher makes the difference between a successful seller and one that is not. A few marquee developers can rise above this and sell games on their own recognizance.

Do licenses, such as "Official NBA," Scooby-Doo, or Star Trek, enhance a game's sales? Why or why not?

Sure, familiarity with the subject makes it much easier to become involved with the game.

Do franchises, such as Resident Evil, Warcraft, Command & Conquer, and Tomb Raider, enhance sales? Why or why not?

Branding breeds familiarity. People know what to expect with those series. Same basic effect as licensed material.

What makes "buzz"?

Excitement and anticipation among the gaming community. It's a bonus if this leaks out and infects a more general consumer market (i.e., Xbox).

Does public relations and marketing sell games?

Yes. They control the flow of information and must in some cases create "buzz" where none exists.

Do journalists sell games?

Some, although they rarely make or break a game.

Does distribution sell games?

Sure, putting copies of games in front of potential customers where they are more likely to purchase them is part of the sales game. This is not always the "no-brainer" software and game stores.

Can they (public relations and marketing) make a bad game sell well? Can they make a good game sell greatly?

Sure. Black & White is a good example of the former, StarCraft the latter.

At what sell point (number of units sold through) is a PC game considered successful? Very successful? How about console games?

It really depends on the development cost. Small, individual developers may find success at a few thousand units. Smaller teams, perhaps 20,000 to 30,000. Major development teams might consider 200,000 a failure. Someone like Blizzard probably counts on well over a million.

What is *the* most important thing that makes games sell?

Familiarity—be it subject matter, theme, paradigm, or prior track record.

What excites you about a new game?

New ideas, developers that take chances, themes and subjects off the beaten path. Precisely the opposite of what the market delivers and what usually sells.

Christina Ginger, Director of Communications, Strategy First

Briefly describe four things that make games sell. Note we are talking about items that make successful games, not necessarily great games.

A decent marketing budget, good packaging, great retail/distribution support, and solid game play in my experience is essential for a game to do well.

Do you feel that great games sell greatly?

Not always. We've had experiences with games that were really good (i.e., they were nominated for numerous awards and even won several of them), but without a large marketing budget or retail support, the games did not sell as well as they could have.

Do you feel that bad games can sell well?

It really depends. I am sure there have been many games that were real stinkers but sold very well once they hit the market. This has a lot to do with the marketing and advertising dollars that are spent on the game and the ensuing hype that surrounds the game's release.

Which do you feel is more important to a game's success, the game's publisher or the game's developer (assuming that the two are different)? Why?

I really think that both have a huge part to play in the success of a game. However, if I had to pick one, it would be the publisher. The publisher is typically the one who is spending the marketing dollars and getting it to market. If all those things aren't done properly, regardless of how well the development team is or how solid the game play, the game will not sell.

Do licenses, such as "Official NBA," Scooby-Doo, or Star Trek, enhance a game's sales? Why or why not?

I don't think they hurt a game's sales, that's for sure. Having a license such as Lord of the Rings, Harry Potter, or Survivor, for example, will help you hit the casual gamer market more so than a game that doesn't have the benefit of an instantly recognized brand. A brand such as Survivor definitely attracts a huge part of the population, and retailers tend to believe these games will do better as well.

Do franchises, such as Resident Evil, Warcraft, Command & Conquer, and Tomb Raider, enhance sales? Why or why not?

Definitely! They create their own brands, which are strong in their own right. Players are more likely to buy a sequel to a good game than an adaptation of a great movie or book.

What makes "buzz"?

Good marketing, PR, community, and retail/distribution support. If I really think about the games that have sold millions of copies, I always come back to the amount of support the game received from the gaming community (i.e., Half-Life). That game has spawned a thriving community of mod creators, which creates a positive feedback loop dragging gamers into spending many hours both playing the game and discussing it on forums. Word of mouth is better advertising than any number of print ads can buy you.

Does public relations and marketing sell games?

I would like to think so, since I work in the public relations industry. People in our office have this argument all the time. Does marketing sell a game? Development people like to think that we don't play that much of a role in the success of a game, and rather that it is the quality of the game that makes it sell. I am big on quality of game play too, but the gaming community would not know about a good game if it wasn't

for PR and/or marketing. It is after all, the press announcements, screen shots, developer diaries, interviews, advertising, POS materials, and packaging that allow the public to learn about the game and then hopefully encourage them to go to the store and purchase it.

Do journalists sell games?

I think journalists have a big part to play in the success of a title. We have read many surveys that suggest that a large percentage of people who buy games will buy a title based on a review they read in a magazine or online. Reviews of games and recommendations play a pivotal role without a doubt.

Does distribution sell games?

Distribution definitely helps sell a game. We had a case where one of our games received tremendous feedback due to the PR and marketing, but the retailers and distributors were wary that it was too much of a niche market title and that it wouldn't sell. Due to our relationship with our distributor, we did get the game placed, but that just goes to show that if retailers and your distribution partner aren't behind the game as well, it could really be a detriment to sales. After all, if the game isn't placed, *no one* will be able to buy the game, regardless of how good it is. Distribution does vary as well. Games that have store standees, co-op, and end caps obviously get more visibility, and that in turn will help you sell more games. Placement has a big part to play too.

Can they (public relations and marketing) make a bad game sell well? Can they make a good game sell greatly?

I think it depends on your marketing and PR team! I really think that a bad game can sell well if the hype is big enough. You may not continue to sell the game well, if it's a bad game, but the initial sell-through in the first couple of weeks can be very big, if you market and promote the game well enough. We've seen that happen in our industry many times.

At what sell point (number of units sold through) is a PC game considered successful? Very successful? How about console games?

I assume it depends on each company's standards. For us, a successful game would sell 50,000+. A very successful game would be over the 100,000 mark. But when a game demonstrates innovative game play, beautiful graphics, and a good solid story line, that's exciting. There are so many games that resemble each other that it is always exciting to see a developer bring something new to the genre.

Pro Sotos, Producer, *Disciples* and *Disciples II*

Do you feel that great games sell greatly?

That's not true; there are probably lots of great games out there that no one has ever played. For a game to sell well, everyone along the way has to their job. It starts with the game developers making a good game, and the marketing department has to make gamers aware of it, the sales department has to sell it to the distributors who then have to sell it to the retailer, and the public relations department has to make the magazines aware of it. It's like in football: The more people that have to touch

the ball to make the play work, the more likely a fumble will occur.

Which do you feel is more important to a game's success, the game's publisher or the game's developer (assuming that the two are different)? Why?

Having worked in both development and publishing, I have to say that the publisher is slightly more important than the developer. A developer can make the best game ever, but if the publisher doesn't get gamers excited about it, the game won't sell as much as it should.

Do licenses, such as "Official NBA," Scooby-Doo, or Star Trek, enhance a game's sales? Why or why not?

Most of the time, licensed games are not nearly half as good as non-licensed games because of the restrictions of working with a license, although sports titles tend to be the exception. A good license will help sell more copies of a game—not to hard-core gamers, but to casual gamers.

Do franchises, such as Resident Evil, Warcraft, Command & Conquer, and Tomb Raider, enhance sales? Why or why not?

All of those games have a huge following because they are associated with great gaming, and that's what hardcore gamers want, great games. Just seeing those titles on a box makes gamers pick them up.

What makes "buzz"?

In my opinion, gamers make buzz. Fans of a game will always look forward to buying the next game in line, but when they start getting their friends interested and they spread the word to others, then you've got buzz.

Do journalists sell games?

If you mean do they help make a game a best seller, I'd say no. I've seen lots of great reviews for great games but all the reviews didn't add up to 20,000 copies sold. The inverse is also true; there are times when a game receives less than great reviews but has great sales. I always research a game before I decide to buy it, but there are times when I'll buy a game regardless of the review, especially if I want to play a game from that genre bad enough.

Does distribution sell games?

Definitely. I was really excited when I went into a store a few days after one of the games I worked on was released and saw that it had sold out. I thought, "That's great, people love it," but at the same time there weren't any copies available for anyone else to buy. If it took one week for them to replenish their stock, there were fewer days for gamers to buy my game from that store. So if a gamer walks into the store and can't find my game, he or she might pick up a similar game and might completely forget about my game.

Can they (public relations and marketing) make a bad game sell well? Can they make a good game sell greatly?

In my opinion, it's much harder to get a bad game to sell well than it is to make a good game sell great, and throwing marketing money at a game title doesn't guarantee success, but to answer your question, I do think that public relations and marketing can sell a game.

At what sell point (number of units sold through) is a PC game considered successful? Very successful? How about console games?

That depends on how many people worked on the game. If two people work on a game for six months, you don't have to sell a million copies to make money on it, but nowadays it's very hard to get a game that small published. For PC games, I'd say 100,000 copies is a hit, and for consoles I'd say between 200,000 and 250,000 copies. Certain publishers won't even consider a game unless it has the potential to sell 200,000 copies, and that's just on the computer.

What excites you about a new game?

That's a really hard question because I like lots of different types of games. The most important thing for me is the fun factor, or as I like to call it, the "funocity level." The kinds of games I always need to have in my library are sports titles (hockey, football, and wrestling), racing games, RPGs, and strategy games, and the only thing they have in common is that they are fun. If a game isn't fun, then who cares how real it is or how great the graphics look? If a game keeps me up until 4:00 A.M., then you can be sure I'll be missing lots of sleep playing it. There's not really one thing that excites me about a game; it's the potential for fun, whether it's a single-player game that I play by myself on the computer or with friends on the couch in the basement.

Dan Clarke, Owner, Gaming Nexus (www.gamingnexus.com)

Briefly describe four thing that make games sell. Note we are talking about items that make successful games, not necessarily great games.

Price, word of mouth, Internet community, and licenses. Price is often overlooked, but look at where most of the NPD list is—under $30 —at least for PC games. Word of mouth and the Internet community

go hand in hand. Look at the most successful games and the fan sites and/or forums about those games. RollerCoaster Tycoon has a huge following. Even the awful Deer Hunter games have quite the following. I think licenses have a role in gaming too—again, more people are likely to buy a Tomb Raider game over an adventure game such as The

Which do you feel is more important to a game's success, the game's publisher or the game's developer (assuming that the two are different)? Why?

Again, it depends on what you mean by success. If you mean quality, I think the developer is key. If we're talking quantity, the game publisher can make a big difference. Something with the EA name can sell quite a bit, regardless of the quality of the game.

Do licenses, such as "Official NBA," Scooby-Doo, or Star Trek, enhance a game's sales? Why or why not?

I think so. When it comes to sports games, not having a license is a game breaker. In other licensed properties, it's a lot more difficult to live up to the hype of a good show/movie in a video game. In my opinion, I know that a movie-licensed game will probably be bad, quality wise. However, I'm sure it'll sell well.

Do franchises, such as Resident Evil, Warcraft, Command & Conquer, and Tomb Raider, enhance sales? Why or why not?

I think they continue a buzz and generate additional sales. I think that many people buy the franchise based on the original game, looking to recreate some of the magic that brought people to that game in the

first place. Unfortunately, the magic rarely happens again.

Do journalists sell games?

I think that journalists do indeed sell games. I personally have bought games based on reviews. I may have regretted those decisions later—but I have done it. Interestingly enough, I have also *not* bought games based on journalists.

Does distribution sell games?

It can. Again, the Wal-Mart/Deer Hunter combination is an example. They knew their market very well and sold through an amazing amount of games.

Can they (public relations and marketing) make a bad game sell well? Can they make a good game sell greatly?

If they are doing their job right, I think so. However, it seems like they can sell bad games better than they can sell good games. That could be because PR lets the good games speak for themselves. Unfortunately, this doesn't always work.

What is *the* most important thing that makes games sell?

I think the game has to appeal to some part of a gamer's mind—the genre and topic have to be something of interest to the gamer in order for them to buy it. You are never going to make a non-sports gamer buy a football game.

Jim Werbaneth, Publisher, *Line of Departure*, Designer of *Inchon* and *Britain Stands Alone*

Briefly describe four things that make games sell. Note we are talking about items that make successful games, not necessarily great games.

The first important thing is a salable genre. As much as I love historical titles and grew up on historical board games, science fiction and fantasy do better, as do hypothetical, current conflict. Second, real-time strategy does better than turn-based games for the most part. Third, a franchise will often sell more than a purely original title, as people are attracted to the "safety" of what they already know or think they understand. Fourth, as in any industry, promotion counts!

Which do you feel is more important to a game's success, the game's publisher or the game's developer (assuming that the two are different)? Why?

The publisher. If either is going to be recognized by the customer, it's going to be the publisher. As a case in point, except for the real cognoscenti, how many Age of Empires series players would be able to figure out that their favorite game is more the work of Ensemble Studios than the great giant Microsoft?

What makes "buzz"?

I see "buzz" as being similar to that in the music business; it's a little bit of word of mouth, more derived from reviews, and arguably the most from advertising and promotion. Suffice to say, buzz is not an impartial counselor to the player.

Does public relations and marketing sell games?

Truly! Don't forget to include the growing phenomenon of movie tie-ins and sound track albums to both the film and the game. The troika of game, movie, and music can be a potent combination for mutually supportive promotion.

Does distribution sell games?

Absolutely. If a game can be distributed to Best Buy or Circuit City or Wal-Mart, it will pick up more sales, much of it from casual walk-through decision making, than a game available only by direct sales from the publisher.

Can they (public relations and marketing) make a bad game sell well? Can they make a good game sell greatly?

Oh yes. Never underestimate the power of the con man or the gullibility of his mark. Besides, as long as record companies can sell contrived boy bands and teen idols with bigger artificial breasts than natural talent, I'll believe that the American entertainment consumer is no more discerning than his car-consuming father who bought piece-of-junk cars from Detroit 30 years ago.

What excites you about a new game?

1) The subject. 2) The reputation of the developer or designer. 3) Evolutionary improvement over proven, past work. 4) Originality.

The Final Question

Of course, the final question (in fact the most important question) is what you think makes a game sell or what you think makes a good game.

Whether you are a potential developer/designer or just a big fan, only you can decide what type of game turns you on.

Chapter 22

Fans Speak Out

ritical to running any business is understanding the customer. Do you want to sell meat? You better understand the man or woman who comes to buy their dinner at your butcher shop. Before, however, you can understand your customer, you must know who that customer is. The developer's customer is not the publisher that holds their purse strings, but rather the gamer that buys their games. Customer confusion can lead to a shoddy product. For example, rushing a design to meet artificial publisher deadlines often leads to low-quality titles with short shelf lives.

Ultimately, the customer must be satisfied. Satisfied customers will lead to satisfied publishers. Of course, satisfying the customer is much easier said than done, especially for first-time developers without a strong reputation to bank on. Publishers often throw withering pressure on unproven developers. It's not that publishers are evil but rather that they may have a different perception of what makes a good game or different goals for the game. As hard as it is to accept, your "game to end all games" may not be a "triple-A" title in the publisher's venue, but rather something to fill the liquidity gap between blockbuster hits. A publisher's market analysis may indicate that a mediocre game released on the Friday after Thanksgiving will sell better than a good game released in January. Under such constraints, new developers hoping to gain recognition must learn to manage their time well, ensuring that they can bring home a top-quality product, and bring it home on time. But I digress.

One way to understand the customer is to ask them what they like. We did just that, surveying 141 gamers and industry veterans. We questioned gamers who frequented several Internet sites, including The Wargamer (www.wargamer.com), Electric Playground (www.electplay.com), and Just Adventure (www.justadventure.com). The Wargamer did an excellent job incorporating the survey into their HTML, making the survey much easier for gamers to take. Accordingly, we received more answers from that location than any other. That in turn slanted the answers toward the strategy side of the spectrum, but they were fascinating nonetheless.

The Questions

We asked each respondent several questions:

- What influences your gaming purchases the most? (Select up to two.)
- Do you believe the publisher (Infogrames, EA, etc.) or the developer (Blizzard, etc.) has a greater impact on how good the game is?
- If you buy a stinker from a publisher, will you buy a subsequent game from the same publisher?
- What is your favorite game you have played in the last 24 months? Why?
- Will you buy a game on impulse if it is connected with a license, such as Star Trek and Star Wars, which you enjoy?
- Does the game's genre strongly influence your purchase?
- What is your favorite genre?
- If you read a glowing review, will you buy the game?

The respondents' answers were intriguing, thought provoking, and more than a little enlightening. Below we examine each question in turn.

What Influences Your Gaming Purchases the Most? (Select up to Two.)

We gave the folks who took the test several options to choose from: genre, cool factor, topic, franchises, developer/publisher. The respondents could choose any two answers, but many chose three. Hey, there's no accounting for...

The results were as follows:

- Genre: 78%
- Cool factor: 15%
- Topic: 50%
- Franchise: 49%
- Developer/publisher: 18%

Obviously, genre is the big winner and appears to be the primary reason that gamers buy games. Nevertheless, topic and franchise are a not-too-distant second and third. None of this is surprising. People are comfortable with familiarity. Furthermore, gamers—especially experienced gamers—know what they like, and it appears that more often than not, a game's genre is indicative of what they like.

By the same token, votes in the franchise column were tantamount to another vote for genre. In fact, 80 percent of those who indicated that franchises influenced their buying decisions also claimed that genre was important. If you compile those who thought franchise significant but didn't check genre, those checking genre includes almost 90 percent of the surveyed gamers.

It only makes sense; for example, No One Lives Forever and its progeny, No One Lives Forever 2: A Spy in H.A.R.M.'s Way, are first-person shooters. It's hard to imagine that the series' next iteration will be a turn-based war game. Hence, first-person shooter aficionados know that the NOLF franchise means good first-person shooter gaming.

The bad news for game designers and their egos is the very few survey takers (15 percent) who claimed to care who designs, develops, and publishes their game. This seems to fly in the face of reason. After all,

anything that Blizzard makes sells like flyswatters in the Alabama summer, doesn't it? No doubt it does, and the firm's reputation for quality certainly enhances their sales, but again the sales are directly linked to strong genres (RTS and action-RPG) and even stronger franchises (Warcraft and Diablo). Although Blizzard created those franchises, it's the name of the game that sticks in gamers' minds.

Also lower than we would have initially expected was the cool factor. Part of this is due to the large number of respondents from the Wargamer web site. Many strategy and wargamers frequent the site, and these gamers have traditionally been players who are older and less influenced by the latest gee-whiz technology or neat game gimmick. Nevertheless, 15 percent is low. Perhaps the illusive cool factor doesn't prompt gamers to pull out the wallet but rather enhances the gamers' experience after they have bought the game. This in turn leads to greater enjoyment, which leads to positive buzz, which leads to better game sales.

Finally, the game's topic was also a big purchase influence. This would seem to indicate that gamers are looking for games about subjects that they enjoy. Although that is true, it is not the primary reason that gamers buy games. Only 17 percent of the surveyed gamers stated that they would buy a game because of an affiliation with a movie license, such as *Star Wars*. Affiliation with a license is first cousin to association with a topic, yet it doesn't seem to get gamers' dollars. Every respondent that chose topic also picked either genre or franchise as an influence on their buying. Obviously, gamers are interested in topics but only when it's in a franchise or genre that they trust.

Do You Believe the Publisher (Infogrames, EA, etc.) or the Developer (Blizzard, etc.) has a Greater Impact on How Good the Game Is?

Not surprisingly, gamers felt that the folks responsible for designing and developing the games (i.e., the development studio) played a larger part in the making of a quality game. Fifty-one percent of those surveyed felt the development studio was king, while only 18 percent opted to go with the publishers. A whopping 31 percent either felt both were equally responsible or weren't sure.

This number is indicative of a general lack of understanding of the roles of developers and publishers. The most common misconception was that the publisher was a heartless group of money mongers. For example, one respondent quipped, "The industry is full of games that

publishers decided to release too soon, push out the door for Christmas, or dumb down and drop features." Although that may be true, fewer gamers seemed to realize that quality publishers can be a boon to the game.

If You Buy a Stinker from a Publisher, Will You Buy a Subsequent Game from the Same Publisher?

But gamers' apathy toward publishers cuts both ways. Nearly 73 percent of the gamers surveyed claimed they would probably buy another game from a publisher that had previously released a piece of junk. In other words, gamers do not seem to hold the publisher accountable for the quality of the game. It makes no difference whether it is good or bad. There were, however, 19 percent who said that they wouldn't buy a subsequent title and even more who stated that they might buy a second title but that would be the publisher's last chance.

There were, however, several respondents who indicated they would not buy a game from a developer that had previously developed a bad game. The feeling seems to be that all publishers can put out a bad title now and again, but a bad game from a developer brands that developer as a failure. Many folks said that they might buy a second game from a publishing company that had publishing company that had previously published a stinker but would only do so after seeing how the journalists reviewed the game—an interesting point since only 35 percent of the surveyed gamers said a glowing review would prompt them to buy a game.

What Is Your Favorite Game You Have Played in the Last 24 Months? Why?

Of course, this question prompted as many replies as there were respondents. Unfortunately, the replies were obviously influenced by the numerous replies from the Wargamer web site, with many respondents choosing strategy titles as their favorite title and none choosing an action-oriented sports title. Nevertheless, the preponderance of strategy favorites cannot be dismissed as merely dictated by wargamers. Strategy games have historically been very strong sellers, and this survey just confirms that.

Will You Buy a Game on Impulse if It Is Connected with a License, such as Star Trek and Star Wars, Which You Enjoy?

Seems not. Only 27 respondents indicated that affiliation with a license would prompt them to buy a game, and two of those 27 stated that

they would buy a game based on its license only if it is a gaming license (a franchise).

That seems to fly in the face of widely accepted game-selling sense. After all, Electronic Arts' Harry Potter and the Sorcerer's Stone turned a widely popular license into a widely popular game (selling nearly a million copies). We feel the disparity results in the type of gamer polled. Harry Potter and the Sorcerer's Stone is widely accepted as a casual gamer's game. Although a solid title, it isn't the type of game that serious gamers (those who game frequently and buy several titles a year) play. Yet serious gamers are exactly the gamers that most often take the time to answer a poll. By definition, serious gamers are interested in their hobby; they are people with a large amount of time invested in the hobby, those who most want to have their voices counted, and hence those most likely to take the poll. So it seems that these "serious gamers" do not care for big-name licenses, but their casual gamer cousins do.

Does the Game's Genre Strongly Influence Your Purchase?

The response to this question was overwhelming. Eighty-eight percent of the surveyed gamers agreed that the genre affected their purchase. It's a common-sense answer if there ever was one. Although most of us genres, we have types of games that we prefer and types that we don't. I love turn-based games. Be they strategy games or role-playing games with a turn-based combat system, I enjoy the mental challenge that turn-based gaming provides. That doesn't mean outstanding titles in other genres won't catch my attention, but all things being equal, I prefer turn-based games. Similarly, I've never met a side-scrolling platform game that kept my attention.

Even gamers that genre doesn't influence are influenced by specific types of games. For example, one respondent stated that although genre did not influence his purchase, he enjoyed war games. It mattered not if the war game was a turn-based title such as The Operational Art of War, an action/adventure such as Operation Flashpoint, or a real-time simulation like Medieval: Total War.

The obvious lesson for those wishing to make games that sell is to make a game in a fast-selling genre, such as real-time strategy. Unfortunately, the discount bins are filled with publishers that tried such a strategy. But as developers and publishers know, to sell well, a game must have more than a popular genre going for it.

Given, however, that a game is innovative, fun, high quality, and well marketed, a title positioned in popular genres will sell well. Even better,

a title that has cross-genre appeal can sell well in multiple genres.

What Is Your Favorite Genre?

Not surprisingly, a combination of real-time and turn-based strategy was the favorite genre of the polled gamers. Most of the respondents took the survey at The Wargamer, a site that focuses on strategy and wargaming. Nevertheless, strategy is a popular genre. NPD Techworld, a corporation that analyzes computer and video game data, states that strategy and sports are two of the fastest-growing genres within the industry. A list of the top-selling PC games for the spring of 2003 places six strategy titles in the top ten, with action/first-person shooters occupying the other four slots.

Forty-eight percent of survey takers named strategy as one of their favorite genres. Of those citing strategy as a favorite, most favored turn-based strategy over real-time strategy. This turn-based preference may just be an anomaly credited to the Wargamer respondents. No turn-based strategy games found their way into NPD Techworld's list of best-selling titles in the spring of 2003.

War games were the second most popular genre, and role-playing games were the third most popular. Bringing up the rear, with only 1.4 percent of the respondents claiming that they preferred the genre, were sports games. Conversely, a poll taken by the Interactive Digital Software Association (IDSA) states that 22 percent of gamers list sports as one of their favorite genre, and an NPD Funworld study shows that almost 20 percent of surveyed video gamers prefer sports games. In the same NPD survey, 27.4 percent of computer gamers listed strategy as their favorite genre. No doubt, there are different views on the subject, but it is also no doubt that strategy gaming is perhaps the strongest genre in both computer and video games.

If You Read a Glowing Review, Will You Buy the Game?

Sixty-seven percent of the gamers surveyed agreed that a glowing review would either prompt them to buy a game or might prompt them to buy a game. Approximately 32 percent claimed that a good review would not prompt them to buy a game.

Good press is a good thing. Don't be stingy with your review copies. Yes, public relations representatives are swamped with requests for games. Many of the requests are bogus, originating from folks who are looking for nothing more than a free game. Yet, despite the swamping, the PR representatives must take the time to sift through the requests to determine which are legitimate or have a chance of being legitimate and get review copies out quickly. It's a very small price to pay for dramatically increasing the buzz that a game generates.

Gamers Speak Out

Now let's see what the gamers had to say. Below is a large sampling of the answers that the gamers sent. You'll find that they are fascinating, insightful, and more than a little bit humorous.

What influences your gaming purchases the most? (Select up to two.)

Cool factor (i.e., Max Payne's Bullet Time) and genre (real-time strategy, etc.)

Do you believe the publisher (Infogrames, EA, etc.) or the developer (Blizzard, etc.) has a greater impact on how good the game is?

The developer has the greater impact since they create the game contents.

If you buy a stinker from a publisher, will you buy a subsequent game from the same publisher?

Yes—if the next game is really good.

What is your favorite game you have played in the last 24 months? Why?

Halo—excellent immersive game with high-quality rendering

Will you buy a game on impulse if it is connected with a license, such as Star Trek and Star Wars, which you enjoy?

No

Does the game's genre strongly influence your purchase?

Yes, a game from a different genre than my favorite must be twice as good.

What is your favorite genre?

Adventure, immersion JDR, sport, replay value war game, historical purpose platform, fun

If you read a glowing review, will you buy the game?

I would read two or more reviews to help me in my choice.

· · · · · · · · · · · · · · · · · ·

What influences your gaming purchases the most? (Select up to two.)

Genre (real-time strategy, etc.)

Do you believe the publisher (Infogrames, EA, etc.) or the developer (Blizzard, etc.) has a greater impact on how good the game is?

The developer, of course. The developer designs the game; the publisher just sells it.

If you buy a stinker from a publisher, will you buy a subsequent game from the same publisher?

Yes. It could have been a fluke.

What is your favorite game that you have played in the last 24 months? Why?

Very tough question. I'd say Airborne Assault because I like historical war games, and this one had an innovative combat system and a good editor.

Will you buy a game on impulse if it is connected with a license, such as Star Trek and Star Wars, which you enjoy?

Never. Star Trek is a perfect example, as almost all of them suck.

Does the game's genre strongly influence your purchase?

Yes, I'm an historical gamer at heart.

What is your favorite genre?

War game

If you read a glowing review, will you buy the game?

Probably; a good review gets me excited about the product, and then I want to try it out for myself.

· · · · · · · · · · · · · · · ·

What influences your gaming purchases the most? (Select up to two.)

Topic (includes era, licenses—Star Trek, franchises—Resident Evil) and genre (real-time strategy, etc.)

Do you believe the publisher (Infogrames, EA, etc.) or the developer (Blizzard, etc.) has a greater impact on how good the game is?

Yes. The publisher is the one with the "go/no go" decision. They decide when or if a game gets released. Assuming the developers "sold" their concept/idea to the publisher, it is the publisher's responsibility to make sure the product maximizes its potential. I've never heard of a developer wanting to "take a shortcut" as far as the quality of their product goes. But the industry is full of games that publishers decided to release too soon, push out the door for Christmas, or dumb down and drop features (actually I'd be interested to know if *any* developer has ever willingly lobotomized his/her latest and greatest, for whatever reason…).

If you buy a stinker from a publisher, will you buy a subsequent game from the same publisher?

No. I generally wouldn't (though there are exceptions…this is kind of a grey area question). Publishers with a good name and reputation certainly make purchasing decisions easier, all things considered.

However, no matter how good the reputation, it only takes one bad apple to make me think a lot longer before buying another of their products.

What is your favorite game that you have played in the last 24 months? Why?

Combat Mission: Beyond Overlord—an AI that makes for a decent solitaire gaming experience. (I don't know the demographics for most gamers, but as a PC game player, most of my gaming is done solitaire. While massively multiplay may be the gaming "rage," there are still a lot of people that (for many reasons) game solitaire, and a good programmed opponent is pretty hard to find in a lot of games.)

Will you buy a game on impulse if it is connected with a license, such as Star Trek and Star Wars, which you enjoy?

No! Licensed products are the easiest ones to, for lack of a better word, "*screw up.*" The lineup of licensed products that were buggy or just did a plain, outright disservice to their respective franchises (through inaccurate representation or whatever) is well known throughout all gaming circles (especially by fans of the genres that have been let down by the string of poorly done licensed products!). Licensed products are the *easiest* to attract buyers to and the *easiest* to ruin (if you're a fan). I don't buy any licensed games without a good deal of research and reading—no matter how much I drool at the magazine ads and the row of boxes in EB!

Does the game's genre strongly influence your purchase?

Yes…computer gaming is a hobby, a hobby that tailors itself to your interests (whatever they may be) exactly.

What is your favorite genre?

I'm a wargamer (and by that defintion, I will also include various sims as well). My first interest is WWII (and the naval and air sims and turn-based games surrounding it). Beyond that, my interests lead down most historical/military avenues. I have neither the time, patience, connection speed, or finances to maintain the PC capable of running most FPSs (in the audio/video splendor and frame rate they were intended to run at!).

If you read a glowing review, will you buy the game?

No! While they may pique my interest and be an interesting read, they don't really influence my purchasing decisions. For *real* information, you have to go to forums and bulletin boards where the players go (although I do read review web sites that encourage/post reader reviews). Buying a game based on a good review is like running out and buying a car after watching a TV commercial.

What influences your gaming purchases the most? (Select up to two.)

Topic or genre

Do you believe the publisher (Infogrames, EA, etc.) or the developer (Blizzard, etc.) has a greater impact on how good the game is?

Not sure

If you buy a stinker from a publisher, will you buy a subsequent game from the same publisher?

No

What is your favorite game that you have played in the last 24 months? Why?

Civilization III, a relaxing and addicting game that stimulates thinking (to some degree) kind of like chess but a whole lot more fun

Will you buy a game on impulse if it is connected with a license, such as Star Trek and Star Wars, which you enjoy?

No

Does the game's genre strongly influence your purchase?

Yes, because I only play strategy games and nothing else. I have played other kinds of games before (racing, sports, action, adventure, puzzle, flight sim, etc.) and decided that the enjoyment that I get out of strategy games is a whole lot more. Thus, I don't waste my time on other

nearly given away, and I still won't buy them.

. . . .

What influences your gaming purchases the most? (Select up to two.)

Topic, franchises, genre, and publisher/developer

Do you believe the publisher (Infogrames, EA, etc.) or the developer (Blizzard, etc.) has a greater impact on how good the game is?

Mostly for the negative as to publishers. Publishers tend to make decisions that are justified on commercial grounds but often diminish the quality and balance of a product. Developers, on the other hand, are essential in transforming one person's vision into a product that is acceptable to a large market. This is perhaps also the role of the publisher, but sadly, I see little evidence that they do it well. Some noteworthy exceptions, such as HPS, exist.

If you buy a stinker from a publisher, will you buy a subsequent game from the same publisher?

Yes, everybody deserves a second chance—but there's a limit. Forget Sierra, for example. Absolutely hopeless and clueless from my point of view.

What is your favorite game that you have played in the last 24 months? Why?

I have a terrible time with a question like that. There is no game I would want to single out. If pressed, I'd fall back on Civilization II—perhaps the most spectacular upgrade of a product ever performed. Too bad about Civ III.

Will you buy a game on impulse if it is connected with a license, such as Star Trek and Star Wars, which you enjoy?

Absolutely not. Games are not movies. Anyway, the more commercial the product, the less likely real quality underlies the concepts in it.

Does the game's genre strongly influence your purchase?

Yes—should be obvious from my response.

What is your favorite genre?

Turn-based strategy or war game. Why? Notwithstanding the canard "real-time," that genre is anything but. To me, a turn-based system is the best way to model real problems and decision-making processes.

If you read a glowing review, will you buy the game?

Maybe. Depends on the reviewer.

. . . .

What influences your gaming purchases the most?

Genre

Do you believe the publisher (Infogrames, EA, etc.) or the developer (Blizzard, etc.) has a greater impact on how good the game is?

Yes—different engines, ideas, etc.

If you buy a stinker from a publisher, will you buy a subsequent game from the same publisher?

No

What is your favorite game that you have played in the last 24 months? Why?

Civ III—good mix of various stuff

Will you buy a game on impulse if it is connected with a license, such as Star Trek and Star Wars, which you enjoy?

No—I only buy games I research and hope they'll pan out (most don't).

Does the game's genre strongly influence your purchase?

Yes—it's the major game element.

What is your favorite genre?

Turn-based strategy and whatever category Fallout Tactics: BoS is. Turn-based strategy offers relaxation, operational (and very basic strategic) planning, and neat little soldiers to move around the map; Fallout (played in real time) offers tension, tactical planning, and the mayhem found there.

If you read a glowing review, will you buy the game?

No. I get info and screen shots from the review. If these point to the

possibility the game may be what I like, I'll first try the demo (if available) and decide after playing it.

· · · · · · · · · · · · · ·

What influences your gaming purchases the most? (Select up to two.)

Genre

Do you believe the publisher (Infogrames, EA, etc.) or the developer (Blizzard, etc.) has a greater impact on how good the game is?

I hold the developer mostly responsible. I am a SW engineer, and I have done both DOD and civilian SW development jobs, and I can make a few observations. Some organizations are inherently incapable of managing a SW engineering operation. Given a billion dollars and a million years, they would still deliver crap. This situation is far more prevelant than might be imagined. There is a serious lack of actual engineering going on in the SW world. There are far too many programmers and coders and far too few engineers. That said, time constraints and pressure to deliver very often cause good engineers that could have produced an excellent product to produce crap. In the end, the commercial SW industry misses an important step in the development of SW. The publisher/developer must have an agreed-upon product description at the start. At the point that the product goes to publication, it must be tested to see if it meets the requirements described by that description. This description must include technical requirements, feature requirements, and reliability requirements. If the delivered product does not fulfill these requirements, it should *not* be published. At that point, the decision must be jointly made to continue development, change the requirements, or cancel. The burden for insisting on this falls on the publisher.

If you buy a stinker from a publisher, will you buy a subsequent game from the same publisher?

Yes. As I said before, I hold the developers responsible more than the publishers. I bought BC 3000 AD, and I will never buy another product by that developer again.

What is your favorite game that you have played in the last 24 months? Why?

Shogun: Total War (in its various incantations). The genre was perfect for me. The "real-time" element was only used where it actually mattered, in a tactical sense. Typical real-time strategy games are idiotic. Napoleon has been quoted as saying "ask me for anything but time," but he didn't say that when deciding to invade Russia, he had plenty of time to decide that. He said it on the battlefield. Shogun captured this perfectly. The game did a lot of other things correct also. The level of detail was a good balance. The map size was good, etc.... The tech tree was excellent. There were discernible differences in the combat performance of the various units (rather than the same performance in a different graphics package). The documentation was adequate; it wasn't verbose, but the game wasn't that complex. Describe chess in one line: Easy to play; difficult to master. Shogun follows that model. Note the sequel Medieval: Total War is not as good a game. It is a case of too much of too many things, which does not equal a good thing. The map is too big, the tech tree is too convoluted, and much of it appears useless. There are 20 different kinds of horsemen in the game, but they all seem to have the same performance (mounted archer, light horse, heavy horse). The game is more complicated, but the documenation is no longer adequate. Now the things left out aren't easily discovered, and they are hidden tricks buried away in the interface.

Will you buy a game on impulse if it is connected with a license, such as Star Trek and Star Wars, which you enjoy?

No. You might as well ask if I would buy a game if Michael Jordan's picture was on the box. Who cares whose picture is on the box? Who cares who the characters are running around in the game. Who cares if the little guys in an RTS game are

Cossacks or stormtroopers. It's still an RTS game. On a side note, most of the physics and combat in movies and TV shows is terrible. This translates to a bad game (i.e., starships running into one another like giant beach balls).

Does the game's genre strongly influence your purchase?

Yes—if someone writes "House Painting the Game," the ultimate simulation of painting. It doesn't matter how well they do it, I still don't want to play. A well-written first-person shooter does nothing for me. I don't play first-person shooters, so I don't care how well done it is.

What is your favorite genre?

Turn-based strategy without a real-time combat element. Simulators go in and out of vogue with me (they are currently out).

If you read a glowing review, will you buy the game?

No. See above. A well-reviewed game on house painting still doesn't interest me.

What influences your gaming purchases the most? (Select up to two.)

Topic, franchises

Do you believe the publisher (Infogrames, EA, etc.) or the developer (Blizzard, etc.) has a greater impact on how good the game is?

I would say the developer. Whether or not one is talking about a computer game or board game, no matter how well it's backed by the publisher, a badly designed game is still bad.

If you buy a stinker from a publisher, will you buy a subsequent game from the same publisher?

It would really depend on the situation; how much money did I spend? Was the hype/advertising way out of line with what the game turned out to be? etc. I would certainly give a publisher a second chance, but I'd be very critical, perhaps more than normal, if the first purchase was a stinker.

What is your favorite game that you have played in the last 24 months? Why?

Computer game: Europa Universalis I. Why? It's the closest I've come to a computer game that replicates the complexity and intelligence of the board games I used to (and would prefer to) play. Board game: None, sadly. Lack of opponents.

Will you buy a game on impulse if it is connected with a license, such as Star Trek and Star Wars, which you enjoy?

No. I'd certainly be enticed to look at the game, but if I bought it, it would be because it was either based on/linked with a previous game I liked and/or my decision would be based on the game's own merits.

Does the game's genre strongly influence your purchase?

Yes, it does. I'm an old-time grognard and still prefer the old pen-and-paper monster games over computer games. So, basically, military, historical, sci-fi, and others of similar bent are what interest me.

What is your favorite genre?

Turn-based strategy/war game. I've always been a huge military history buff.

If you read a glowing review, will you buy the game?

Possibly. A lot would depend on if the game was of a subject matter that interested me and whether or not it was of a genre I liked. If a game does fall within my preferred subject matter or genre, a review will certainly influence my decision.

What influences your gaming purchases the most? (Select up to two.)

Genre

Do you believe the publisher (Infogrames, EA, etc.) or the developer (Blizzard, etc.) has a greater impact on how good the game is?

I don't believe that this is a question that can be wholly answered in a yes/no format. Realistically, it is a combination of several factors from both sides. When a game is bad because it was rushed, it could either be because the publishers pressed for a strategic release date or wanted their invested money back immediately and pushed for an early release. On the flip side, it may have needed to be rushed since the developer spent too much time designing rather than making the game, or perhaps they told the publisher an unrealistic ship date at the start of development. Factors from both sides of the pond are responsible for success and failure in every game, no matter the scenerio. Half-Life's success is equally attributable to Valve's performance, getting the game finished and refined when they did, while Sierra made it possible by funding the game, and not releasing it until it was done. If a game fails because it was simply an idea that could never work, then it is the fault of the developer for saying it could and the fault of the publisher for telling the public it would.

If you buy a stinker from a publisher, will you buy a subsequent game from the same publisher?

Absolutely. While I would not buy a game before good reviews, I would not blame the publisher for it being bad. The quality of a game doesn't rely solely with the publisher; it also lies with the developer. It is also not often that a publisher doesn't learn from a bad release. It is likely, in my opinion, that a bad game will only induce the publisher to take more care when selecting games to back in an attempt to avoid a black tag being put on their name by several bad releases. A single bad game does not say enough about a developer to make me avoid it. Everyone makes mistakes and falters at times, and there is no reason to not play a good game simply because of who put it in the stores.

What is your favorite game that you have played in the last 24 months? Why?

Combat Mission: Beyond Overlord. To start, it is a game that brought commanding military units during conflict to a whole new level. It gave the game player a close-up perspective of the unfolding events. Its innovation and ease of use allowed many new people to enter the wargaming genre. It had an interface that displayed large amounts of data in a manageable format and gave the ability to make complex orders in little time and with great ease. The

tactical AI also meant that units did not have to be cradled and added further to the realism. The we-go turn system employed the uncertainty of warfare and sometime loss of control while in command in battle, yet it allowed the player to continually keep a firm grasp of the situation with its unlimited playback and continually save their units once things had gone sour—no sitting for an entire turn while you get pummeled, only occasionally returning fire. It was also user-definable to the largest extent possible (with the exception of changing weapons). A professional scenerio editor allowed the greenest of players to make their own battles, resulting in the ability to only play the game how you wanted, if you so desired. Operations allowed for prolonged play, letting a player enjoy the thrill of victory and defeat for longer than a single battle but maintaining the historical accuracy of the combat system and the ability to change every single sound and graphics texture resulting in the ability to make the game sound and look exactly as you wanted. You could have vibrant colors and crystal-clear sound to contrast the panic that you would feel as your forces reeled from a counterattack, or you could have dull sounds and washed-out color to comply with the tired and grotesque face of war. It was the greatest war game ever because it allowed the player to dictate what kind of war game it was.

Top-down or on-the-ground, small engagements or big engagements, short or long engagements…it was a true milestone, pushing good graphics with an intricate and detailed mathematical engine, while being the most user-friendly war game to date.

Will you buy a game on impulse if it is connected with a license, such as Star Trek and Star Wars, which you enjoy?

No. I buy nothing on impulse for any reason whatsoever. I do not see a point in spending money on something that is not at least a somewhat assured thing. Product or name tie-ins say nothing about who made the game, what they did while making it, how well they made it, how long they took making it and for what reasons, or anything. I will only buy a game once I have read reviews and public opinion; I will then use those facts (not biases) to decide my purchases.

Does the game's genre strongly influence your purchase?

Yes. I will not buy anything outside of the genres I play. I have tried all genres, and know the ones I like. If a game is genre-blending, I will give the demo a try. With my past experience, I have been able to discern my gaming tastes, and I have no reason not to listen to years of experience.

What is your favorite genre?

War game. I find it intensely rewarding to pluck victory from the hands of defeat or happily humbling to be beaten into a smear for the purposes of further learning. War games also allow me to take part in what I research as another hobby—military history. By knowing the subject, I can apply knowledge to the games. On several occasions, I have learned something interesting from playing the games. War games allow me to cross the boundaries of my two major hobbies, and the enjoyment of two hobbies in one is all I need to have a great deal of fun.

If you read a glowing review, will you buy the game?

No. I read many glowing reviews of games in genres I do not play, or it may be a good game to that one reviewer, but what does the whole say? Or what were my experiences with the demo? I never make my decisions based on single sources (something learned from studying history). A glowing review will have most likely been written by someone who has spent time with the game; it took them time to learn it wholly, and get full enjoyment from it. The time spent with the game may vary from reviewer to reviewer, and so multiple people playing it for multiple lengths of time need to be weighed to understand the learning curve or how much of a gamer the reviewer really is. Without an included biography of the reviewer, biases cannot be known to the reader and therefore cannot be judged as to how they affected the end scoring. A single source will never be enough.

What influences your gaming purchases the most? (Select up to two.)

Topic, franchises

Do you believe the publisher (Infogrames, EA, etc.) or the developer (Blizzard, etc.) has a greater impact on how good the game is?

The developer. The publisher does very little and often messes it up with stupid marketing tactics. The developers are the ones with the vision, and they create the actual game. Look at something like Net-Hack or more recently the Combat Mission series. No publisher, just the developers creating the game and marketing themselves and releasing high quality products. Publishers often do more harm than good.

If you buy a stinker from a publisher, will you buy a subsequent game from the same publisher?

Yes, unless *every* game they publish is a stinker.

What is your favorite game that you have played in the last 24 months? Why?

Planescape: Torment—fantastic plot and character, great graphics and sound, and a great game engine. It's probably the best game of all time.

Will you buy a game on impulse if it is connected with a license, such as Star Trek and Star Wars, which you enjoy?

No. I read reviews of it first. Too many atrocious games are based on great licenses.

Does the game's genre strongly influence your purchase?

Yes, there are some genres I can't stand. I hate real-time strategy, so all games in that genre are immediately struck off my list. I love RPGs and games based on WWII, so they immediately go to the top of the list.

What is your favorite genre?

My favorite genre is probably RPGs. I like developing my character and having a good plot, so they take the cake with me.

If you read a glowing review, will you buy the game?

Only if it is from a source I respect, and then I often buy the game sight unseen, without trying any demos. Otherwise I will try the demo first.

What influences your gaming purchases the most? (Select up to two.)

Topic, franchises, and genre

Do you believe the publisher (Infogrames, EA, etc.) or the developer (Blizzard, etc.) has a greater impact on how good the game is?

The publisher. A good example would be a Psygnosis/Take 2/Zono game called Metal Fatigue. Psygnosis pulled out major support for the game after release, and the game never got the bug/patch support it really needed, and the game was good yet very buggy. Developer Take 2 tried but failed to provide help to gamers, which ended in failure also.

If you buy a stinker from a publisher, will you buy a subsequent game from the same publisher?

Yes. I have bought and will still buy games that turned out to be stinkers from a publisher/developer, and I find games that turned out to be wonderful; Ubi Soft would be a good stinker and sleeper company such as Dark Planet: Battle for Natrolis (stinker) and Pool of Radiance: Ruins of Myth Drannor (a could-be stinker until they patched the problems, and then it turned into a game I could not stop playing, until I got Morrowind).

What is your favorite game that you have played in the last 24 months? Why?

This is unfair to ask; I have so many. Xbox: Blood Rayne, because of the blood, the gore, the lady vampire. Plus if you are a guy and love *The Man Show*, you got to love this game.

It has a cheat system where if you input *Man Show* quotes, you get funny comebacks! The FMV, CGI, whatever you want to call it is very eye-popping in more ways then one! The game graphics could have been better, but the good things outweight the less-than-Xbox (Halo) standard graphics. PC: Morrowind, hands down! This game I can play over and over again, I am able to DL (download) plug-ins others have made or make my own with the editor to make the game new and different and replayable!

Will you buy a game on impulse if it is connected with a license, such as Star Trek and Star Wars, which you enjoy?

Yes and no. I am a Star Wars fan (I have a copy of Star Wars Monopoly for the PC), but I drift. I purchased Star Wars: Force Commander the day it hit the shelves—WOW a Star Wars RTS WOWOOO. Well it turned out to be a stinker! Now I am more selective. I waited for Star Wars: Galactic Battlegrounds to come down in price before I bought, and the day the expansion came out I bought it and enjoyed it! Every Star Trek game that has come out I have bought on impulse and enjoyed it!

Does the game's genre strongly influence your purchase?

Yes and no. I will play most games, but I end up getting RPGs, FPSs (first-person shooters), and RTSs.

What is your favorite genre?

RPGs, FPSs, and RTSs. I love the thrills a good FPS can give you or someone out to prove they are the best in the business of killing the enemy! The power to control larger or smaller forces that can stomp one another into the ground will always keep me coming back to a good RTS! D&D to AD&D, back to D&D, once a diehard Half-Elf Ranger with a Long Sword of a Green Basilisk, always a Half...you get the point!

If you read a glowing review, will you buy the game?

Yes and no. Reviews are good when you know the person writing the review understands what a gamer looks for in a game. Sometimes, a game gets a Five Star rating, and you get your new game home, unwrap the plastic or cut the security tape, pull out the instructions and CD(s), install, start a game, and you lose interest after one or two missions or the game play is strained, unbalanced, etc. Yet, sometimes reviews bash a game until it's dead and pleading for you to stop, yet otherwise would have turned out to be a great game (i.e., Reach for the Stars got bad reviews in a few magazines and online so I did not get it, until I found it for $9.99 on the clearance rack, and it turned out to be really fun!).

What influences your gaming purchases the most? (Select up to two.)

Topic, franchises, genre

Do you believe the publisher (Infogrames, EA, etc.) or the developer (Blizzard, etc.) has a greater impact on how good the game is?

Most games from the more well-known publishers and developers are better, as they have more money behind them, but the less-known company's games are good but could be better if they had more money behind them. Some of the games are really good and don't need to be changed at all.

If you buy a stinker from a publisher, will you buy a subsequent game from the same publisher?

Yes, I would if the game got good reviews and if I had played it before and liked it.

What is your favorite game that you have played in the last 24 months? Why?

Warcraft III. It is a really good game, and I haven't had much time to play many others.

Will you buy a game on impulse if it is connected with a license, such as Star Trek and Star Wars, which you enjoy?

No, I usually play all games once or twice before I buy them, so I know I'm not wasting my hard-earned money (which is very little).

Does the game's genre strongly influence your purchase?

Yes, I really like strategy but I don't like simulations and adventure.

What is your favorite genre?

All genres are good; I don't know why but I get lost in them and play them for hours. I can't stop even if it is 5 A.M. and I have been playing all night and I then have to go to school in three hours.

If you read a glowing review, will you buy the game?

Yes and no—depends if I have the money for it and like it from what I have seen.

What influences your gaming purchases the most? (Select up to two.)

Topic, franchises, genre

Do you believe the publisher (Infogrames, EA, etc.) or the developer (Blizzard, etc.) has a greater impact on how good the game is?

Developer; it's their baby. Publisher has the lesser influence in general.

If you buy a stinker from a publisher, will you buy a subsequent game from the same publisher?

Yes—the development team has more influence on the quality of game than publisher. Bad support/attitude is more important for quality of publisher.

What is your favorite game that you have played in the last 24 months? Why?

Russo-German War. It's an in-depth and detailed look at WWII Eastern front, yet it's playable enough with a lot of replayability with optional rules and 52 scenarios and superb developer support and forum presence.

Will you buy a game on impulse if it is connected with a license, such as Star Trek and Star Wars, which you enjoy?

No—game genre and quality are more important than license.

Does the game's genre strongly influence your purchase?

Yes. Because of limited time, I focus on my preferred genre.

What is your favorite genre?

War game. It's connected with my interest in history—I learn and play at the same time.

If you read a glowing review, will you buy the game?

No. Genre and feedback from newsgroups are more important than reviews.

What influences your gaming purchases the most? (Select up to two.)

Cool factor, genre

Do you believe the publisher (Infogrames, EA, etc.) or the developer (Blizzard, etc.) has a greater impact on how good the game is?

To an extent, yes. Most publishers today find themselves publishing in niches; EA is largely about EA Sports, Blizzard does nothing but RTS click games, and so forth. Smaller developers find themselves devoted to one idea or game engine, which isn't necessarily a bad thing. Matrix Games uses different game engines but primarily makes war games in a somewhat traditional mold. The same can be said for HPS and Shrapnel.

If you buy a stinker from a publisher, will you buy a subsequent game from the same publisher?

I might consider another purchase, but I'll be on my guard. After both Gangsters games and Hitman, Eidos is on my *out* list.

What is your favorite game that you have played in the last 24 months? Why?

None really

Will you buy a game on impulse if it is connected with a license, such as Star Trek and Star Wars, which you enjoy?

Sometimes. There are plenty of licensed games I do not own. I love Star Wars, but I do not own any of the Jedi Knight games; I have enough shooters already and I'm an Imperial fan anyway. I don't own the RTS games based on SW either, since I don't like RTS. For me, the license is usually icing on the cake. If someone made a turn-based, detail-heavy SW war game or an RPG, I'd be all over it. But on the other hand, I do not like multiplayer or online games, yet when the SW online game comes out, I am sure to try it solely because of the license.

Does the game's genre strongly influence your purchase?

Yes. I like first-person shooters to an extent but find even the good ones extremely repetitive. Yet, I own innumerable war games that all simulate the same historic battles. It can be argued that HOMM is loosely based on Warlords, yet I own all of the HOMMs and Warlords games (except the RTS one). It's really all about genre and how the game expresses it.

What is your favorite genre?

Turn-based strategy, action, some RPGs, and on consoles, sports

If you read a glowing review, will you buy the game?

A glowing review will convince me to buy only if I am interested in the genre to begin with or if I am "on the fence" and in the mood for something different. I'm sure the usual suspects will slobber all over StarCraft II when it ever gets developed, but you wouldn't catch me spending money on that. I got bored with Diablo and didn't bother with Diablo II. I wasn't crazy about Tomb Raider.

What influences your gaming purchases the most? (Select up to two.)

Genre, publisher/developer

Do you believe the publisher (Infogrames, EA, etc.) or the developer (Blizzard, etc.) has a greater impact on how good the game is?

It's both really; the publisher chooses what is sold under its name, while the developer does the ground work to make a good game.

If you buy a stinker from a publisher, will you buy a subsequent game from the same publisher?

Yes, I would buy another game most of the time. All companies seem to have bad games from time to time. I buy more on the subject matter of the game rather than on the publisher.

What is your favorite game that you have played in the last 24 months? Why?

Delta Force series, currently Task Force Dagger. I have played the games in this series since the day the original Delta Force came out and love the action it gives—not so complex and unforgiving as Ghost Recon (which I do play from time to time). I also spent tons of time playing Civilization III for a while.

Will you buy a game on impulse if it is connected with a license, such as Star Trek and Star Wars, which you enjoy?

On occasion...it will get my attention, although I have never played a game with a contract for long that I am aware of.

Does the game's genre strongly influence your purchase?

Oh yes. I only play certain types of games.

What is your favorite genre?

I like both first-person shooters for a little excitement and war games for the mental workout. It just depends on my mood.

If you read a glowing review, will you buy the game?

Yes, most of the time I will try a game out in my genres if it has a glowing review, although most of the time if the game is that good I have heard about it before it is out and purchased it anyway.

What influences your gaming purchases the most? (Select up to two.)

Topic, franchises, genre

Do you believe the publisher (Infogrames, EA, etc.) or the developer (Blizzard, etc.) has a greater impact on how good the game is?

Integrity. Some simulations and historic RTSs do not lend themselves to the mass market. If a publisher has a reputation for compromising accuracy and "dumbing down" a product to increase sales, I won't touch them with a barge-pole.

If you buy a stinker from a publisher, will you buy a subsequent game from the same publisher?

Yes but not until the finished game had been comprehensively and positively reviewed by a magazine or web site that I respect.

What is your favorite game that you have played in the last 24 months? Why?

Combat Mission: Barbarossa to Berlin (non-European version) and IL-2 Sturmovik. Both are beautifully presented, historically accurate, and a challenge to play for completely different reasons. The one thing they do have in common is that the developer did not compromise the content for mass-market appeal.

Will you buy a game on impulse if it is connected with a license, such as Star Trek and Star Wars, which you enjoy?

No. Licenses come at a cost. Those costs have to be recovered, and chances are that this means

shortcuts have been taken with the development. I have had very few good experiences with "licensed" games.

Does the game's genre strongly influence your purchase?

Yes. I enjoy historical simulations.

What is your favorite genre?

Simulation and RTS. I do not like games that take a linear approach to the subject by stringing together a series of "missions" with limited ways of accomplishing them. I prefer a more free-form approach that is not repetitive and allows the player to attempt different approaches each time.

If you read a glowing review, will you buy the game?

Yes—but only if the subject matter appeals to me

. . . .

What influences your gaming purchases the most? (Select up to two.)

Topic, franchises, genre

Do you believe the publisher (Infogrames, EA, etc.) or the developer (Blizzard, etc.) has a greater impact on how good the game is?

Yes. Some developers just seem to have that extra something that turns anything they touch to gold. Generally, they have to have had multiple games of good quality before I'll give a developer benefit of the doubt. This is less true of publishers, though long-time publishers who seem to have a knack for backing good games might get a similar benefit of the doubt with regards to a game.

If you buy a stinker from a publisher, will you buy a subsequent game from the same publisher?

Yes. Often a publisher will learn more from mistakes than from successes.

What is your favorite game that you have played in the last 24 months? Why?

Neverwinter Nights. While I feel there have been many excellent games over the course of the past two years, this game stands out for its excellent single-player *and* multiplayer experiences, good graphics, and excellently paced game play. This is a game I'll keep coming back to as new modules are released.

Will you buy a game on impulse if it is connected with a license, such as Star Trek and Star Wars, which you enjoy?

No. Licenses are nice, but game content, play, and overall quality are more important. A license might influence me slightly toward a game, but it won't make me outright jump in and buy the game.

Does the game's genre strongly influence your purchase?

Yes. I just like RPGs, turn-based strategy, and action. On the other

hand, I'm not a big fan of real-time strategy or adventure games, so I'm very unlikely to purchase something from those genres.

What is your favorite genre?

Role playing. I like the story, character development, exploration, and combat aspects of this genre.

If you read a glowing review, will you buy the game?

Yes and no. After one glowing review, I might think about buying a game. After several glowing reviews, I will at least seriously think about buying a game, sometimes even if it's in a genre I have no interest in.

What influences your gaming purchases the most? (Select up to two.)

Topic, franchises, genre

Do you believe the publisher (Infogrames, EA, etc.) or the developer (Blizzard, etc.) has a greater impact on how good the game is?

I don't really know the differences from the example above; but I expect that the guys who demand something go to print (to hit the shelves) too soon have the most influence, mostly negative.

If you buy a stinker from a publisher, will you buy a subsequent game from the same publisher?

Yes, but I will be more wary on the next go-around.

What is your favorite game that you have played in the last 24 months? Why?

The Ardennes Offensive 2. I'm a boardgamer at heart, and this game is very easy to play PBEM, which is the method that best suits my lifestyle. It's a clean, well-thought-out, bug-free war game and on one of my favorite topics.

Will you buy a game on impulse if it is connected with a license, such as Star Trek and Star Wars, which you enjoy?

No, at least not to date. This isn't a religious issue for me. I'm more interested in war games, and these typically don't follow from licenses. If one came along that I was interested in, I would buy it.

Does the game's genre strongly influence your purchase?

Yes, my gaming interests typically are following my other interests. I have an interest in military history, therefore in military history games.

What is your favorite genre?

War games. It follows from an interest in history in general and military history in particular. Psychologically, it probably follows from growing up with wargaming in the family since I was age three or so (a way to participate in family activities and get attention as a youngster).

If you read a glowing review, will you buy the game?

It is only one of many factors in the decision to buy the game. On the other hand, if I read a bad review, it has caused me not to buy a few games.

What influences your gaming purchases the most? (Select up to two.)

Genre, publisher/developer

Do you believe the publisher (Infogrames, EA, etc.) or the developer (Blizzard, etc.) has a greater impact on how good the game is?

I do believe that the publisher/developer does affect the outcome of a game. Some companies are known for their releases—Id, Blizzard, and Firaxis, for example. When they release a title, people take notice. The people usually buy them too. That said, releasing a game that is not complete also affects the status of a company.

If you buy a stinker from a publisher, will you buy a subsequent game from the same publisher?

A stinker would definitely make me reluctant to purchase from them again. My money supply is not endless. Each game that I purchase is based on research and reviews that pay particular attention to game play or the need for patches. In my opinion, patches should be banished.

What is your favorite game that you have played in the last 24 months? Why?

My most favorite game is Thief. It was a gift from my brother, and I hesitated installing it on my hard drive. I am not a fan of shooters and when it started, my worst fears were swept away by a game of surprising ingenuity and some good scares. Thief forced me to rethink the first-person genre and allowed me to get lost in the world that Looking Glass so lovingly created. It's a shame that they are no longer here to supply us with that caliber of games.

Will you buy a game on impulse if it is connected with a license, such as Star Trek and Star Wars, which you enjoy?

No, I never buy games associated with a movie or a book. They operate on different levels than games do, and they cannot be compared to one another. I tire of developers who try to fit their game designs into an existing world. The examples of successful games based on such hybrids are rare indeed. It shows the lack of creativity in the game world at present. Games that make their own places to dwell in or fight in are always more compelling.

Does the game's genre strongly influence your purchase?

There are many games that are of interest because of the concept or appearance. The genre does influence my decision, even though I purchase other titles as well. No single game can do it all.

What is your favorite genre?

Of the many games I own and play, I go back to turn-based strategy games and will seek them out over all other genres because they provide an experience that no other game can duplicate. Heroes, Lords of Magic, Alpha Centauri, Disciples II, all remain on my hard drive because they are excellent games.

If you read a glowing review, will you buy the game?

No, and that's because I have read conflicting reviews on the same game on several occasions. If reviewers have a different opinion, there is no problem. When their reviews sound as if they are writing about different games, I wonder if one of them is being honest or has played the game all the way through.

What influences your gaming purchases the most? (Select up to two.)

Genre

Do you believe the publisher (Infogrames, EA, etc.) or the developer (Blizzard, etc.) has a

greater impact on how good the game is?

Unsure

If you buy a stinker from a publisher, will you buy a subsequent game from the same publisher?

No

What is your favorite game that you have played in the last 24 months? Why?

Operation Flashpoint

Will you buy a game on impulse if it is connected with a license, such as Star Trek and Star Wars, which you enjoy?

No

Does the game's genre strongly influence your purchase?

Yes

What is your favorite genre?

Simulation

If you read a glowing review, will you buy the game?

Yes

What influences your gaming purchases the most? (Select up to two.)

Genre, publisher/developer

Do you believe the publisher (Infogrames, EA, etc.) or the developer (Blizzard, etc.) has a greater impact on how good the game is?

Developer

If you buy a stinker from a publisher, will you buy a subsequent game from the same publisher?

No. It is OK if they offer stinkers, but I want to be able to judge before buying.

What is your favorite game that you have played in the last 24 months? Why?

Tropico. Very relaxing.

Will you buy a game on impulse if it is connected with a license, such as Star Trek and Star Wars, which you enjoy?

No, never.

Does the game's genre strongly influence your purchase?

Yes, I am able to hear *each* Russian soldier's "hurrah" when two 4-3 Corps with NATO-Infantry markers assault. And, yes, this is very noisy.

What is your favorite genre?

War games, RPG, Tropico

If you read a glowing review, will you buy the game?

No. I try to read between the lines.

What influences your gaming purchases the most? (Select up to two.)

Topic, franchises, genre

Do you believe the publisher (Infogrames, EA, etc.) or the developer (Blizzard, etc.) has a

greater impact on how good the game is?

The developer. They have a greater stake in their product. They are concerned not only with sales and profit but with quality. Developers appear to be persons who are/were gamers and still know why we play and purchase games. Developers are like the film director and writer who make their masterpiece and then have to sell it to a studio to have it seen.

If you buy a stinker from a publisher, will you buy a subsequent game from the same publisher?

Yes, I might, but I will be much more cautious. For example, I will seek out more and varied reviews. I will also seek out a demo. For the most part, no demo equals no sale.

What is your favorite game that you have played in the last 24 months? Why?

I guess that would be Ghost Recon. I find it immersive. I also like the "real world" take. The game also has lots of action but makes you think.

Will you buy a game on impulse if it is connected with a license, such as Star Trek and Star Wars, which you enjoy?

No, not very often. My dollars are precious to me and impulses usually lead to a waste of them.

Does the game's genre strongly influence your purchase?

Yes. Certain genres hold no interest for me. Even if I occasionally branch out, I quickly come back.

What is your favorite genre?

Simulation, war game, and turn-based strategy. They all make me think without wearing out my thumb.

If you read a glowing review, will you buy the game?

Only if the subject interests me, but rarely if I have not played a demo

What influences your gaming purchases the most? (Select up to two.)

Topic, franchises, genre

Do you believe the publisher (Infogrames, EA, etc.) or the developer (Blizzard, etc.) has a greater impact on how good the game is?

Publisher because they have the money

If you buy a stinker from a publisher, will you buy a subsequent game from the same publisher?

Yes—but next time I will avoid the developer. A publisher might have some cool games depending on different developers.

What is your favorite game that you have played in the last 24 months? Why?

IL-2 Sturmovik—great graphics and game play, cool topic, physics, excellent artificial intelligence

Will you buy a game on impulse if it is connected with a license, such as Star Trek and Star Wars, which you enjoy?

No. A good license does not equal a good game.

Does the game's genre strongly influence your purchase?

Yes. I don't want to waste money on a title I might not like because of its genre.

What is your favorite genre?

Simulations; I like flight simulations.

If you read a glowing review, will you buy the game?

Yes—if the reviewer seems to be an expert in gaming

What influences your gaming purchases the most? (Select up to two.)

Cool factor, genre

Do you believe the publisher (Infogrames, EA, etc.) or the developer (Blizzard, etc.) has a greater impact on how good the game is?

Oftentimes the publisher because good publishers have good distribution, making the game easier to find.

If you buy a stinker from a publisher, will you buy a subsequent game from the same publisher?

Yes, but I'll avoid the developer.

What is your favorite game that you have played in the last 24 months? Why?

Medieval: Total War. It is just so much fun—the perfect balance between realism and fun.

Will you buy a game on impulse if it is connected with a license, such as Star Trek and Star Wars, which you enjoy?

No, I learned that lesson the hard way.

Does the game's genre strongly influence your purchase?

Yes, I basically only play strategy games.

What is your favorite genre?

Real-time strategy

If you read a glowing review, will you buy the game?

No, I learned that lesson too.

What influences your gaming purchases the most? (Select up to two.)

Topic, franchises, genre

Do you believe the publisher (Infogrames, EA, etc.) or the developer (Blizzard, etc.) has a greater impact on how good the game is?

Developer. It's up to the software people to actually bring all the good ideas of the game designers into fruition. A badly designed game without any bugs might be playable, if boring. A well-designed game riddled with errors will be frustrating. If you don't get the engineering right, you won't get a good game.

If you buy a stinker from a publisher, will you buy a subsequent game from the same publisher?

Yes. I take very little note of who publishes (or even develops) a game. I always check a number of reviews online before I buy a game in order to assess how much I think I will enjoy a game. If my assessment indicates that I'll enjoy the game, I'll buy it regardless of publisher/developer and their previous reputation.

What is your favorite game that you have played in the last 24 months? Why?

I think the game I've played the most in the last two years is probably Angband [A freeware RPG—author]. I like it partly because it's free. It also has a massively addictive random item/map feature that can keep you playing for hours, just for the chance to find another artifact/greater vault or whatever. If you die in Angband, you have to start all over

again, which makes it massively challenging. Plus, it offers just the right balance of entertaining hacking/tactical consideration in combat. It's a masterpiece. I just wish someone would improve the graphics :).

Will you buy a game on impulse if it is connected with a license, such as Star Trek and Star Wars, which you enjoy?

No. Games cost a lot of money, and a lot of licensed games are dreadful. I'd rather spend a little time making sure I'm going to enjoy the game before I buy.

Does the game's genre strongly influence your purchase?

Yes. I know I like certain genres, so I tend to stick with games that fall into that category. Similarly, I avoid ones I don't like.

What is your favorite genre?

Although I play a lot of different games, I have a lasting fondness for turn-based games. I enjoy the fact they require some mental planning but don't have the brain-teasing puzzles associated with adventure games. They also (generally) offer the most replayability in my experience. A well-designed turn-based game can also have a massive "hook," inspiring you to keep playing to gain new powers/things/areas.

If you read a glowing review, will you buy the game?

Depends. I won't on the basis of one review, but if I see consistently good reviews, I'll buy a game. I don't buy every game that gets great reviews of course; I tend only to have one or two games on the go at any one time, and I only buy a new one once I'm bored with my old ones.

. . . .

What influences your gaming purchases the most? (Select up to two.)

Topic, franchises, publisher/developer

Do you believe the publisher (Infogrames, EA, etc.) or the developer (Blizzard, etc.) has a greater impact on how good the game is?

Certain publishers are simply more reliable at making sure that a game is good before it is released, and others will simply release buggy crap. Not a hard-and-fast rule, but a trend at least.

If you buy a stinker from a publisher, will you buy a subsequent game from the same publisher?

No. Fool me once, shame on you. Fool me twice, shame on me.

What is your favorite game that you have played in the last 24 months? Why?

Operation Flashpoint: Cold War Crisis mainly for the multiplayer. It's a game where strategy and tactics actually make a difference—in fact a huge difference.

Will you buy a game on impulse if it is connected with a license, such as Star Trek and Star Wars, which you enjoy?

No, because historically such games are crappy and count on the license to sell the game.

Does the game's genre strongly influence your purchase?

Not really. I play all sorts of games.

What is your favorite genre?

In general, probably equal time spent on shooters, turn-based strategy, and war games but with a bit of the other genres thrown in.

If you read a glowing review, will you buy the game?

Depends on where the review is coming from. If it's from somewhere that I trust (Gamesdomain or the Wargamer), then that's enough for me. Other than that, no.

. . . .

What influences your gaming purchases the most? (Select up to two.)

Genre

Do you believe the publisher (Infogrames, EA, etc.) or the developer (Blizzard, etc.) has a greater impact on how good the game is?

Developer, although a publisher can screw things up by releasing a game before it's done and tested.

If you buy a stinker from a publisher, will you buy a subsequent game from the same publisher?

No. They obviously don't have sufficient QA.

What is your favorite game that you have played in the last 24 months? Why?

Panzer Elite. It kept my attention and didn't get boring. I got it for free at CompUSA (on sale for $20, with a $20 rebate)!

Will you buy a game on impulse if it is connected with a license, such as Star Trek and Star Wars, which you enjoy?

No. I don't do anything on impulse.

Does the game's genre strongly influence your purchase?

Yes. I mostly like war games. However, I do sometimes purchase other genres if the reviews are excellent. Right now I'm playing Baldur's Gate. It's a good game but too long for someone like myself who has maybe five to ten hours a week to play.

What is your favorite genre?

War games. I used to play board war games. It's hard to find players. Even mediocre AI is better than playing against oneself.

If you read a glowing review, will you buy the game?

Perhaps. However, a bad review will make me not buy a game. For example, I like castles, and Stronghold seemed to be an interesting title. It received mediocre reviews, so I didn't purchase it.

What influences your gaming purchases the most? (Select up to two.)

Cool factor, topic, franchises

Do you believe the publisher (Infogrames, EA, etc.) or the developer (Blizzard, etc.) has a greater impact on how good the game is?

Publisher—among the first things I look at is whether it's an established, reputable publisher that avoids putting out buggy, low-quality games. Only recently have I begun focusing in on the developer (although, admittedly, they have more of an impact than the publisher, it's the latter's "seal of approval" that is typically the easiest way to gauge a new game's quality).

If you buy a stinker from a publisher, will you buy a subsequent game from the same publisher?

Yes, but only if the subject material is sufficiently engaging.

What is your favorite game that you have played in the last 24 months? Why?

Halo on the Xbox. I play war and strategy games on my computer, allowing for careful deliberation and reflection, but I reserve the console for action and adventure games. By far, Halo had the right mix of challenge and immersive action to fascinate me for hours on end.

Will you buy a game on impulse if it is connected with a license, such as Star Trek and Star Wars, which you enjoy?

Yes—Star Wars games still end up in my collection, even if they look so-so.

Does the game's genre strongly influence your purchase?

Yes—I tend to stick to the same genres, rarely branching out.

What is your favorite genre?

War games

If you read a glowing review, will you buy the game?

Yes, but only if the review is detailed, and offers comparisons to other games (giving a frame of reference). Unqualified raves have little to no impact on my purchase decisions.

What influences your gaming purchases the most? (Select up to two.)

Genre

Do you believe the publisher (Infogrames, EA, etc.) or the developer (Blizzard, etc.) has a greater impact on how good the game is?

I have played a lot of strategy games and most often the ones I like are from a small developer/publisher.

Generally, I buy games which appear realistic, *not* games like StarCraft and Battlefield 1942 (I wouldn't play that game even if you gave me money to do it... okay a lot of money might persuade me).

If you buy a stinker from a publisher, will you buy a subsequent game from the same publisher?

Generally, I'll be very suspicious of any games from an unreputable publisher, but if they do come up with a good game, I usually try to check it out before I buy it. For example, Battlefield 1942 was a great idea but a rotten game.

What is your favorite game that you have played in the last 24 months? Why?

Napoleon 1813. Why? Well, because I enjoy the strategic feel to the game (too bad they didn't develop it fully and give it an intelligent artificial intelligence) and the tactical battles.

Will you buy a game on impulse if it is connected with a license, such as Star Trek and Star Wars, which you enjoy?

Generally no, but I have been known to do it if it's a type of game that I like. I could easily be persuaded by a good review or some interesting info on the box....

Does the game's genre strongly influence your purchase?

Yes, generally it does. I'm really into realistic war games (strategic, tactical, and 3D), space simulations (Freelancer), and games like The Sims.

What is your favorite genre?

Simulation, turn-based strategy, real-time strategy, and war games are the group of games that I really like, as long as they are, or appear to be, realistic!

If you read a glowing review, will you buy the game?

Yes, and I have regretted it more times than not, I'm sorry to say....

What influences your gaming purchases the most? (Select up to two.)

Genre

Do you believe the publisher (Infogrames, EA, etc.) or the developer (Blizzard, etc.) has a greater impact on how good the game is?

Yes and no to both. Yes because some companies have above-average quality and others below average. Some vary depending of the game. No because above average doesn't mean the quality is good enough.

If you buy a stinker from a publisher, will you buy a subsequent game from the same publisher?

Not necessarily

What is your favorite game that you have played in the last 24 months? Why?

Diablo II. I don't play many games now because it's hard to find a quality game that fits my needs. Diablo II is simple, works relatively well, and has some depth.

Will you buy a game on impulse if it is connected with a license, such as Star Trek and Star Wars, which you enjoy?

No

Does the game's genre strongly influence your purchase?

Yes (sometimes no). I'm not interested in some genres, but there are always exceptions. It's always a pleasure to play a great product.

What is your favorite genre?

Action. It needs to move without many clues to resolve (I do this all day long so I want to take a break).

If you read a glowing review, will you buy the game?

If I know the series (MechWarrior, for example), yes. Otherwise, I try a demo first (my decision is almost always based on reviews *and* demo).

What influences your gaming purchases the most? (Select up to two.)

Genre

Do you believe the publisher (Infogrames, EA, etc.) or the developer (Blizzard, etc.) has a greater impact on how good the game is?

Developer. I stay with Blizzard because of great quality check. But I also keep in mind that Space Empires IV (Shrapnel Games) is a fantastic game.

If you buy a stinker from a publisher, will you buy a subsequent game from the same publisher?

Yes because I own 600 games. You have to try the next.

What is your favorite game that you have played in the last 24 months? Why?

Warcraft III because of its multiplayer balance and, again, Fallout 2 because of its great freedom.

Will you buy a game on impulse if it is connected with a license, such as Star Trek and Star Wars, which you enjoy?

No, because most of them are real crap.

Does the game's genre strongly influence your purchase?

Yes, I hate action-adventure but love RTS and RPGs.

What is your favorite genre?

RTS and RPGs

If you read a glowing review, will you buy the game?

Yes, when collaborated with other reviews

What influences your gaming purchases the most? (Select up to two.)

Topic, franchises, publisher/ developer

Do you believe the publisher (Infogrames, EA, etc.) or the developer (Blizzard, etc.) has a greater impact on how good the game is?

Developer—both the company and the actual person leading the development. They primarily determine the content and quality of the game.

If you buy a stinker from a publisher, will you buy a subsequent game from the same publisher?

Probably—but it depends on why it was a stinker and what the publisher did about it. If the design was hopeless, then that's the developer's problem so the publisher is partially off the hook (of course, they did let it loose on the world so they're not completely guiltless). If the game was buggy, then the publisher should see to it that fixes get made and distributed promptly, and the fixes better work. If they just promise lots of action and nothing happens, the publisher takes the hit and my money will tend to go elsewhere.

What is your favorite game that you have played in the last 24 months? Why?

Civilization III because I'm hooked on TBS games!

Will you buy a game on impulse if it is connected with a license, such as Star Trek and Star Wars, which you enjoy?

Probably not. I pay more attention to the designer and genre than any association with something non-gaming.

Does the game's genre strongly influence your purchase?

Yes

What is your favorite genre?

Turn-based strategy (TBS) and war games

If you read a glowing review, will you buy the game?

Not likely, unless it was a game I was likely to buy anyway, but a bad review might keep me from buying one.

What influences your gaming purchases the most? (Select up to two.)

Topic, franchises, genre

Do you believe the publisher (Infogrames, EA, etc.) or the developer (Blizzard, etc.) has a greater impact on how good the game is?

I would imagine the developer has a greater impact on how good a game actually is; they create the game. The publisher is responsible for how well a game is advertised.

If you buy a stinker from a publisher, will you buy a subsequent game from the same publisher?

Publisher gets three strikes with me, and then they are out.

What is your favorite game that you have played in the last 24 months? Why?

Quite frankly, I don't believe in the phrase "favorite"—but if I had to mention the game I've played the most in the past 24 months, it would be The Campaign Series of games by Talonsoft (Take 2). This series has most of what I want in a military simulation. There's always room for improvement, of course.

Will you buy a game on impulse if it is connected with a license, such as Star Trek and Star Wars, which you enjoy?

Never. I won't buy hype.

Does the game's genre strongly influence your purchase?

I purchase historical games that I can learn from.

What is your favorite genre?

War game (military simulation)

If you read a glowing review, will you buy the game?

Actually, it depends on the reviewer. There are only a couple of reviewers that I enjoy reading, and I take their opinions seriously.

Whether I would buy it or not based on that review is another matter. Had the reviewer said good things about the game, I might be inclined to try a demo.

What influences your gaming purchases the most? (Select up to two.)

Topic, franchises, genre

Do you believe the publisher (Infogrames, EA, etc.) or the developer (Blizzard, etc.) has a greater impact on how good the game is?

The developer. If my knowledge is correct, the developer determines how well the game works.

If you buy a stinker from a publisher, will you buy a subsequent game from the same publisher?

No, unless the new game is rated much better than the stinker

What is your favorite game that you have played in the last 24 months? Why?

Medal of Honor: Allied Assault. I was totally committed to the game from the start, until I finished the game. I normally get bored quickly and then come back to a game weeks later. Not this one.

Will you buy a game on impulse if it is connected with a license, such as Star Trek and Star Wars, which you enjoy?

Yes, if its predecessor was a good game. No, if I don't have a previous connection.

Does the game's genre strongly influence your purchase?

Yes. Certain genres I like, and others that I don't like, I don't look at.

What is your favorite genre?

Turn-based strategy—I've played these since childhood and still love them the most. Shooter—I enjoy the fast-paced thrill.

If you read a glowing review, will you buy the game?

Yes, I depend on reviews. If the genre and style match my interest, and the reviews are good, I am usually happy with my purchase.

What influences your gaming purchases the most? (Select up to two.)

Genre

Do you believe the publisher (Infogrames, EA, etc.) or the developer (Blizzard, etc.) has a greater impact on how good the game is?

Publisher. Developers have to conform to the publisher's wishes. The quality of the game doesn't matter in the slightest to the publisher; it's what will sell that matters.

If you buy a stinker from a publisher, will you buy a subsequent game from the same publisher?

Yes. Publishers are caught up in the moment and always will be. Just because they make a stinker now doesn't mean they won't publish a jewel later. Publishers don't create; they publish and market. You don't hold them responsible; you hold the shoddy developers responsible.

What is your favorite game that you have played in the last 24 months? Why?

Civilization III. Good graphics, great game play, actually challenges you.

Will you buy a game on impulse if it is connected with a license, such as Star Trek and Star Wars, which you enjoy?

No. I did when I was younger but found most developers use these licenses as a reason to make a sub-par game because they know there is a large market for just the name. See Star Fleet Battles (real game) vs. Starfleet Command (video game).

Does the game's genre strongly influence your purchase?

Yes. Regardless of other peoples responses, everybody should say yes. If they honestly didn't care, they would never have bought a game system and would be sitting home playing a game with a rock and a stick. Genre matters … it's also called preference. Personally though it's not that I can't find a gem in any genre, it's just that I find certain genres conform to my idea of a gem more than others. For example, a turn-based strategic game has a solid chance of me finding it enjoyable while anything real-time has a pretty solid chance of me not enjoying it. I have tried both and found what I like. Occasionally I buy other genres but not too often.

What is your favorite genre?

Turn-based strategy

If you read a glowing review, will you buy the game?

No. All review sites are businesses. You get business by advertising. You can't afford to honestly review a game. Don't bite the hand that feeds you and all. I am not condemning it; it's the way the world will always work. This isn't just gaming; this is any product. I didn't exactly just wake up and see this either. It took me a couple years of buying games with glowing reviews that were junk before I developed this cynicism.

What influences your gaming purchases the most? (Select up to two.)

Topic, franchises, genre

Do you believe the publisher (Infogrames, EA, etc.) or the developer (Blizzard, etc.) has a

255

greater impact on how good the game is?

The development team because it's their job. Without them, the game will be soulless.

If you buy a stinker from a publisher, will you buy a subsequent game from the same publisher?

No

What is your favorite game that you have played in the last 24 months? Why?

Sub Command. Realistic, great editor, lots of scenarios, polished, and the love of the design team for submarines is evident.

Will you buy a game on impulse if it is connected with a license, such as Star Trek and Star Wars, which you enjoy?

No. Most license games are poor quality. Licenses tend to be purchased by large publishers who don't care.

Does the game's genre strongly influence your purchase?

Yes. I don't like some genres, such as mindless shooters.

What is your favorite genre?

Strategy (turn or real)

If you read a glowing review, will you buy the game?

No. It depends on what the review says. Arcanum received glowing reviews, but I strongly disliked it.

What influences your gaming purchases the most? (Select up to two.)

Genre

Do you believe the publisher (Infogrames, EA, etc.) or the developer (Blizzard, etc.) has a greater impact on how good the game is?

You cannot really say.

If you buy a stinker from a publisher, will you buy a subsequent game from the same publisher?

No; it is up to them to put their name on a good product if they want me to come back to them again.

What is your favorite game that you have played in the last 24 months? Why?

Delta Force: Land Warrior. It was a good year for killing terrorists.

Will you buy a game on impulse if it is connected with a license, such as Star Trek and Star Wars, which you enjoy?

No, especially if it connected with a license because they frequently rely on the license to sell a game and put no thought into game play.

Does the game's genre strongly influence your purchase?

Yes; I love a good strategy game.

What is your favorite genre?

Real-time strategy/war game

If you read a glowing review, will you buy the game?

Depends on who wrote it

What influences your gaming purchases the most? (Select up to two.)

Genre

Do you believe the publisher (Infogrames, EA, etc.) or the developer (Blizzard, etc.) has a greater impact on how good the game is?

With the rare exception of the truly innovative game engine, it is the "bells and whistles" that make you buy and keep you playing.

If you buy a stinker from a publisher, will you buy a subsequent game from the same publisher?

Yes, games are not yet commodities. Each game stands or falls on its own merit, and you don't buy the brand; you buy the game.

What is your favorite game that you have played in the last 24 months? Why?

Medieval: Total War. The mix of strategy and tactics was right, and the engine and graphics gave you a feeling of involvement. As a solo gamer, you need some help in driving your imagination and immersion in the game to keep you playing it.

Will you buy a game on impulse if it is connected with a license, such as Star Trek and Star Wars, which you enjoy?

No

Does the game's genre strongly influence your purchase?

Yes. My personal interest in military history makes me want to see if I could have done "better." Also, I am a solo gamer of "mature" years and my reflexes aren't up to some shooters and real-time games where the fastest mouse wins.

What is your favorite genre?

War games. I have been lucky to be able to "advance" over the years from books and model soldiers to Avalon Hill and GDW map and counter games to PC-based games where I don't need an extra room in the house to battle Waterloo, etc.

If you read a glowing review, will you buy the game?

Yes, if it is in the genre I am interested in. I ride motorcycles, but a glowing review of a touring bike will not make me swap my Supersports. I decided a number of years ago what I wanted in biking, and the same goes with gaming.

What influences your gaming purchases the most? (Select up to two.)

Topic, franchises, genre

Do you believe the publisher (Infogrames, EA, etc.) or the developer (Blizzard, etc.) has a greater impact on how good the game is?

I think the developer has a greater influence. The original ideas, concept, design, and implementation are critical factors. If these all come together, then a game will almost certainly be a good game. Alternatively, if the developers fail in any of these areas, the game is also likely to be a failure, irrespective of the input from the publishers.

If you buy a stinker from a publisher, will you buy a subsequent game from the same publisher?

Yes, I am willing to give a publisher a second chance, although I will be a lot more wary. I would certainly wait to see some reviews of any future games. A bad experience will rule out buying a game on blind faith, but I wouldn't automatically never buy from the same publisher again.

What is your favorite game that you have played in the last 24 months? Why?

Probably the Championship Manager series of games. Realism is the key to this—the games feel so close to reality and immerse you in the world of managing a soccer team. It does this without lots of graphics or audio cues; a lot is left to the imagination, yet it seems to work. I also get a lot of pleasure "outside" the game (for example, by watching a soccer game you are constantly thinking of how you could integrate the players you are watching into "your" Championship Manager team). The online community is also terrific, meaning there is a lot more that can be discovered by surfing the web. A close second would be European Air War. This game has also captured my imagination for a number of reasons. It is relatively simple, but has a great immersion factor. The flexibility it offers is also terrific—you can adapt the game to your needs or tastes. A huge supporter base is what makes the game. User mods have been critical in extending the game's life. I think the ability to modify a game is an important factor in judging whether it is a success. It ensures that the gamer is not restricted to the developer's vision for the game.

Will you buy a game on impulse if it is connected with a license, such as Star Trek and Star Wars, which you enjoy?

No, in my experience, games with licenses can be extremely poor. The use of a license is no guarantee of a quality game. A poor game can ruin the enjoyment you have from the particular franchise in question. I prefer to wait for reviews and the judgment of fellow fans.

Does the game's genre strongly influence your purchase?

Yes, I rarely buy games to experience the latest graphics or sound if it is not in the genre I like. These games will only have a limited appeal—once the "wow" factor is gone, there is nothing of substance left. Purchasing games based on the genre is as close as you can get to a guarantee that the game will hold some lasting appeal for the gamer.

What is your favorite genre?

Turn-based strategy and/or war games. I like the fact that these games rely more on your ability to think than your reflexes or ability to click quickly. These games offer the most scope for your imagination to play a part in your enjoyment of the game. I do like a variety of genres though, including simulations and sports.

If you read a glowing review, will you buy the game?

Yes, but only if the game is one that normally attracts my interest, either because it is of a certain genre or I had independently developed an interest in the game.

What influences your gaming purchases the most? (Select up to two.)

Publisher/developer

Do you believe the publisher (Infogrames, EA, etc.) or the developer (Blizzard, etc.) has a greater impact on how good the game is?

Developer

If you buy a stinker from a publisher, will you buy a subsequent game from the same publisher?

Yes, it's the developer that counts.

What is your favorite game that you have played in the last 24 months? Why?

Europa Universalis, different topic from earlier games but quite realistic and extremely replayable.

Will you buy a game on impulse if it is connected with a license, such as Star Trek and Star Wars, which you enjoy?

Never

Does the game's genre strongly influence your purchase?

Yes

What is your favorite genre?

Turn-based strategy or some real-time if it has enough strategy in it. So no Command & Conquer, but some Europa Universalis, Tropico, or Railroad Tycoon. Sometimes RPGs.

If you read a glowing review, will you buy the game?

Yes, I trust totally the reviews of *Pelit* (a Finnish magazine).

What influences your gaming purchases the most? (Select up to two.)

Genre, publisher/developer

Do you believe the publisher (Infogrames, EA, etc.) or the developer (Blizzard, etc.) has a greater impact on how good the game is?

Both. For publishers, some houses throw out their games too early; the result is the lack of quality and many patches. Developers do the main design of the game.

If you buy a stinker from a publisher, will you buy a subsequent game from the same publisher?

Yes, but I will take my lesson and think twice about it. Everybody could make a mistake (even a publisher).

What is your favorite game that you have played in the last 24 months? Why?

My favorite games the last 24 months are Call to Power II and The War Engine (I cannot decide which is better). I like good Civilization-like games, and I like also generic war games because with such basic war rules you can simulate a lot of war game genres (say, Ogre or Warhammer 40k). And the best of it is they are both turn based.

Will you buy a game on impulse if it is connected with a license, such as Star Trek and Star Wars, which you enjoy?

No, I am not an impulse buyer. First I visit the home sites of the games that have my interest. Then I follow the development path and read previews and reviews. If they are good, I buy the game.

Does the game's genre strongly influence your purchase?

Yes, I am buying only turn-based games.

What is your favorite genre?

Turn-based war games or strategy games. I prefer to think and plan a long time, before taking my turn. I have a board war game background. A good computer game is, for me, a board game that has several features that a normal board game could not easily have (like real fog of war, etc.)

If you read a glowing review, will you buy the game?

No, I will buy a game if it is interesting for me (turn-based strategy or war game), not because some guy is writing a review. A review is for me a support for a buying decision. But there are some other reasons for my buying habits.

What influences your gaming purchases the most? (Select up to two.)

Topic, franchises, genre

Do you believe the publisher (Infogrames, EA, etc.) or the developer (Blizzard, etc.) has a greater impact on how good the game is?

Don't really know—certainly either can screw it up.

If you buy a stinker from a publisher, will you buy a subsequent game from the same publisher?

I tend to approach their products with much greater caution.

What is your favorite game that you have played in the last 24 months? Why?

Fallout. I actually have all three Fallout games, but now I finally have the time to actually get into them. It's an enthralling universe with much to see and do. There are plot devices to move you in certain directions, but you have great freedom to explore. The second game is European Air War, a good game made really special by the after-market efforts of enthusiasts.

Will you buy a game on impulse if it is connected with a license, such as Star Trek and Star Wars, which you enjoy?

Probably not, as I don't know of a "license" that I am attached to.

Does the game's genre strongly influence your purchase?

Yes, some genres totally disinterest me, although there are one or two new RTS that I might try out

because the back stories look very interesting.

What is your favorite genre?

Turn-based war game. The best is Steel Panthers: World at War. Historical equipment and situations. Simulation—European Air War—(ditto)

If you read a glowing review, will you buy the game?

Maybe—depends on if the review provides meat or only fluff.

What influences your gaming purchases the most? (Select up to two.)

Topic, franchises

Do you believe the publisher (Infogrames, EA, etc.) or the developer (Blizzard, etc.) has a greater impact on how good the game is?

Some publishers have a brand with consistent quality.

If you buy a stinker from a publisher, will you buy a subsequent game from the same publisher?

Rarely. I don't have a lot of time. I reinforce success, not failure, especially if it is a QA failure. I see those as marketing choices that a company makes.

What is your favorite game that you have played in the last 24 months? Why?

TacOps v4. Good simulation. It didn't waste a lot of effort on BS 3D graphics.

Will you buy a game on impulse if it is connected with a license, such as Star Trek and Star Wars, which you enjoy?

No

Does the game's genre strongly influence your purchase?

No, I like realistic simulations.

What is your favorite genre?

Simulation, war game

If you read a glowing review, will you buy the game?

No, I don't care for reviewers' opinions. I look for facts and then make up my own mind.

What influences your gaming purchases the most? (Select up to two.)

Genre, publisher/developer

Do you believe the publisher (Infogrames, EA, etc.) or the developer (Blizzard, etc.) has a greater impact on how good the game is?

The publisher can make all the difference. Companies that offer continued active support of their titles are the best. Companies that seem to offer the title just to make a quick buck on a game and drop it into bargain bins are the worst. Most fall between the extremes, but my preference is companies that tolerate (and encourage) mods.

If you buy a stinker from a publisher, will you buy a subsequent game from the same publisher?

No, I learn my lessons easily. No second chances. I hate wasting money.

What is your favorite game that you have played in the last 24 months? Why?

Close Combat III: The Russian Front. I *love* this game but I must qualify this by saying I usually play it heavily mod. I have played this game for *years* and still love it.

Will you buy a game on impulse if it is connected with a license, such as Star Trek and Star Wars, which you enjoy?

No

Does the game's genre strongly influence your purchase?

Yes

What is your favorite genre?

Turn-based strategy

If you read a glowing review, will you buy the game?

Yes, I really like to be "sold" on a game. I prefer that someone else let me know what a game is about.

What influences your gaming purchases the most? (Select up to two.)

Topic, licenses, franchises

Do you believe the publisher (Infogrames, EA, etc.) or the developer (Blizzard, etc.) has a greater impact on how good the game is?

I believe the developer has the greater impact. While a publisher can muck up a game with a rushed production schedule, ultimately it is up to the developer to release a worthy product, with or without the pressure/input of the publisher.

If you buy a stinker from a publisher, will you buy a subsequent game from the same publisher?

Yes, if the quality is there. Ultimately, I judge each game on an individual basis. A publisher can publish garbage one year and release a real winner the next.

What is your favorite game that you have played in the last 24 months? Why?

Combat Mission (both Beyond Overlord and Barbarossa to Berlin). Why? It is a quality product with solid wargaming (i.e., game play) with terrific graphics/sound. Isn't that the secret of every good game? Good content with a pleasing presentation? It is a simple formula but one that many developers/publishers seem to have forgotten.

Will you buy a game on impulse if it is connected with a license, such as Star Trek and Star Wars, which you enjoy?

No, a license does not guarantee quality. Again, for me, quality is everything. I could care less if the game deals with *Star Trek* or *Saving Private Ryan*, for that matter. If the game play isn't there, who cares? With so much garbage being released today, buying a game based upon the license will lead to much wasted money!

Does the game's genre strongly influence your purchase?

Yes, over the years, I have developed certain definite preferences in my genres. For example, wargaming fascinates me, largely because of my interest in military history. So I stick with the genres that reflect my preferences.

What is your favorite genre?

Wargaming! I love it because, as H.G. Wells once commented, it allows the student of military history to explore war without gore or death (I paraphrase here). Wargaming also has a strong intellectual component. Mindless shooting is not for me. I want to play a game that engages my mind like a tense chess match. A mental victory will always be superior to a physical victory (i.e., click-fest).

If you read a glowing review, will you buy the game?

If the game deals with a topic that interests me, a glowing review will get me to buy the game 75 percent of the time. Reviews from credible sources carry a lot of weight with me. Advertisements have almost no influence on my buying decision.

What influences your gaming purchases the most? (Select up to two.)

Genre, publisher/developer

Do you believe the publisher (Infogrames, EA, etc.) or the developer (Blizzard, etc.) has a greater impact on how good the game is?

Both, because some are just simply known to produce top-quality products.

If you buy a stinker from a publisher, will you buy a subsequent game from the same publisher?

Yes, because one bad game does not mean they will all be bad. Also, it depends largely on the developer and not the publisher.

What is your favorite game that you have played in the last 24 months? Why?

Civilization III because it is extremely different every playing, very interesting, and just plain hardcore fun!

Will you buy a game on impulse if it is connected with a license, such as Star Trek and Star Wars, which you enjoy?

No, I am not into movie-type games.

Does the game's genre strongly influence your purchase?

Yes, because I prefer strategy or war games.

What is your favorite genre?

Turn-based strategy

If you read a glowing review, will you buy the game?

Probably so.

What influences your gaming purchases the most? (Select up to two.)

Cool factor, genre

Do you believe the publisher (Infogrames, EA, etc.) or the developer (Blizzard, etc.) has a greater impact on how good the game is?

The guy doing the coding has the greater effect. If the publisher is forcing the product out to meet a schedule, he is definitely decreasing the quality of the product. I believe it is better to delay the game than to publish something that causes the buying public to be "beta" testers.

If you buy a stinker from a publisher, will you buy a subsequent game from the same publisher?

Most probably not. It depends on the support that the publisher provides on its web site to correct the problems with a game.

What is your favorite game that you have played in the last 24 months? Why?

I like John Tiller's Squad Battles series because the action is fast, the play time is low, and the AI is very good. I also liked Freedom Force for basically the same reasons.

Will you buy a game on impulse if it is connected with a license, such as Star Trek and Star Wars, which you enjoy?

Generally not. I find that after sale support for both these specific areas is bad. S&S is the worst.

Does the game's genre strongly influence your purchase?

Yes, I tend to buy only war (and generally non-RTS) games. The subject must really grab me to go outside this box.

What is your favorite genre?

War game

If you read a glowing review, will you buy the game?

It depends on the subject matter and in some cases where the review is found. I definitely do not buy things that have been panned by multiple reviewers.

What influences your gaming purchases the most? (Select up to two.)

Genre, publisher/developer

Do you believe the publisher (Infogrames, EA, etc.) or the developer (Blizzard, etc.) has a greater impact on how good the game is?

The developer. They are the creators. The publisher is the funder and marketing tool.

If you buy a stinker from a publisher, will you buy a subsequent game from the same publisher?

No, absolutely not. One strike and they are out. Too many bad games hit the shelves.

What is your favorite game that you have played in the last 24 months? Why?

Civilization III and predecessors

Will you buy a game on impulse if it is connected with a license, such as Star Trek and Star Wars, which you enjoy?

Never. Too much of a risk.

Does the game's genre strongly influence your purchase?

It is the main factor. Strategy. Turn-based first, and then selected real-time strategy.

What is your favorite genre?

Although I have sampled all other genres over the last 11 years, I keep going back to my strategy roots— A-H board war games and strategy games from 40 years ago, anything that challenges and exercises my mind. PC arrival automated an enjoyable distraction.

If you read a glowing review, will you buy the game?

Depends on the source of review. The more respected, the more credible, hence valuable. I have done it.

What influences your gaming purchases the most? (Select up to two.)

Topic, franchises, genre

Do you believe the publisher (Infogrames, EA, etc.) or the developer (Blizzard, etc.) has a greater impact on how good the game is?

The developer has more impact because its focus is on producing a viable product while the publisher gives more emphasis to sales-enhancing peripherals.

If you buy a stinker from a publisher, will you buy a subsequent game from the same publisher?

Yes, because I give more credence to subject matter and the developer's track record.

What is your favorite game that you have played in the last 24 months? Why?

Medieval: Total War because of its beauty, replayability, excellent AI, and the fact that it is the best game to date to allow real-time recreation of historical and hypothetical battles.

Will you buy a game on impulse if it is connected with a license,

such as Star Trek and Star Wars, which you enjoy?

Not if that is the sole reason. Too many poor games have been published on that hook. I would still rely on previews and reviews.

Does the game's genre strongly influence your purchase?

Yes

What is your favorite genre?

Favorite is real-time historical military simulation. Why?... for the same reason I don't like science-fiction shooters... I'm 80 years old.

If you read a glowing review, will you buy the game?

Yes, if the review has the ring of truth and also points out some weaknesses.

What influences your gaming purchases the most? (Select up to two.)

Cool factor, topic, franchises, genre

Do you believe the publisher (Infogrames, EA, etc.) or the developer (Blizzard, etc.) has a greater impact on how good the game is?

Yes, a lot of publishers know how to sell games to people and what people want. They make suggestions to developers on how to make their game better. More experienced developers also know what is good and what is bad in games.

If you buy a stinker from a publisher, will you buy a subsequent game from the same publisher?

Yes, I really don't pay attention to who publishes the games in the first place.

What is your favorite game that you have played in the last 24 months? Why?

My favorite game is C&C: Renegade. It has a good netcode, and the game itself is very fun to play online.

Will you buy a game on impulse if it is connected with a license, such as Star Trek and Star Wars, which you enjoy?

No, I have to be interested in the genre, and it has to look interesting to me.

Does the game's genre strongly influence your purchase?

Yes, I like certain genres a lot more than others.

What is your favorite genre?

I enjoy first-person war games like Operation Flashpoint. It is more immersive when it is realistic, and I love major battles and action.

If you read a glowing review, will you buy the game?

If it is the right genre

What influences your gaming purchases the most? (Select up to two.)

Topic, franchises

Do you believe the publisher (Infogrames, EA, etc.) or the developer (Blizzard, etc.) has a greater impact on how good the game is?

Yes, in this industry, a game comes from the ideas of the developer. There is very little input into the game outside them.

If you buy a stinker from a publisher, will you buy a subsequent game from the same publisher?

Yes, first it would be unlikely for me to buy a stinker. I research my buys pretty well. As I stated above, the developer is far more important in making a stinker.

What is your favorite game that you have played in the last 24 months? Why?

Combat Mission. Hands down. I loved Squad Leader (the board game), and it is a more realistic Squad Leader. Real tactics are pretty effective. You don't get much of a gaminess feeling playing it.

Will you buy a game on impulse if it is connected with a license, such as Star Trek and Star Wars, which you enjoy?

No, a license tells you nothing about the genre of a game, much less the quality.

Does the game's genre strongly influence your purchase?

Yes, I get bored quickly with games that are primarily reflex. I like deep-thinking games. I'm a history fanatic. I like to learn from my games. I also like a deep mental challenge. The only game on my PDA is chess.

What is your favorite genre?

Turn-based strategy, real-time strategy, war game

If you read a glowing review, will you buy the game?

No, not just based on one review. There is no way to tell what prejudices, either way, a reviewer might have.

What influences your gaming purchases the most? (Select up to two.)

Genre

Do you believe the publisher (Infogrames, EA, etc.) or the developer (Blizzard, etc.) has a greater impact on how good the game is?

The developer has the greatest impact on the game, since they are the ones doing the actual work, creative and otherwise. However, the publisher has an effect as well, since they are the ones giving the money, setting deadlines, and giving the final yes or no for the game. So a patient publisher might give the developer good time to finish the game up properly, whereas an impatient one will cause the developer to make a rush job of the thing.

If you buy a stinker from a publisher, will you buy a subsequent game from the same publisher?

Yes. I think publishers nowadays have such a large variety of developers under their wings that it really doesn't matter if one single game sucks.

What is your favorite game that you have played in the last 24 months? Why?

Thief. The environment and the feeling of being there is excellent, and lighting and sounds create a good illusion of the player as a thief.

Will you buy a game on impulse if it is connected with a license, such as Star Trek and Star Wars, which you enjoy?

No

Does the game's genre strongly influence your purchase?

Not really. As long as the game is good, it doesn't matter what the genre is.

What is your favorite genre?

Role-playing and strategy games. Gives you more to think about, rather than just turning off all brain-activity and shooting everything. Though once in a while it's good to play games like that as well. In that sense, I can't really say any genre is better than another one. I wouldn't play only strategy games just as much as I wouldn't want to play first-person shooters all the time.

If you read a glowing review, will you buy the game?

Yes, if it works properly on my computer and my budget allows for it.

What influences your gaming purchases the most? (Select up to two.)

Genre

Do you believe the publisher (Infogrames, EA, etc.) or the developer (Blizzard, etc.) has a greater impact on how good the game is?

Yes and no. The impact of the publisher's money is important, but the developers are responsible for how good the game is at first. At least I think so...

If you buy a stinker from a publisher, will you buy a subsequent game from the same publisher?

Perhaps, if a game is a part of a series and if I like it...

What is your favorite game that you have played in the last 24 months? Why?

The Campaign series from HPS because it is a unique series with real flavor.

Will you buy a game on impulse if it is connected with a license, such as Star Trek and Star Wars, which you enjoy?

No. A license doesn't guarantee a good game.

Does the game's genre strongly influence your purchase?

Yes. It must be a turn-based one. I don't like rushes; the game must be as realistic as possible

What is your favorite genre?

Turn-based strategy war game

If you read a glowing review, will you buy the game?

I don't look at reviews too much—only to see what kind of game it is.

What influences your gaming purchases the most? (Select up to two.)

Topic, franchises, genre

Do you believe the publisher (Infogrames, EA, etc.) or the developer (Blizzard, etc.) has a greater impact on how good the game is?

It seems to me the developers have the greater impact on how "good" a game is. They are the creative force behind the game, performing the historical research (e.g., Uncommon Valor vs. Pacific General), establishing the user interface ("smooth" vs. "clunky"), writing the artificial intelligence routines for folks who can't (or won't) play a human opponent, developing the user documentation (e.g., "clear" or "obtuse"), adding features, and removing bugs, etc. On the other hand, the publisher's role is to move the project along, which by its nature imposes limitations on the creative team in the form of project deadlines, funding limits, etc., that will sometimes result in a poor or bug-ridden product going to market, where people will (sometimes) wait patiently for all the bug fixes and features that didn't make the initial release. In a way, the developer is responsible for "how good the game is"; the publisher has the greater impact on "how good the game could have been."

If you buy a stinker from a publisher, will you buy a subsequent game from the same publisher?

Yes, but only after reading a lot of reviews. I generally read a lot of reviews anyway to avoid this problem in the first place.

What is your favorite game that you have played in the last 24 months? Why?

I can't say there's *one* favorite, but two: 1. Uncommon Valor, from (2x3) and Matrix Games. An outstanding operational simulation of the fighting in the Solomons and New Guinea from May 1942 to December 1943. The game appears to be historically accurate (e.g., order of battle, Japanese logistical woes) and has the "feel" of carrier combat as described in history books (groping for the enemy and then trusting to luck as to whether your air formations even find the enemy task force). The game has had outstanding support from the publisher (bug fixes; active

support of online forums; updates and improvements). I have had board games that covered this campaign (Avalon Hill's FLATTOP, etc.), but their realism suffered somewhat without an umpire to help implement the "fog of war" effects that feature so prominently in historical accounts of the period. The computer handles this nicely, either as an opponent or as an umpire between two opponents. 2. America's Army, from the U.S. Army. A reasonably good first-person shooter, you can't beat the price (free). This game also has outstanding support in terms of continuous updates, new features, game maps, and bug fixes, as well as support for online forums. I had avoided FPS games because my hand-eye coordination can't compete with others (getting old, you know), but this game seems to reward teamwork over individual "Rambo-esque" heroics, and so it seemed more suited to my style of play, as well as reflecting the values and behaviors that I've observed in real combat soldiers and Marines. You'll notice the common thread: "support." Games seem without exception to be released in a semi-finished state, so it seems to me only logical that to get the most from the game, one needs a developer/publisher team that's willing to continue actively working to amend and fix its products after the initial release date.

Will you buy a game on impulse if it is connected with a license, such as Star Trek and Star Wars, which you enjoy?

No. Mere connection with a franchise is no guarantee of quality. A good example of this is the Star Trek franchise, which went through a whole series of dreary fiascoes before Starfleet Command computerized a successful board game (Starfleet Battles) based on the Star Trek series.

Does the game's genre strongly influence your purchase?

Yes. My hand-eye coordination doesn't allow me to do very well on the shooters and other "simulations" that require that ability, so I tend to focus on games where I can use thinking and strategy to win instead of relying on how fast I can click the mouse button or slap around a joystick.

What is your favorite genre?

Turn-based strategy and war games (war games being a subset of turn-based games like chess).

If you read a glowing review, will you buy the game?

No, not if there's only one review. I will review several online sources before I'll buy a game. If they're all pointing in the same direction, I'll go ahead and buy it.

What influences your gaming purchases the most? (Select up to two.)

Topic, franchises, genre

Do you believe the publisher (Infogrames, EA, etc.) or the developer (Blizzard, etc.) has a greater impact on how good the game is?

Developer. These people actually make the game fun to play or not fun.

If you buy a stinker from a publisher, will you buy a subsequent game from the same publisher?

No, reputation will be ruined. A good example is SSI's last game Pool of Radiance.

What is your favorite game that you have played in the last 24 months? Why?

Morrowind III—depth of play, good interface, easy to play and awesome graphics

Will you buy a game on impulse if it is connected with a license, such as Star Trek and Star Wars, which you enjoy?

No. Many "license" games in the past have been mediocre releases.

Does the game's genre strongly influence your purchase?

Yes. Personal preference to specific genre, due to fun factor.

What is your favorite genre?

Turn-based strategy; this genre appeals to my creative thinking and planning to the execution side of my intellect, with the reward of seeing a grand strategy come together.

If you read a glowing review, will you buy the game?

Yes, these reviews are a good indicator of the game's fun factor as it was played by a gamer such as myself.

What influences your gaming purchases the most? (Select up to two.)

Topic, franchises, genre

Do you believe the publisher (Infogrames, EA, etc.) or the developer (Blizzard, etc.) has a greater impact on how good the game is?

I mostly pay attention to the developer because they actually make the game. There are some publishers, however, that have a good reputation. I only buy EA sports games because they have been solid in the past, for example. I'll also occasionally buy a game from small publishers/developers that I don't necessarily need (Schwerpunkt, Battlefront, Matrix) to "support the cause."

If you buy a stinker from a publisher, will you buy a subsequent game from the same publisher?

It depends on the type of publisher.

What is your favorite game that you have played in the last 24 months? Why?

It's a close call between Uncommon Valor and Europa Universalis II. The same reasoning applies to both. I'm a fiend for tons of behind-the-scenes detail in an elegantly presented game. Both have lots of options and are fairly open-ended. Basically letting me do what I want, that type of game stays on the computer for a long time. A couple games I bought outside of my usual genre were Independence War 2 and Black & White. Independence War was great, Black & White horrible, but a couple more examples of the kind of thing I like. I've had a hankering to buy Battle Cruiser for the longest time but haven't, given the absolutely awful reputation of that fellow that's in charge over there.

Will you buy a game on impulse if it is connected with a license, such as Star Trek and Star Wars, which you enjoy?

No, especially considering how bad most licensed games are. I will buy a game on impulse if Sid Meier, Gary Grigsby, or Norm Koger had something to do with it. But in those cases, it usually turns out well. SimGolf, for example, just looked horrible.

Does the game's genre strongly influence your purchase?

Yes. Mostly because over time I have learned through the pain of an empty wallet which type of game to avoid. Under no circumstances will I buy an RTS, FPS, adventure, or sports/racing (for the PC) game. Games in the strategy (grand or otherwise), war, simulation, or anything turn based will get extra consideration from me.

What is your favorite genre?

Grand strategy. I explained this above, but to reiterate I like the open-ended, conquer-the-world, micro-management, keep-you-awake-for-days-on-end type of thing.

If you read a glowing review, will you buy the game?

I only read reviews to see if the game has elements I like. As to the "final score," I don't really care. So I guess the answer is maybe, but only as a corollary.

What influences your gaming purchases the most? (Select up to two.)

Genre

Do you believe the publisher (Infogrames, EA, etc.) or the developer (Blizzard, etc.) has a greater impact on how good the game is?

Developer

If you buy a stinker from a publisher, will you buy a subsequent game from the same publisher?

Possibly, but it will make me think twice.

What is your favorite game that you have played in the last 24 months? Why?

Uncommon Valor, Matrix games. Very detailed but also very playable. Shows that you don't need top of the range graphics for a good game.

Will you buy a game on impulse if it is connected with a license, such as Star Trek and Star Wars, which you enjoy?

No. I would read a review first. Although I must admit, I did buy the whole X-Wing series of games. I think that was because I really enjoyed the first game I bought though.

Does the game's genre strongly influence your purchase?

Yes, I usually only buy strategy games, turn based, or real-time.

What is your favorite genre?

Strategy war games of World War II. I just think it's so interesting.

If you read a glowing review, will you buy the game?

Yes, if the review goes into enough detail and it says things that the game has that I am interested in. Also the reviewers, for Wargamer and Military Gamer, etc., are mostly interested in the same games as I am and are therefore better than the mainstream magazines who just generalize.

What influences your gaming purchases the most? (Select up to two.)

Genre

Do you believe the publisher (Infogrames, EA, etc.) or the developer (Blizzard, etc.) has a greater impact on how good the game is?

No. Certain publishers put out better games but are still prone to putting out a stinker now and then. It doesn't really make a difference.

If you buy a stinker from a publisher, will you buy a subsequent game from the same publisher?

Maybe…I am leery of getting suckered twice though.

What is your favorite game that you have played in the last 24 months? Why?

Close Combat 4 and Close Combat 5. I continue to play these two games to death! Why that series ever got discarded is beyond me.

Will you buy a game on impulse if it is connected with a license, such as Star Trek and Star Wars, which you enjoy?

No. I have thrown away far too much money on crap. I now play the demos, and only after a good

experience will I decide if the full version is worth purchasing and playing.

Does the game's genre strongly influence your purchase?

Yes

What is your favorite genre?

WWII squad-based, real-time combat. Pretty focused, I know. I would love to see a revival of the older Atomic WWII games, like the V for Victory series. I would love to see what these games do with today's technology (especially for multiplayer TCP/IP support). Can you imagine having online battles where multiple players are controlling whole battalions and regiments?

If you read a glowing review, will you buy the game?

No, but I will try the demo.

What influences your gaming purchases the most? (Select up to two.)

Cool factor, topic, franchises

Do you believe the publisher (Infogrames, EA, etc.) or the developer (Blizzard, etc.) has a greater impact on how good the game is?

Publishers. Although they do not make the games, they pick and choose what is worth publishing and as a result of these decisions there are some publishers I like better than others.

If you buy a stinker from a publisher, will you buy a subsequent game from the same publisher?

Yes. They do not actually make the game. I will however think twice about buying a game from the same company.

What is your favorite game that you have played in the last 24 months? Why?

Battlefield 1942. It is an amazing game that mixes both action, tactics, and strategy. And with the open nature of the scenarios, the replayability factor is through the roof, not to mention the rapidly developing mod community.

Will you buy a game on impulse if it is connected with a license, such as Star Trek and Star Wars, which you enjoy?

Yes, but only from the Mech-Warrior series because I have come to trust their game creation over several years.

Does the game's genre strongly influence your purchase?

No, I enjoy a variety of games ranging from RPG, strategy, war game, FPS, simulation, and even some sports games.

What is your favorite genre?

It would have to be a tie between the action-packed adrenaline-pumping hours of an FPS and the methodical and tactical thinking of a strategy game.

If you read a glowing review, will you buy the game?

No, but depending on the source of the review it may greatly influence my judgment of the game.

What influences your gaming purchases the most? (Select up to two.)

Genre, publisher/developer

Do you believe the publisher (Infogrames, EA, etc.) or the developer (Blizzard, etc.) has a greater impact on how good the game is?

I would believe the developer would have greater impact due to its influence in game design, playability, and realism (on the assumption the publisher is providing only financial and marketing guidance).

If you buy a stinker from a publisher, will you buy a subsequent game from the same publisher?

No—the publisher is obviously not committed to providing quality games.

What is your favorite game that you have played in the last 24 months? Why?

ANGV—real-time simulation, graphically good, good AI

Will you buy a game on impulse if it is connected with a license, such as Star Trek and Star Wars, which you enjoy?

No, but I will be favorably predisposed to purchasing a game based on a familiar, well-liked license.

Does the game's genre strongly influence your purchase?

Yes. I purchase only strategic, history-based games with a preference for real-time strategy games.

What is your favorite genre?

Real-time strategy

If you read a glowing review, will you buy the game?

If the reviewer bases his review on similar game play criteria to which I use to evaluate the playability of a game, then his review would affect my purchase. The ultimate review would be from a friend with whom I've played. Normally the more the reviews, the more confidence I have in the game panning out.

What influences your gaming purchases the most? (Select up to two.)

Topic, franchises, genre

Do you believe the publisher (Infogrames, EA, etc.) or the developer (Blizzard, etc.) has a greater impact on how good the game is?

The developer has a bigger impact, as they are responsible for what goes into the game. The publisher just tries to sell copies.

If you buy a stinker from a publisher, will you buy a subsequent game from the same publisher?

Yes. Just because one game is a flop does not mean the next one will be.

What is your favorite game that you have played in the last 24 months? Why?

Computer World in Flames. I play the board game and enjoy it greatly, and although it is not complete, the PC version does cover WWII across the entire world. I enjoy grand strategy with corps or divisional level combat and movement

Will you buy a game on impulse if it is connected with a license, such as Star Trek and Star Wars, which you enjoy?

Maybe, depends on the previous version/quality, but before I buy I always look for reviews and previews to help me decide.

Does the game's genre strongly influence your purchase?

Yes, if a game is a turn-based WWII war game, I'll buy it. I will at least always look at turn-based games, and any WWII game or for that matter any tactical games will get my interest.

What is your favorite genre?

I prefer turn-based war and strategy games. These are 85 percent of my purchases. I buy others for downtime or for a distraction.

If you read a glowing review, will you buy the game?

Maybe. Much still depends on the subject and how the reviewer discusses the game. Often reviewers focus on looks and not the depth of the game.

What influences your gaming purchases the most? (Select up to two.)

Topic, franchises, genre

Do you believe the publisher (Infogrames, EA, etc.) or the developer (Blizzard, etc.) has a greater impact on how good the game is?

The developer certainly has the greater impact. A good example is Operation Flashpoint. With that game, a previously unknown developer produced an excellent title.

If you buy a stinker from a publisher, will you buy a subsequent game from the same publisher?

Generally I would say no, but some usually good publishers have released real stinkers—for example, SSI with their Luftwaffe Commander.

What is your favorite game that you have played in the last 24 months? Why?

I have to say Operation Flashpoint. An excellent campaign, with a logical line of events from one scenario to another. Bad squad leader and armored scenarios, but the basic infantry scenarios are very good.

Will you buy a game on impulse if it is connected with a license, such as Star Trek and Star Wars, which you enjoy?

No, as a fanatic boardgamer I was close to buying Squad Leader, but didn't as a result of reading a review. Conclusion: Reviews have a large impact on me.

Does the game's genre strongly influence your purchase?

Yes. The sense of realism is important. It doesn't have to be historically accurate, though—Op Flashpoint is a good example of this.

What is your favorite genre?

Simulations (mainly flight and tank) as well as turn-based strategy (the Steel Panthers series is still a favorite)

If you read a glowing review, will you buy the game?

As stated above, I probably will.

What influences your gaming purchases the most? (Select up to two.)

Genre

Do you believe the publisher (Infogrames, EA, etc.) or the developer (Blizzard, etc.) has a greater impact on how good the game is?

Yes. Production is very important. Not as much as design, but yes enough to provide a good look to the final game.

If you buy a stinker from a publisher, will you buy a subsequent game from the same publisher?

Yes, I have done it. Many times the publisher repeats the factors that make a game a good one (same designer team or genre). A good game may be the link to very good sequels and a good engine too. A bad one is usually the last mistake.

What is your favorite game that you have played in the last 24 months? Why?

Stronghold. It is a very good mixture of RTS, adventure and sim-style game.

Will you buy a game on impulse if it is connected with a license, such as Star Trek and Star Wars, which you enjoy?

Not necessarily. If it's the genre I like, maybe. But not any action or adventure game just because it's based on a license I enjoy.

Does the game's genre strongly influence your purchase?

Yes. It's the main influence. I love wargaming and it's the kind of game I spend my time on. No other.

What is your favorite genre?

War game, turn-based strategy, RTS

If you read a glowing review, will you buy the game?

No. I try to read more than one review and then look at the minimum requirements.

What influences your gaming purchases the most? (Select up to two.)

Promotions, genre

Do you believe the publisher (Infogrames, EA, etc.) or the developer (Blizzard, etc.) has a greater impact on how good the game is?

I think (hope) that the developers are trying to make the game as perfect as possible before releasing it, while the publishers are hurrying the developers to complete the game in time for the deadline (we can always patch it later…).

If you buy a stinker from a publisher, will you buy a subsequent game from the same publisher?

Maybe, if it has good reviews and a great demo, but I won't queue on the day it's released.

What is your favorite game that you have played in the last 24 months? Why?

Sid Meier's Civilization III. It really makes the hours fly away. (Just another turn…) It's fun, addictive, changing, editable, and so on.

Will you buy a game on impulse if it is connected with a license, such as Star Trek and Star Wars, which you enjoy?

No, not before reading reviews and, if possible, playing the demo. I've learned that some companies spend more money on the license than on the game.…

Does the game's genre strongly influence your purchase?

Yes, I wouldn't buy a game about knitting because I'm not interested in that.

What is your favorite genre?

Oooh, it's a mix with first-person shooters/sword wielding, (combat) flight simulators, real-time, and turn-based strategy games. I like games where you get to build things, cities, armies, characters, or blow them to pieces.

If you read a glowing review, will you buy the game?

If the review is exclusive and published before the game is released, I'd be alerted because the reviewer might not be allowed another exclusive if they say that the game is a stinker and are thus forced to say it's a great game…remember Daikatana?

What influences your gaming purchases the most? (Select up to two.)

Genre

Do you believe the publisher (Infogrames, EA, etc.) or the developer (Blizzard, etc.) has a greater impact on how good the game is?

Developer—they are they ones that make the game!

If you buy a stinker from a publisher, will you buy a subsequent game from the same publisher?

It depends. I'm not too bothered about who publishes or develops the game. I'll judge each game as it comes.

What is your favorite game that you have played in the last 24 months? Why?

Masters of Orion II. It's a great blend of strategy and tactics, with technology and design included.

Will you buy a game on impulse if it is connected with a license, such as Star Trek and Star Wars, which you enjoy?

I'd buy a game on impulse but not because of its branding.

Does the game's genre strongly influence your purchase?

Yes. I like strategy games and not much else.

What is your favorite genre?

Strategy—turn based

If you read a glowing review, will you buy the game?

No, not based on the review. I'm more interested in screen shots. You can tell a lot about a game from the UI.

What influences your gaming purchases the most? (Select up to two.)

Topic, franchises, genre

Do you believe the publisher (Infogrames, EA, etc.) or the developer (Blizzard, etc.) has a greater impact on how good the game is?

Publishers, because they can afford to give a title additional resources that other companies may not be able to supply. Also, they will attract the best talented coders, graphic artists, etc. They also have an idea on what options gamers want in a game, but this is limited to the genre that they produce. While SSI would produce great war games based around game play and average graphics, Blizzard produces RTS with high energy graphics, simple game and strategy concepts—the basis of this is that they stick to a winning formula. Thus, a purchaser will know what they are getting before they hand over the cash for the next title.

If you buy a stinker from a publisher, will you buy a subsequent game from the same publisher?

Yes. I hate to say it. The reason is that the game offered a genre that I was interested in. It was usually based upon an earlier game that was great, and they jazz up with graphics and forget the game play. Perhaps next time they will get the mix right.

What is your favorite game that you have played in the last 24 months? Why?

Panzer General. I have every subsequent title but for pure game play—forget the graphics—this is the best. This game is almost pure strategy—yes, a limited AI, but enough. I have played many others, but I have a DOS boot disk just for this game.

Will you buy a game on impulse if it is connected with a license, such as Star Trek and Star Wars, which you enjoy?

Yes, but generally it would have to be discounted or specific to a title type that I like. Generally, role-playing games associated with a license attached to TV shows cannot match what the show provides. A graphic of Spock just isn't the same, especially when the voices are different. I am more likely to buy on impulse when purchasing for another as a gift—the more famous the show, the greater the appeal.

Does the game's genre strongly influence your purchase?

Yes, these games cost a lot of money. My interest mainly is in strategy-type games. First-person shooters—no matter how graphic—involve a simple plot. I play them but put them away. Later when I see them collecting dust on the book shelf, I can think of the wasted money. This reinforces my decision to stick to what I know what I will play, not just like.

What is your favorite genre?

I like multiple genres—turn-based strategy and real-time strategy war games. While they align to my job as a soldier—I think they relate to more why I became a soldier opposed to the fact that is the job that I do. They make me think, plan—yet no real consequences.

If you read a glowing review, will you buy the game?

Yes, but this is more of a support role. If I want a game, a review can be the final justification to buying it. A review attacking game play has a big effect. But a bad review does not hurt my decision if it is clear that the reviewer does not understand the genre.

What influences your gaming purchases the most? (Select up to two.)

Genre, publisher/developer

Do you believe the publisher (Infogrames, EA, etc.) or the developer (Blizzard, etc.) has a greater impact on how good the game is?

No, anyone can have a good idea or make a great game (Big Time Software rings a bell), but after finding a developer that does well, I will at least give them a chance and try the new demo....

If you buy a stinker from a publisher, will you buy a subsequent game from the same publisher?

Yes. No one bats a thousand. Some outfits do better than others... so I will look more closely at their games, but no one is perfect.

What is your favorite game that you have played in the last 24 months? Why?

Combat Mission: Barbarossa to Berlin. It's historical based, no bugs (few bugs), great editor, and makes for lots of re-play ability.

Will you buy a game on impulse if it is connected with a license, such as Star Trek and Star Wars, which you enjoy?

No. I have been playing PC games for ten years...

Does the game's genre strongly influence your purchase?

Yes. I just like strategy games, can't help myself...

What is your favorite genre?

Strategy/war games...

If you read a glowing review, will you buy the game?

Yes, sometimes, but not often, as I will also check out the forums...

What influences your gaming purchases the most? (Select up to two.)

Genre

Do you believe the publisher (Infogrames, EA, etc.) or the developer (Blizzard, etc.) has a greater impact on how good the game is?

Developer...the publisher is not *doing* the game; they're just supervising and giving deadlines...

If you buy a stinker from a publisher, will you buy a subsequent game from the same publisher?

Yes. Everybody makes mistakes.

What is your favorite game that you have played in the last 24 months? Why?

Medieval: Total War, a game that is so deep that I will never be able to play it through. I like strategy games that are realistic and require thinking!

Will you buy a game on impulse if it is connected with a license, such as Star Trek and Star Wars, which you enjoy?

No. I have only bad experiences with that.

Does the game's genre strongly influence your purchase?

Yes. I want to use my brains when playing, and with real-time strategy games like Command & Conquer, etc., it's almost impossible.

What is your favorite genre?

Turn-based strategy and real-time strategy (I don't mean click-fests)

If you read a glowing review, will you buy the game?

Depends on its genre, etc. I won't buy certain games even if they get 99/100 reviews in every magazine.

What influences your gaming purchases the most? (Select up to two.)

Topic, franchises

Do you believe the publisher (Infogrames, EA, etc.) or the developer (Blizzard, etc.) has a greater impact on how good the game is?

No, a good game is a good game, no matter who makes it.

If you buy a stinker from a publisher, will you buy a subsequent game from the same publisher?

Yes. All games are different.

What is your favorite game that you have played in the last 24 months? Why?

Uncommon Valor—excellent game, good support

Will you buy a game on impulse if it is connected with a license, such as Star Trek and Star Wars, which you enjoy?

Yes. Only if the game is good.

Does the game's genre strongly influence your purchase?

Real-time strategy is garbage. I never even consider buying real-time strategy games. They are all the same.

What is your favorite genre?

Turn-based strategy—actual strategy (thinking) involved, not just click and dragging.

[I wonder if this guy ever actually played an RTS game.—author]

If you read a glowing review, will you buy the game?

Not always, depends on game

. . . .

What influences your gaming purchases the most? (Select up to two.)

Topic, franchises, genre

Do you believe the publisher (Infogrames, EA, etc.) or the developer (Blizzard, etc.) has a greater impact on how good the game is?

I expect the developer to have the greater impact. If the game engine

(the rules, mechanisms, etc.) is sound, the game stands a good chance of being a winner. Good graphics and sound are necessary too, but ultimately second in importance. I guess the developer develops the game engine, while the producer dictates how much glamour and glitz should be added to it.

If you buy a stinker from a publisher, will you buy a subsequent game from the same publisher?

Why not? But I should add I never buy a game on impulse.

What is your favorite game that you have played in the last 24 months? Why?

Shogun: Warlord Edition. It combines a simple and elegant rule set with a lot of freedom of choice for the player. At its level of abstraction, it seems fairly realistic. The good graphics and sound get me in the right mood. It is the kind of game that gives the impression of being a labor of love.

Will you buy a game on impulse if it is connected with a license, such as Star Trek and Star Wars, which you enjoy?

No. At least I cannot remember having done that. I usually read a lot of reviews on the Internet, see what kind of following a game attracts, and finally decide if it is something I want to buy.

Does the game's genre strongly influence your purchase?

Yes, it does. Barring a few "one-night stands," I typically end up with flight simulations, turn-based strategy, and war games in the medium to hard-core realism range. That is usually the kind of game I look for and read about.

What is your favorite genre?

I guess ultimately I want a game to make me think, but it should not play out in a completely logical way. If it were that logical (á là chess), personally I could not see it as a game but only as a competition. The random processes and the fog of war make war games entirely different from chess. Also, I have an interest in the history of war, its technical, political, and human aspects. Flight simulations, strategy games, and war games usually cater for at least one if not more of these aspects by providing some sort of test lab. Nevertheless, I enjoy this because ultimately I see these games as just that: games.

If you read a glowing review, will you buy the game?

It certainly is a bonus to a game if it receives glowing reviews. But it also depends on who wrote the review, for what (Internet) magazine, and what exactly the reviewer liked/disliked. I review the review and then decide what to make of it.

What influences your gaming purchases the most? (Select up to two.)

Cool factor

Do you believe the publisher (Infogrames, EA, etc.) or the developer (Blizzard, etc.) has a greater impact on how good the game is?

Yes, as they have the resources and the money to really make a game good, both in development and game design. Plus, they know what sells and what doesn't by the response of consumers who buy it. If they like it, they'll be hooked!

If you buy a stinker from a publisher, will you buy a subsequent game from the same publisher?

Yes, just because one game is not up to par, it might just be who worked on the game and how long they spent developing it. The next game out might be great—just have to wait and see!

What is your favorite game that you have played in the last 24 months? Why?

Steel Panthers III. It is a great war strategy game that is realistic, keeps you hooked, and is fun to play. Plus you get to blow things up! It also has an editor, so you can design your own battlefields and the game stays fresh.

Will you buy a game on impulse if it is connected with a license,

such as Star Trek and Star Wars, which you enjoy?

Yes, especially some license that I am a fan of. I'll buy the game just to see how it compares to the TV show or movie...

Does the game's genre strongly influence your purchase?

Yes, I tend to like strategy games that challenge your mind, not unlike some shooters or action games that are just mindless challenges and boring after a while!

What is your favorite genre?

Turn-based strategy. It is very challenging, it stimulates your mind, and it makes you think, sometimes several turns ahead! I also like RPGs for the same reason.

If you read a glowing review, will you buy the game?

Yes

What influences your gaming purchases the most? (Select up to two.)

Topic, franchises, genre

Do you believe the publisher (Infogrames, EA, etc.) or the developer (Blizzard, etc.) has a greater impact on how good the game is?

I believe that the developer has a greater impact on how good a game is. It is the developer, not the publisher, who brings the creative and intellectual talent to the table. While the publisher is important in terms of marketing and distribution, it is the developer that shapes the game's identity and ultimately its success or failure. Big publishers like EA bring a wide variety of games to the marketplace—some good, some bad. The consistency of performance, either good or bad, is linked to the developer. I believe it is more important to look at who is the developer. I am more willing to have "brand loyalty" to a proven developer than to any given publisher.

If you buy a stinker from a publisher, will you buy a subsequent game from the same publisher?

Yes, I would. In my opinion, most of the larger publishers deal with a variety of developers. As stated previously, these publishers team with both good and not-so-good developers. The publishers are middlemen. It is the consistency of the developer that matters. I am willing to try a new or unproven developer, yet by the same token, I would shy away from a proven bad developer.

What is your favorite game that you have played in the last 24 months? Why?

I would say the entire Campaign Series (West Front, East Front II, and Rising Sun) by TalonSoft in its various incarnations. The Campaign Series uses a proven game engine that has been improved with time. There are a myriad of third-party scenarios and mods available, an extremely high replay value, and there are plenty of sites that cater to the Campaign Series and capitalize on the Play By E-Mail and Head to Head aspect of the series.

Will you buy a game on impulse if it is connected with a license, such as Star Trek and Star Wars, which you enjoy?

Yes and no. Certain licenses are connected with proven developers, while others are not. For example, the AD&D license owned by Wizards of the Coast is associated with Ubi Soft and Black Isle. Ubi Soft turned out the biggest stinker that this license has ever known when they produced Pool of Radiance: Ruins of Myth Drannor. Bad game engine, bad interface, totally unbalanced game play. This game did a great injustice to the AD&D license. On the other hand, there is Black Isle. Black Isle produced the Baldur's Gate series, the Ice Wind Dale series, and Neverwinter Nights. All of these were great successes. Outstanding game engine, excellent interface, balanced play, and gripping story line. On the other hand, in regards to Star Trek, I will buy any Starfleet Command title unseen. Interplay has consistently done an outstanding job in conjunction with 14 East and Taldren to produce an excellent series.

Does the game's genre strongly influence your purchase?

Yes, it does. I tend to stay away from twitch games and first-person shooters. I love real-time strategy because of the challenge of managing the entire battle as a whole, all at once. I love turn-based strategy games because of the thought and planning that must go into the game play and the ability to play human opponents via head to head or PBEM play. I will take a gamble and purchase either a real-time strategy game or a turn-based strategy game from an unknown or unproven developer/publisher just because of the genre. On the other hand, I will stay away from other genres that I am not interested in, no matter how popular the game/series or how great the reviews.

What is your favorite genre?

I love turn-based strategy, real-time strategy, and war games more than any other types of games. I like war games in general, WWII war games in particular. Turn-based or real-time strategy, it really does not matter. In real-time strategy games, I am a big Sudden Strike, C&C, Warcraft, and StarCraft fan. In turn-based strategy games, I am a big TalonSoft Campaign Series and HPS Squad Battles series fan. Turn-based strategy games are great because they lend themselves to head to head or PBEM play. It's great to be able to pit your skills against another human instead of against the computer AI. Real-time strategy games are great because you have to approach the battle problem as a whole, all at once. Multiplayer gaming is a plus also. The new generation of WWII first-person/vehicle shooter games is very interesting also. Games like Battlefield 1942, Medal of Honor: Allied Assault, and GI Combat are intense because of the feeling of being immersed in the battle, and these games tend to be historically accurate and have an authentic feel.

If you read a glowing review, will you buy the game?

Not necessarily. Again, it depends on the genre, license, and developer. Certain genres I tend to stay away from due to lack of interest. I'm not really into twitch games or first-person shooters. Certain licenses have a great deal of appeal (Star Trek, AD&D), while others don't (Star Wars … I love Star Wars as a movie series, but I don't care for Star Wars as a gaming license). Finally, the developer makes or breaks a game. Rave reviews about a game by a bad developer will not motivate me to make a purchase, no matter how glowing the review.

What influences your gaming purchases the most? (Select up to two.)

Topic, franchises, publisher/developer

Do you believe the publisher (Infogrames, EA, etc.) or the developer (Blizzard, etc.) has a greater impact on how good the game is?

The publisher. They bring a certain feel or ambience to the game that is unique to each publisher. It simplifies choices for the buyer, knowing what to expect from any one developer.

If you buy a stinker from a publisher, will you buy a subsequent game from the same publisher?

Yes, depending on the genre. A bad FPS publisher may be a great RTS publisher.

What is your favorite game that you have played in the last 24 months? Why?

Medal of Honor: Allied Assault. Realism. Nobody has a weapon that will fire 100 bazillion laser-guided exploding, heat-seeking projectiles at aliens from the planet Trug. Gimme something based somewhere in the realm of possibility, please.

Will you buy a game on impulse if it is connected with a license, such as Star Trek and Star Wars, which you enjoy?

No. Not an impulsive guy.

Does the game's genre strongly influence your purchase?

Yes. FPS with tactical or strategic elements and RTS are my faves.

What is your favorite genre?

FPS, RTS

If you read a glowing review, will you buy the game?

Yes, depending on the reviewer. If I feel they are too subjective, I'll find another review. Dispassionate observation is what I look for.

What influences your gaming purchases the most? (Select up to two.)

Topic, franchises, genre

Do you believe the publisher (Infogrames, EA, etc.) or the developer (Blizzard, etc.) has a greater impact on how good the game is?

Publisher. It appears that no matter how good the content, how deep the programming, how successful the effort, it all comes down to the whims of the publisher and what they foresee for the product. It's not always good for the hobby, but it's how things work.

If you buy a stinker from a publisher, will you buy a subsequent game from the same publisher?

Yes. Even bad publishers have linked with excellent developers to produce a fine product.

What is your favorite game that you have played in the last 24 months? Why?

What a question! Too hard to answer, though I enjoy strategy/war games over all others.

Will you buy a game on impulse if it is connected with a license, such as Star Trek and Star Wars, which you enjoy?

No. The Star Trek license is an excellent example of the possibility for a horrible product. It's in the detail, not the name.

Does the game's genre strongly influence your purchase?

Sure, I prefer games that make me think. For me, that's the challenge.

What is your favorite genre?

I've dabbled in and purchased all of them. Strategy (of all types) gives me the most satisfaction. Real time can be incredible but there are plenty of worthless efforts that do nothing for the hobby.

If you read a glowing review, will you buy the game?

Possibly, I may seek out a second opinion from a competing magazine. For me, it's not different from buying anything else. You get what you pay for, but I only pay for what I want.

What influences your gaming purchases the most? (Select up to two.)

Topic, franchises, genre

Do you believe the publisher (Infogrames, EA, etc.) or the developer (Blizzard, etc.) has a greater impact on how good the game is?

Occasionally. It, of course, all depends on the publisher's/developer's previous record of success. For example, I would trust anything coming from Blizzard. They have an extremely good lineup, not a bad apple in the crop. I might not purchase it, depending on the genre, but I would know it's still a good game. However, I would be a little more skeptical when considering something from a "bargain bin" company such as Activision. They've had a few OK hits, but the majority of their games are not worth looking at, and so a little more research would be necessary. That takes up my time, so I would probably not buy any more games from them.

If you buy a stinker from a publisher, will you buy a subsequent game from the same publisher?

It really depends on what the other game is! In general terms, it really wouldn't matter too much because the publisher isn't the one programming the game, and they have little effect on the overall quality (Contradiction: WarBirds, pushed to an early release from Wal-Mart pressure on publisher).

What is your favorite game that you have played in the last 24 months? Why?

I have particularly enjoyed Max Payne. It was amazingly easy to master, and there were a bunch of new features that made it particularly worthwhile and distinguished it from the rest of the FPS genre. There was an actual plot, and while the story line was linear, it never really seemed like it was.

Will you buy a game on impulse if it is connected with a license, such as Star Trek and Star Wars, which you enjoy?

Probably not. It has been my experience that franchise-related games are mostly money-makers and wouldn't exist without their parent idea. Take Harry Potter, for instance. Would that game have *ever* been made if there were no books? I think not. Licensed games have a short shelf life and an even shorter development time. Enough said.

Does the game's genre strongly influence your purchase?

Yes, mostly for the fact that when I purchase a game I am "in the mood" for a particular genre. Sometimes I shy away from a certain genre, but it's usually based on what I want.

What is your favorite genre?

That's a tough question! :) Actually, I might have to go with two. I really like RTS games, especially when they're particularly realistic and offer a wide range of features and nice graphics. They can also be played as a mindless shooter or as a drawing-you-in, tactical simulator. I'm also a big fan of RPGs, but not the MMORPGs. I'm practically in love with games like Baldur's Gate II and Diablo II, and I can't really even tell you why. I love seeing who—and what—you'll encounter next, solving puzzles, and putting all the pieces together to come to a gripping conclusion.

If you read a glowing review, will you buy the game?

Sometimes, and it depends whether I was going to buy the game or not. If I was planning to, and I see a good review for it, I will definitely go ahead with the purchase. However, if I was not planning to, and I see a good review, then maybe I'll play a demo and look into it a little further before coming to a decision.

What influences your gaming purchases the most? (Select up to two.)

Topic, franchises, genre

Do you believe the publisher (Infogrames, EA, etc.) or the developer (Blizzard, etc.) has a greater impact on how good the game is?

Yes, all companies are competing with each other, and some will work harder to create high-quality games, while others will believe in quantity and price. A high-quality game will cost more and will be fewer and far

between, while with quantity, you get a new game every month.

If you buy a stinker from a publisher, will you buy a subsequent game from the same publisher?

Yes, some games are better than others.

What is your favorite game that you have played in the last 24 months? Why?

Hearts of Iron. This game has grasped the timeline that it was in and held it firmly. You find yourself in charge of a nation during one of the darkest times in history, and in many instances, you make a rather large impact on world history (well, at least in the game).

Will you buy a game on impulse if it is connected with a license, such as Star Trek and Star Wars, which you enjoy?

Yes, well, I'm a Star Wars fan.

Does the game's genre strongly influence your purchase?

Yes, some things are more fun to me than others. Same with everybody I suppose.

What is your favorite genre?

War games are more likely to catch my eye than any others.

If you read a glowing review, will you buy the game?

Yes. Reviewers, at least in many instances, have to give an honest opinion of a game, at least if they want to keep their job.

What influences your gaming purchases the most? (Select up to two.)

Topic, franchises, genre

Do you believe the publisher (Infogrames, EA, etc.) or the developer (Blizzard, etc.) has a greater impact on how good the game is?

Ultimately, the publisher. Development can determine potential "hows," but that won't matter unless the publisher is behind the project 110 percent.

If you buy a stinker from a publisher, will you buy a subsequent game from the same publisher?

No, there's enough variety in games to where loyalty to one house is not necessary if they disappoint severely.

What is your favorite game that you have played in the last 24 months? Why?

Just for the play of the game, all the WizKids products—the combat dial system is great and could really enhance the wargaming hobby.

Will you buy a game on impulse if it is connected with a license, such as Star Trek and Star Wars, which you enjoy?

No, the game has to be good too.

Does the game's genre strongly influence your purchase?

Yes, I like variety and specifically look for certain genres that cover what I don't have a lot of.

What is your favorite genre?

All, I like them all. They all have a place as games and strategic/tactical challenges.

If you read a glowing review, will you buy the game?

No, I want to research the game more or sample it if possible for myself.

What influences your gaming purchases the most? (Select up to two.)

Cool factor, genre

Do you believe the publisher (Infogrames, EA, etc.) or the developer (Blizzard, etc.) has a greater impact on how good the game is?

Any publisher or developer brings something to the table. Whether it makes the game better or not is in the eye of the gamer. A majority of people may buy a game done by EA simply because they like what they've done in the past. In my case, there are a couple of companies where I'll follow this "buy now, ask later" attitude—Blizzard and most monogamously Ensemble Studios.

If you buy a stinker from a publisher, will you buy a subsequent game from the same publisher?

I might, although I'll do a hell of a lot more research than I usually would before buying it. Once I'm satisfied I'm not wasting my money again. Then yes I would.

What is your favorite game that you have played in the last 24 months? Why?

I've had many favorite games in the last two years, but the ones that rise above all the rest for me would have to be the Age series from Ensemble. At the moment, I'm hooked on the newest installment, Age of Mythology, but before that it went all the way back to the original Age of Empires. I enjoy lots of different genres, but RTS has always been the one I favor the most, and the Age series just does every one of them so well, outdoing themselves every time. Not to mention as RTSs go, these are probably the most balanced.

Will you buy a game on impulse if it is connected with a license, such as Star Trek and Star Wars, which you enjoy?

Nope. Unless it's already a series of games that I've liked flawlessly every time, I won't buy anything on impulse. Especially because of a TV or movie license. In my opinion, TV/movie games are often stricken with flaws, so I would pay attention before I bought.

Does the game's genre strongly influence your purchase?

Most definitely. I know what kind of games I like and don't like. I'm way, way more likely to buy a real-time strategy over a flight simulator. That is, unless there's something the game is offering that nothing else is.

What is your favorite genre?

I've got a few of them, but based on my favorite game, I'd say the top of the list is real-time strategy. Others would be online war games, role-playing games (if they're done right), shooters, and a few sports games at the end of the ladder. I'm sure I've missed a few, but those are the major ones.

If you read a glowing review, will you buy the game?

Not unless the glowing review has a whole family of glowing reviews following it. Just because one reviewer likes it doesn't mean the next is going to. If one of my friends says, "This game rocks!," there's bound to be at least a few others who think it sucks. I try and listen to reviewers who have steered me right in the past, as well as the reviews of the ones who haven't.

· · · · · · · · · · · · · ·

What influences your gaming purchases the most? (Select up to two.)

Topic, franchises

Do you believe the publisher (Infogrames, EA, etc.) or the developer (Blizzard, etc.) has a greater impact on how good the game is?

Developer—publisher only looks at marketability

If you buy a stinker from a publisher, will you buy a subsequent game from the same publisher?

Yes—publisher doesn't do the game, just pushes it

What is your favorite game that you have played in the last 24 months? Why?

Tigris & Euphrates, but for computer gaming, Age of Wonders II. It gets Master of Magic right.

Will you buy a game on impulse if it is connected with a license, such as Star Trek and Star Wars, which you enjoy?

No. A license doesn't impress me.

Does the game's genre strongly influence your purchase?

Yes. I need to specialize. There is simply too much out there. Holding to a few themes lets me compare and learn more.

What is your favorite genre?

Turn-based strategy—closer to the games I used to play FTF

If you read a glowing review, will you buy the game?

No. No one publishes anything but good reviews, so I don't even bother to read them anymore.

What influences your gaming purchases the most? (Select up to two.)

Promotions, genre

Do you believe the publisher (Infogrames, EA, etc.) or the developer (Blizzard, etc.) has a greater impact on how good the game is?

Yes. I think that a developer has a degree of skill in a particular area and you can rely on that skill if they are developing a particular style of game.

If you buy a stinker from a publisher, will you buy a subsequent game from the same publisher?

Yes—if it looks good and reviews say it is good. Or the demo is good.

What is your favorite game that you have played in the last 24 months? Why?

Steel Panthers: World at War—this has so many different options to play with and has near endless playability. It's also free.

Will you buy a game on impulse if it is connected with a license, such as Star Trek and Star Wars, which you enjoy?

No. Just because it is connected with a license doesn't mean it's any good. I will take a look to see if it sounds interesting, but it doesn't mean I will buy it.

Does the game's genre strongly influence your purchase?

Yes. I enjoy particular genres and not others. So, I will be looking for that particular type of game. I do try all types of games, but I will primarily be looking for the types I prefer.

What is your favorite genre?

Turn-based or real-time strategy. I like these games, as they require you to think about what you are doing. There is a bit more than just blasting away mindlessly, although the destruction factor in any game is always enjoyable. It's more enjoyable when you have to work for it.

If you read a glowing review, will you buy the game?

No. I will only buy a game if it suits my playing tastes, even if it got a glowing review. If I was considering buying it in the first place and it got a glowing review, then it might push me further to buy it, but I don't buy every game that gets a glowing review.

What influences your gaming purchases the most? (Select up to two.)

Genre

Do you believe the publisher (Infogrames, EA, etc.) or the developer (Blizzard, etc.) has a greater impact on how good the game is?

The publisher has a much greater impact on how good the game is because of the time constraints they put on the developers. The developers are not controlled by the Christmas season. The publishers are in this to make money, not for the love of the game.

If you buy a stinker from a publisher, will you buy a subsequent game from the same publisher?

Yes. One can always hope they will have learned something. However, I will read the reviews carefully before I purchase another from them.

What is your favorite game that you have played in the last 24 months? Why?

Medieval: Total War! It has everything—strategy, tactics, and an interesting subject matter.

Will you buy a game on impulse if it is connected with a license, such as Star Trek and Star Wars, which you enjoy?

I have done so in the past, but I have slowed down, as I have more games than I currently play.

Does the game's genre strongly influence your purchase?

Yes. There are certain types of games that I like and many I don't like.

What is your favorite genre?

War game, turn-based strategy

If you read a glowing review, will you buy the game?

Probably, depending on if it was something I was interested in.

What influences your gaming purchases the most? (Select up to two.)

Topic, franchises, genre

Do you believe the publisher (Infogrames, EA, etc.) or the developer (Blizzard, etc.) has a greater impact on how good the game is?

The developer has the greater impact.

If you buy a stinker from a publisher, will you buy a subsequent game from the same publisher?

Yes

What is your favorite game that you have played in the last 24 months? Why?

Civilization III

Will you buy a game on impulse if it is connected with a license, such as Star Trek and Star Wars, which you enjoy?

No, except for MechWarrior/BattleTech

Does the game's genre strongly influence your purchase?

Yes

What is your favorite genre?

Turn-based strategy, war game

If you read a glowing review, will you buy the game?

No. I prefer to see a variety of actual players' opinions.

What influences your gaming purchases the most? (Select up to two.)

Topic, franchises, genre

Do you believe the publisher (Infogrames, EA, etc.) or the developer (Blizzard, etc.) has a greater impact on how good the game is?

The developer. If a game is good, then it is good, no doubt about it, and it'll get good reviews and such.

If you buy a stinker from a publisher, will you buy a subsequent game from the same publisher?

Yes, because people screw up all the time.

What is your favorite game that you have played in the last 24 months? Why?

Steel Panthers: World at War because I like wargaming and it is the kind of wargaming I enjoy, beside its free.

Will you buy a game on impulse if it is connected with a license, such as Star Trek and Star Wars, which you enjoy?

I don't know; this question is hard to answer.

Does the game's genre strongly influence your purchase?

Yes because nobody who likes to play Counter-Strike would go and buy a puzzle game about Counter-Strike.

What is your favorite genre?

War game. I like war games because it puts me as the commander in chief of a group of men. I must care for them, but yet do my duty. It's very fun. Besides since I'm into war histories, it's about the easiest way to reenact many of the famous battles of the world.

If you read a glowing review, will you buy the game?

Maybe if the game is about topics I like or genres I like

What influences your gaming purchases the most? (Select up to two.)

Topic, franchises, genre

Do you believe the publisher (Infogrames, EA, etc.) or the developer (Blizzard, etc.) has a greater impact on how good the game is?

Publishers because of build quality and reputation

If you buy a stinker from a publisher, will you buy a subsequent game from the same publisher?

No. Leopards seldom change their spots.

What is your favorite game that you have played in the last 24 months? Why?

Europa Universalis II—originality and depth

Will you buy a game on impulse if it is connected with a license, such as Star Trek and Star Wars, which you enjoy?

No; these games trade more on the "franchise" than the substance of what is an interesting game.

Does the game's genre strongly influence your purchase?

Yes; I can't buy them all, but I know what appeals to me.

What is your favorite genre?

No absolute, but ones that you have to think about and that immerse you in their virtual world.

If you read a glowing review, will you buy the game?

Yes, particularly if there are many glowing reviews and the game's genre suits me.

What influences your gaming purchases the most? (Select up to two.)

Topic, franchises, genre

Do you believe the publisher (Infogrames, EA, etc.) or the developer (Blizzard, etc.) has a greater impact on how good the game is?

In some cases, yes. Some vendors have a history of releasing quality games that install and run out of the box, while others release a piece of junk. The prime example I'd use is Fallout from Interplay—it was amazing at the time that it would work as installed from the CD. Contrast that with Battlecruiser from Take 2 Entertainment; the game advertised as better than sex. Indeed.

If you buy a stinker from a publisher, will you buy a subsequent game from the same publisher?

No. After the Battlecruiser debacle, I have actively avoided Take 2 products.

What is your favorite game that you have played in the last 24 months? Why?

Civilization III. Hours of play, plenty of variety. Gives one time to consider strategy, unlike first-person shooters or real-time strategy games.

Will you buy a game on impulse if it is connected with a license, such as Star Trek and Star Wars, which you enjoy?

No. Perhaps when I was younger, but I have been burned way too many times by license-based games (especially early Star Trek titles). Now it's read the reviews first before dropping $50 on a new game.

Does the game's genre strongly influence your purchase?

Yes. I won't buy a game if it doesn't look interesting.

What is your favorite genre?

Turn-based strategy, especially hex-based board game style games.

If you read a glowing review, will you buy the game?

If it appears the reviewer is credible, this will influence my buying decision.

What influences your gaming purchases the most? (Select up to two.)

Genre

Do you believe the publisher (Infogrames, EA, etc.) or the developer (Blizzard, etc.) has a greater impact on how good the game is?

Producer. Based on the previous titles they have created, you come to expect a certain quality of their software to be the same, if not better. They have the resources to help players via services that they have and the staff to create good quality products on a regular basis.

If you buy a stinker from a publisher, will you buy a subsequent game from the same publisher?

Yes. If a publisher creates a terrible game, I would have to give them one more chance to see if they learned from their mistake(s). However, only one chance...

What is your favorite game that you have played in the last 24 months? Why?

Medal of Honor: Allied Assault. Very stable, very fun (multiplayer). Medieval: Total War… simply a lot to do and a lot to think about without the real-time factor.

Will you buy a game on impulse if it is connected with a license, such as Star Trek and Star Wars, which you enjoy?

Yes. If the game sounds interesting enough and it's what I enjoy… why not? I impulse buy a lot.

Does the game's genre strongly influence your purchase?

Yes

What is your favorite genre?

Turn-based strategy

If you read a glowing review, will you buy the game?

Yes, but only if several reviews are consistent

What influences your gaming purchases the most? (Select up to two.)

Cool factor, genre

Do you believe the publisher (Infogrames, EA, etc.) or the developer (Blizzard, etc.) has a greater impact on how good the game is?

I don't even look at who the developer or publisher is when I buy a game. They both usually put out as much junk as they do good stuff.

If you buy a stinker from a publisher, will you buy a subsequent game from the same publisher?

Yes, it all just depends on the game. If one game was bad, it doesn't mean that any of the other games they make are bad.

What is your favorite game that you have played in the last 24 months? Why?

Max Payne. It had an awesome story line and did for computer games what *The Matrix* did for the movies. By far the best game play of a third-person shooter of all time. Nothing has matched it yet.

Will you buy a game on impulse if it is connected with a license, such as Star Trek and Star Wars, which you enjoy?

No, I always go for the game or the game play instead of the license. In fact, most of the license games have quite a few horrible games to their names.

Does the game's genre strongly influence your purchase?

No. I buy what I like, and that's just about everything.

What is your favorite genre?

I like all of these types of genres, but by far war games are the most enticing to me due to the fact that they are usually historically accurate, and you want to see if you can match up to the great leaders of the past.

If you read a glowing review, will you buy the game?

No, I usually download the demo (if there is one).

What influences your gaming purchases the most? (Select up to two.)

Topic, franchises, genre

Do you believe the publisher (Infogrames, EA, etc.) or the developer (Blizzard, etc.) has a greater impact on how good the game is?

I have no idea. I would hope (in my naiveté) it would be the developers. I feel they would be more likely to be gamers and know what makes a good game and be aware of the gripes raised in reviews not just in magazines, but through other sources. Publishers are more likely to rely on surveys and market analysis. That said, do publishers override developers with regard to the final product?

If you buy a stinker from a publisher, will you buy a subsequent game from the same publisher?

Yes. If I buy a stinker, it'll most likely be my fault. I read reviews before buying and buy on the basis of that and the criteria listed in [the first] question.

What is your favorite game that you have played in the last 24 months? Why?

My favorites are: Ghost Recon—it's fun, though challenging. I prefer Hidden & Dangerous, but that's out of the date range. The modding ability is nice. Deus Ex—good for a bit of a mindless blast. Jane's FA/18—I love flight sims. Being a techie type, it's fun playing a game that needs you to push loads of buttons, even if you are abysmal at it.

Will you buy a game on impulse if it is connected with a license, such as Star Trek and Star Wars, which you enjoy?

No. I bought TIE Fighter because it was basically a flight sim (of sorts), but wouldn't but one of the FPS/console-style ones, like Rogue Squadron. The franchise thing is getting ridiculous now.

Does the game's genre strongly influence your purchase?

Yes. Some I enjoy, some I don't. This can be overridden by the game itself (for example, Deus Ex, Hidden & Dangerous are FPS), but I hate Quake because it's just about big guns.

What is your favorite genre?

Adventure, simulation (flight) sometimes shooter…depends on my mood. To be honest, I don't think you can have a single favorite genre or game.

If you read a glowing review, will you buy the game?

No—reviews are inevitably subjective. However, it would make me look more closely at the game.

. . . .

What influences your gaming purchases the most? (Select up to two.)

Topic, franchises, genre

Do you believe the publisher (Infogrames, EA, etc.) or the developer (Blizzard, etc.) has a greater impact on how good the game is?

I believe the publisher has a greater impact on how good a game is. In most cases, the publisher, who holds the purse strings, controls the pace of development either positively (by supporting the developer) or negatively (by pushing deadlines). There are a few exceptions to this. The game "gods" who have proven themselves may have more to say over the development company. Ultimately, the publisher can always pull the plug.

If you buy a stinker from a publisher, will you buy a subsequent game from the same publisher?

Yes, possibly. A "stinker" from a publisher probably means more than the company is a bad publisher. They may have released early to try to break even, for example. A publisher with a track record of stinkers might make me think twice.

What is your favorite game that you have played in the last 24 months? Why?

Neverwinter Nights. First, I am a huge fantasy/RPG player, and NWN is a great RPG. Second, the game has allowed me to recreate some of those nights sitting around a table with a bunch of dice playing pen and paper with the guys, even though we all live in four different states now.

Will you buy a game on impulse if it is connected with a license, such as Star Trek and Star Wars, which you enjoy?

No. A good license doesn't make a good game. There have been some very bad Star Wars games. License is a lure, not a hook.

Does the game's genre strongly influence your purchase?

Yes. While I have crossed genres from time to time, I generally stick to the genres in which I have an interest.

What is your favorite genre?

Turn-based strategy. I grew up on SSI and SSG turn-based war games for the Apple II. My first love.

If you read a glowing review, will you buy the game?

No. I will usually buy a game based on more than one reviewer's opinion. I also consult friends for their feelings about a game.

. . . .

What influences your gaming purchases the most? (Select up to two.)

Topic, franchises, genre

Do you believe the publisher (Infogrames, EA, etc.) or the developer (Blizzard, etc.) has a greater impact on how good the game is?

The developer. Some of the most innovative games have come from smaller outfits. For example, look at the Combat Mission series or IL-2.

If you buy a stinker from a publisher, will you buy a subsequent game from the same publisher?

Perhaps, depends on whether they get their act together and if others who buy the subsequent game have good things to say about it.

What is your favorite game that you have played in the last 24 months? Why?

Simulations—love the machines

Will you buy a game on impulse if it is connected with a license, such as Star Trek and Star Wars, which you enjoy?

No. A license does not a good game make.

Does the game's genre strongly influence your purchase?

No. I'm open minded and will try any game as long as the game play is good and the subject matter appeals to me.

What is your favorite genre?

Flight simulation

If you read a glowing review, will you buy the game?

Perhaps … the subject matter has to appeal to me.

What influences your gaming purchases the most? (Select up to two.)

Cool factor, genre, publisher/developer

Do you believe the publisher (Infogrames, EA, etc.) or the developer (Blizzard, etc.) has a greater impact on how good the game is?

Different companies have different goals. Some are geared toward realism, while others steer to the more user fun games.

If you buy a stinker from a publisher, will you buy a subsequent game from the same publisher?

Yes. It would be stupid to think that one bad game reflects the company as a whole.

What is your favorite game that you have played in the last 24 months? Why?

My favorite game is Gettysburg.

Will you buy a game on impulse if it is connected with a license, such as Star Trek and Star Wars, which you enjoy?

Absolutely not

Does the game's genre strongly influence your purchase?

Not really

What is your favorite genre?

I like them all; no favorites here.

If you read a glowing review, will you buy the game?

Well, it depends on how many other glowing reviews I read. If it sounds good, I try and find a demo first.

What influences your gaming purchases the most? (Select up to two.)

Topic, franchises, genre, publisher/developer

Do you believe the publisher (Infogrames, EA, etc.) or the developer (Blizzard, etc.) has a greater impact on how good the game is?

I think that the developer is the base for the quality of the game. Infogrames has published some really horrible games and some really good ones, but if a developer does a good game, you can usually believe that their games will always be good.

If you buy a stinker from a publisher, will you buy a subsequent game from the same publisher?

Yes, because the developer is the one who affects the quality of the game. All the publisher does is advertise, oversee, and fund.

What is your favorite game that you have played in the last 24 months? Why?

Hearts of Iron. It's hard. I'm tired of little five-minute skirmishes in RTSs where you could possibly win with your eyes closed. HOI is *hard* and *long*. I've been playing the game I'm on right now for the past five days and have only taken over Mexico, half of South America, the Carribean, and one province in Spain as a starting point for my war in Europe.

Will you buy a game on impulse if it is connected with a license, such as Star Trek and Star Wars, which you enjoy?

No. I always research a game before purchasing it.

Does the game's genre strongly influence your purchase?

Yes. I hate turn-based games. They are just too slow for me. It seems you spend most of your time just waiting so you can have a five-second turn.

What is your favorite genre?

RTS, with FPS in a real close second (MOHAA: Spearhead)

If you read a glowing review, will you buy the game?

I need to see a good review on at least two sites or in two magazines. I generally check out my *PC Gamer*, Gamesdomain.com, and of course Wargamer.com.

What influences your gaming purchases the most? (Select up to two.)

Genre, publisher/developer

Do you believe the publisher (Infogrames, EA, etc.) or the developer (Blizzard, etc.) has a greater impact on how good the game is?

I may be fooled once, but with all the reviewers on the "net" and in magazines, to be fooled even once is because you rushed in to buy. The publishers or developers also know what makes a winning combination to a true gamer. We, the gamers, want the meat of the game. If we are going to put out $70 to $80 CDN for a game (which is still okay), then I need to know I'm not wasting my time or my money because it will not happen twice. Some gamers have their preferences as to which publisher/developer they will migrate to, but when it come down to the meat of the game, the juiciest meat wins.

If you buy a stinker from a publisher, will you buy a subsequent game from the same publisher?

No! See above. Now, having said that, I will read discussion boards and reviews to see if the publisher/developer has learned some new coding and will give them a second chance.

What is your favorite game that you have played in the last 24 months? Why?

Medal of Honor: Allied Assault. I know it can get repetitive, but for what I've paid, it has given me hours and hours of entertainment until I trade it in on a new version or new game.

Will you buy a game on impulse if it is connected with a license, such as Star Trek and Star Wars, which you enjoy?

Yes, sometimes. But I know I might be taking a chance on the coding and might end up with a dog.

Does the game's genre strongly influence your purchase?

Yes, I'm a wargamer, but sometimes I do venture out into the real world.

What is your favorite genre?

War game. Real time and get outta my way.

If you read a glowing review, will you buy the game?

I will put it on my short list to buy and go do some research. I know enough about journalistic opportunities and affiliations to know that anyone can have their favorites.

What influences your gaming purchases the most? (Select up to two.)

Topic, franchises, publisher/developer

Do you believe the publisher (Infogrames, EA, etc.) or the developer (Blizzard, etc.) has a greater impact on how good the game is?

I believe this varies greatly depending on the game and the relationship between the publisher and developer.

If you buy a stinker from a publisher, will you buy a subsequent game from the same publisher?

Only if the publisher is a mainstream publisher with titles from multiple developers.

What is your favorite game that you have played in the last 24 months? Why?

My favorite game has been Operation Flashpoint. I enjoy it mostly because of continued support from the publisher featuring new add-ons and engine improvements, as well as the community that exists around the game. It also features an extremely easy to learn editing system that still produces pro-quality results without the need for advanced coding.

Will you buy a game on impulse if it is connected with a license, such as Star Trek and Star Wars, which you enjoy?

Most likely no. These games are almost always bad or limited and predictable. The only exception is the Jedi Knight series perhaps, and even

this did not faithfully follow the Star Wars genre.

Does the game's genre strongly influence your purchase?

No. If a game is good, I will play it.

What is your favorite genre?

I have no favorite genre. But my least favorite are console-style platform jumping games.

If you read a glowing review, will you buy the game?

No. At most, it would make me consider finding out more about the game and maybe trying a demo.

· · · · · · · · · · ·

What influences your gaming purchases the most? (Select up to two.)

Topic, franchises, genre

Do you believe the publisher (Infogrames, EA, etc.) or the developer (Blizzard, etc.) has a greater impact on how good the game is?

The developer should, in theory, have the greater impact on how good the game is. They are the creators looking to put forward the game ideas, feel, and playability. Regrettably, the real world has to intrude and publishers frequently have to "tone down" the developer's more grandiose schemes/plans to produce a commercially viable product suitable for a wide audience. It follows therefore that publishers have the final say as to how close the game reaches its full potential (i.e., how good it is). I personally feel that this is a real shame, but games have to have commercial appeal—if not, the industry dies.

If you buy a stinker from a publisher, will you buy a subsequent game from the same publisher?

No, not without a damn good recommendation from someone who has actually played the second game.

What is your favorite game that you have played in the last 24 months? Why?

On the computer—Activision's Medieval: Total War combines all the elements of strategy (overall campaign), tactics (battles), and diplomacy in a realistic and historical setting. Graphics are outstanding and game play is second to none.

Will you buy a game on impulse if it is connected with a license, such as Star Trek and Star Wars, which you enjoy?

Yes, unfortunately, I will and do, if the game looks to be able to capture the feel of the setting (be it Star Wars, Star Trek, or a historical subject, say, Band of Brothers in WWII). I admit that in this instance it is usually the game blurb and packaging that does the dirty deed in persuading me to buy.

Does the game's genre strongly influence your purchase?

Definitely. If I'm not interested in the basic type, the game stays on the shelf. Flight simulations leave me totally cold, first-person shooters don't usually provide enough mental challenges—i.e., basically they consist of "get in there, shoot anything that moves, grab the right bit of equipment, complete the job and get out"—once you have completed the mission, that's it. There is no real fresh approach to take.

What is your favorite genre?

Turn-based strategy

If you read a glowing review, will you buy the game?

More than likely if the subject matter appeals to me

Index

www.GameInstitute.com
A Superior Way to Learn Computer Game Development

The Game Institute provides a convenient, high-quality game development curriculum at a very affordable tuition. Our expert faculty has developed a series of courses designed to teach you fundamental and advanced game programming techniques so that you can design and develop your own computer games. Best of all, in our unique virtual classrooms you can interact with instructors and fellow students in ways that will ensure you get a firm grasp of the material. Whether you are a beginner or a game development professional, the Game Institute is the superior choice for your game development education.

Quality Courses at a Great Price

- ◯ **Weekly Online Voice Lectures** delivered by your instructor with accompanying slides and other visuals.

- ◯ **Downloadable Electronic Textbook** provides in-depth coverage of the entire curriculum with additional voice-overs from instructors.

- ◯ **Student-Teacher Interaction** both live in weekly chat sessions and via message boards where you can post your questions and solutions to exercises.

- ◯ **Downloadable Certificates** suitable for printing and framing indicate successful completion of your coursework.

- ◯ **Source Code** and sample applications for study and integration into your own gaming projects.

"The leap in required knowledge from competent general-purpose coder to games coder has grown significantly. The Game Institute provides an enormous advantage with a focused curriculum and attention to detail."

—Tom Forsyth
Lead Developer
Muckyfoot Productions, Ltd.

● Graphics Programming
th Direct3D

3D Graphics Programming
With OpenGL

Advanced BSP/PVS/CSG
Techniques

mines the premier 3D graphics
gramming API on the Microsoft
dows platform. Create a
nplete 3D game engine with
nated characters, light maps,
cial effects, and more.

An excellent course for newcomers
to 3D graphics programming. Also
includes advanced topics like
shadows, curved surfaces, environment mapping, particle systems, and
more.

A strong understanding of spatial
partitioning algorithms is important
for 3D graphics programmers. Learn
how to leverage the BSP tree data
structure for fast visibility processing
and collision detection as well as
powerful CSG algorithms.

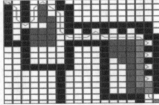

al-Time 3D Terrain
ndering

Path Finding Algorithms

Network Game Program-
ming With DirectPlay

e your 3D engine into the great
doors. This course takes a
ious look at popular terrain
neration and rendering algorithms
uding ROAM, Rottger, and
dstrom.

Study the fundamental art of maneuver in 2D and 3D environments.
Course covers the most popular
academic algorithms in use today.
Also includes an in-depth look at the
venerable A*.

Microsoft DirectPlay takes your
games online quickly. Course
includes coverage of basic network-
ing, lobbies, matchmaking and
session management.

ONLY 100
WILL BE CHOSEN
FOR THE QUEST
of a
LIFETIME

Twice a year the challenge is raised — and 100 of the best are admitted to the Hart eCenter at SMU Digital Games Guildhall. The Guildhall is designed to train talented students to become immediately productive digital games developers. The program is just like the industry — intense, results oriented, and only for the dedicated few.

The Guildhall grants membership to those who complete the 18-month certificate program, designed by industry professionals to train the next generation of game developers. High-profile industry leaders from top name development companies have designed the courses and take special interest in the Guildhall as teachers, mentors, and craft experts.

For more information and details on how to apply, contact David Najjab at **214-768-9903** or email **najjab@smu.edu**.

Check out the website at **guildhall.smu.edu**.